Table of Contents

Acknowledgments	ix
Preface	1
Introduction	3
1. Place and Space: Miami—Havana, USA?	23
2. Spanish- and English-Language Newspapers in Miami	39
3. Miami's Cuban American Radio Scene	67
4. Spanish-Language Television, Cuban Americans and Hispanic Audiences	84
5. The Internet: An Emerging Transnational Sphere?	107
6. The Politics of Memory: Pre-Revolutionary Cuba	124
Conclusion	140
Epilogue	150
Appendix A	155
Appendix B	175
Appendix C	178
Chapter Notes	179
References	186
Index	197

Cuban Americans
and the Miami Media

Cuban Americans and the Miami Media

CHRISTINE LOHMEIER

McFarland & Company, Inc., Publishers
Jefferson, North Carolina

LIBRARY OF CONGRESS CATALOGUING-IN-PUBLICATION DATA

Lohmeier, Christine, 1978–
    Cuban Americans and the Miami media / Christine Lohmeier.
        p.   cm.
    Includes bibliographical references and index.

    ISBN 978-0-7864-6894-2 (softcover : acid free paper) ♾
    ISBN 978-1-4766-1339-0 (ebook)

    1. Cuban Americans in the mass media industry—Florida—Miami. 2. Mass media—Social aspects—Florida—Miami.
3. Cuban Americans—Florida—Miami—Ethnic identity.
I. Title.
P94.5.C83L65 2014
302.23089'687291—dc23   2013050954

BRITISH LIBRARY CATALOGUING DATA ARE AVAILABLE

© 2014 Christine Lohmeier. All rights reserved

No part of this book may be reproduced or transmitted in any form or by any means, electronic or mechanical, including photocopying or recording, or by any information storage and retrieval system, without permission in writing from the publisher.

Cover image: Miami skyline (photograph by Marc Averette)

Manufactured in the United States of America

McFarland & Company, Inc., Publishers
   Box 611, Jefferson, North Carolina 28640
   www.mcfarlandpub.com

For my parents

Acknowledgments

Although this book has been written by only one author, there are numerous people without whom this project would not have come to fruition. I would like to express my sincere gratitude to all informants in the field who took the time to patiently answer my questions. Special thanks are due to Donn Tilson of the University of Miami, who was my first port of call and established valuable contacts. Barbara Gutierrez of the University of Miami kindly put me in touch with potential interviewees. Esperanza de Varona, Gladys Gómez-Rossié and Annie Sansone Martínez of the Cuban Heritage Collection at the Richter Library of the University of Miami were extremely helpful during times of field work and always made me feel welcome.

I am extremely grateful to Philip Schlesinger and Raymond Boyle for continuous support, inspiration and insightful comments. Throughout the years of research and writing Philip's support has encouraged me to keep going when I was ready to give up. Raymond's pragmatic and up-beat approach has given this project momentum, particularly in the final stages. Thanks are also due to Jairo Lugo for his encouragement and advice and to Myra Macdonald, who supervised this work in its earlier incarnation as a PhD thesis when I was based at the University of Stirling, Scotland. Special thanks go to Anna Reading and Christine Geraghty for their critical reading of an earlier version. I would like to thank the Carnegie Trust for the Universities of Scotland for the financial support of research phases in Miami in 2007 and 2008.

There have been many friends and colleagues who have offered inspiration and support. I would particularly like to thank Daniela Gabor, Nichola Mayer, Diane Waugh, Ruth Walker, Heather Porteous,

Acknowledgments

Lynne Hibberd, Isabel Awad, Joyce Neys, and Sara Avant Stover. Special thanks go to Caitriona Noonan, Jiska Engelbert, Seian Al-Jebali, Caro Paulus, Michael Ertl, Christian Pentzold, and Thomas Herbert for their help with the manuscript and their insightful comments.

My family has been a great network of encouragement; Sylvia, Martin and Sarah Kobelt, Inge Lohmeier as well as my grandparents, Sophie and Wilhelm Lohmeier, have always taken an interest in my work while simultaneously providing much-needed opportunities to leave the "academic realm" behind from time to time.

My deepest gratitude goes to my parents, Christhild and Dieter Lohmeier, for unconditional love, invaluable support and an unshakable belief in my abilities. My mother has been with me through it all as a constant source of whatever was needed. Thank you.

Preface

The idea for this project grew out of my curiosity about what it means to live in exile. How does having to leave one's home for whatever reason influence feelings of belonging and community? How can we feel at home and create a home when everything around us has changed? What does going into exile mean for our social contacts, our relations to others and the world around us? In essence, these were the questions that fascinated me as an aspiring PhD student. For me, these issues are as intriguing today as they were when I first started contemplating my dissertation topic in 2005.

No doubt this project owes itself to another of my fascinations: Cuba—Caribbean culture, spicy food, cigars, rum and intoxicating rhythms. These were the associations in most people's minds when they heard about my research interest. Upon further reflection an equally captivating, if perhaps a bit less colorful, topic would occur to them: the bilateral relationship between Cuba and the United States. Cuban history and the country's relations to its big northern neighbor, the United States, is packed with exotic and exciting tidbits. Think poisoned cigars and CIA agents in linen suits. These are the types of stories that we find featured in the media on a regular basis. A recent example was provided by the *New Yorker* with a longish essay on William Alexander Morgan, "The Yankee Commandante" (Grann 2012). It seems that Cuba, despite its partly violent history that tore so many families apart and some would argue even drew a line of separation across an entire nation, nevertheless continues to ignite wild, yet forgiving, fantasies about rebels and rum. Pins, T-shirts and hats with the iconic picture of Ernesto Ché Guevara, the Argentinian doctor who became one of the most well-known figures

Preface

of the Cuban revolution, are popular around the world. And even though those wearing Ché's image may consider him more of a pop icon than a political hero, this differentiation matters little to those whose lives have been negatively affected by the Cuban revolution.

The image triggered by the pearl of the Caribbean is mirrored to some extent by people's ideas of the exile community. Miami and the Cuban Americans based there have received a lot of attention over the past five decades; some of it good, some of it bad, and a lot of it rather one-dimensional. The Cuban American community is typically considered strongly right-wing, so the shades of grey within it often get lost. Hopefully, this book will be helpful in painting a more nuanced picture of the Cuban American community.

The overriding theme this book addresses is the impact and significance of media for and on an exile community; this encompasses everything between the interaction of individual media outlets and members of the Cuban American community and others based in Miami and the media's potential to afford transnational encounters. Even from a distance (at the time I was based in Scotland) it was easy to see that the Cuban American community in Miami and South Florida would provide an excellent case study for such a research project. It is a vibrant community with a well-established relationship to a diverse media landscape in Miami. And despite ongoing political gridlock, there is a lively exchange on various levels between the island and the exile community. On a wider scale, this publication makes a contribution to the academic debate on diasporas and media, as well as highlights the significance of media in cultural encounters, transnational processes and issues of home and belonging.

Introduction

> You wanna do research on the Cuban exile?—Well, you've come to the right place.[1]—Interview, June 2006

This book brings together two main fields of interest; that of migration and that of communication. Its primary aim is to examine and analyze the communicative spaces and functions of the media for a diasporic community. More specifically, this work focuses on the experience of the Cuban American community based in Miami, Florida. It investigates the evolution and purpose of different Miami-based media, in particular the press, radio, television and the internet,[2] in relation to incoming migrants from Cuba and other countries. It explores these changes in the context of established communities and in relation to changing demographics in Miami. It focuses on generational differences in media use and the shifting allegiances and power structure within the Cuban American community. The findings presented in the following chapters point toward the complexity of the Cuban American community, toward the power struggles between different segments of the community, and toward generational shifts regarding media use as well as to a dynamic relationship between Cuban exiles and Cubans based on the island.

It would go beyond the scope of this monograph to offer a complete analysis of all Spanish- and English-language media to be found in Miami and South Florida. Instead, this book examines specific media, developments and events that can be viewed as insightful and were signaled in the field as occupying a central position in the communication patterns of the Cuban American community in Miami. The significance

Introduction

of transnational communication and transnational media shared with other Cuban American communities based elsewhere, and indeed with Cubans living in Cuba, is alluded to frequently. In addition to continuous desk research, the bulk of data was gathered during field work that was carried out in Miami in 2006, 2007 and 2008. This included over 40 in-depth interviews with journalists and selected members of the Cuban American and Hispanic communities.

Figures from the U.S. Census Bureau (2006) indicate that 44.3 million Hispanics are now living in the United States, 14.8 percent of the total population. Between 2000 and 2006, the growth rate of the Hispanic population was 24.3 percent in contrast to the total U.S. population's growth rate of 6.1 percent. It is no surprise then that "immigration" is one of the buzz words of everyday life in the United States today. Similarly, European countries can be observed in an ongoing struggle regarding policies toward incoming migrants with discourses ranging from threats of "the other" and fears of terrorism and cultural clashes à la Samuel Huntington to economic arguments about migrants allowing for the continuing functioning of pension systems.

Over recent decades, topics such as integration, transnational communication, minority media and generational shifts in relation to media use and cultural change have thus found a secure place in academic as well as public (Western) discourses. This work can be situated within these themes. It contributes a thorough analysis of the functions played by the media for the Cuban American and other communities based in Miami in terms of identity negotiation and construction. It demonstrates how certain media are used for political purposes by specific segments of the community and how individuals and groups with different age and migration backgrounds have reacted to and influenced existing structures. Moreover, outcomes of this investigation show that later migrants purposefully employed other media than earlier arrivals to move away from dominant narratives. The choice of language has a significant role to play here too. The findings demonstrate that some media institutions were extremely reluctant to take certain groups and viewpoints into account. Furthermore, some migration waves had a much greater influence on the development of Miami's media scene than others. Finally, the cool casualness of everyday life in Miami perhaps sug-

Introduction

gests that hybrid identities and transnational belongings can imply a greater problem for theorists than for the individuals in question.

Following these themes and interests, there were three main questions that guided the development of this study and the writing process of this book:

1. What role do media have for negotiations of identity and community, notions of exile, and politically contested issues among a group of migrants?
2. How have the media in Miami developed and changed in response to the arrival of Cuban migrants?
3. What differences can be observed between distinct media, i.e., the press, radio, television and the internet?

Historical Background and Waves of Migration

The histories of Cuba and the United States are tightly knit. After the island achieved separation from the Spanish Empire in December 1898, it was the United States who took over the reins.[3] Although Cuba was nominally independent at the beginning of the twentieth century, historians agree that it was under the aegis of Washington, D.C., when it came to political decision-making processes (Benjamin 1990; Pérez Jr. 2009).[4] But this uneven relationship experienced a radical U-turn after 1959. Having forced the previous government under Fulgencio Batista out of power, Fidel Castro and his bearded warriors took to the streets of Havana accompanied by the cheers of the masses. Many of them, some close allies and friends during the revolution and the time spent in the woods of *El Oriente* Province, would eventually end up in Miami as his fiercest enemies. Some scholars assert that it was Fidel's younger brother, Raúl Castro, who made the initial move toward turning Cuba into a communist country.[5] But irrespective of which Castro brother first harbored communist sentiments, Cuba became a close ally of the Soviet Union in the 1960s. This association remained in place until the fall of the Iron Curtain in the early 1990s. The Cold War between the United States and the Soviet Union thus brought the island into a

Introduction

precarious situation. It was situated in the front garden of the U.S.—a strategically attractive position that the Soviet Union made good use of, for example, during the Cuban Missile Crisis of 1962.

Migration from Cuba to the U.S., in particular to South Florida, was not a new phenomenon. There had been a vivid exchange between the two countries in terms of art, trade and tourism. But the waves of migration that started with the advent of the Cuban revolution in 1959 were of unprecedented dimensions.[6] While Miami and Miami-Dade, the county it forms part of, was home to only 50,000 Hispanics in 1960, the figure rose to over 1.4 million by the year 2005, though it is worth remembering that illegal immigrants are not included in these figures (see Appendix B for a detailed overview). In addition, census methods of defining and identifying Hispanics have changed through the decades. Of the Hispanics based in Miami-Dade, people of Cuban origin form the clear majority with 794,883, followed by Nicaraguans (105,415), Colombians (94,511) and Puerto Ricans (94,264).[7] The Cuban American community undoubtedly formed a nucleus which to a great extent attracted more Spanish-speaking migrants with other national backgrounds to settle in Miami. The global community of people with Cuban origin living outside the island is estimated to be 1.5 million.

Migration from Cuba to Miami has been characterized by distinct migration waves. The people arriving in the early 1960s were members of Cuba's upper and middle classes. Mostly white and well-educated, they were welcomed by Miami's Anglo community. The shared understanding between early exiles and the host community was that a swift return to the island was likely. Soon after Fidel Castro's takeover of Havana, secret missions, plots and espionage began. It was during these early years of the exile that some segments of the community got involved with the CIA. One example of the CIA's cooperation with members of the exile community was the failed Bay of Pigs Invasion of 1961. Still today, many Cuban Americans believe that President Kennedy abandoned their men during the invasion by refusing to send air support. It is this incident that is said to have driven great parts of the historic exile away from the Democratic Party and turned the Cuban American community into a stronghold for the Republicans.

Instead of Cubans in Miami making a quick return, more Cuban

Introduction

migrants made their way to the United States in the 1970s. The year 1980 brought the Mariel Boatlift, named after the Cuban port of Mariel. In an act of defiance, Fidel Castro allowed for Miami's Cuban Americans to approach the island in boats to pick up relatives and friends. However, things were not as straightforward as they had sounded initially. Cuban Americans did not always have a choice regarding whom they actually got to take with them. In addition to friends and family, they were forced to take prisoners, mentally ill people, homosexuals and others who—according to the Cuban government—were unwanted on the island. The Mariel Boatlift was a significant turning point in the relationship between the white Anglo community and Cuban Americans. It became apparent that the Cuban American community was likely to stay for good. In addition, the city of Miami and Miami-Dade County were having great difficulty in dealing with the high numbers of incoming migrants. Between April and October 1980, circa 124,000 Cubans migrated to South Florida. Crime statistics rose and gave Miami a bad national and international reputation. In contrast to the historic exiles, later migration waves had less cultural capital and were of darker skin color. Their motivation to leave the island was rooted more in economic than in political considerations. The historic exiles were often first- or second-generation Cubans with a Spanish heritage. Their history and affiliation was closer to Europe than to South America. While the early exiles were mainly Catholic, later migrants had lived most if not all of their lives in a country strongly influenced by communist ideology and often thus had an a-religious upbringing or one that was characterized by less rigidly organized traditions. Mariel marked not only a turning point in the relations between the Anglo and the Cuban American community, it also brought home some fundamental truths about the changing make-up of Cuban society and life on the island.

Despite these difficulties, the Cuban Adjustment Act, which had first been issued in 1966, allowed Cuban migrants a comparatively easy way into legal residency in the United States as well as into obtaining U.S. citizenship. In the history of Cuban migration to South Florida, the 1990s became known for the rafters (*balseros*) crisis. The downfall of the Soviet Union and its allies had serious economic repercussions in Cuba. The Castro government therefore termed those years the "special

Introduction

period." Increasing deprivation on the island was followed by an increase in migrants who tried to make it across the Florida Straits on makeshift boats. In turn, the Clinton administration decided to revisit the Cuban Adjustment Act. The legislative changes became known as the "wet foot/dry foot policy." Now Cubans who were found at sea had to be returned to the island, while those who touched foot on U.S. soil were allowed to stay. Although the "wet foot/dry foot policy" added a significant hurdle for rafters, it has not let to an overall halt of people trying.

Finally, the current agreement between the U.S. and Cuba allows the Cuban government to issue exit visas for those wishing to leave the island, though the practicalities of this way of emigration are subject to the willingness toward cooperation on both sides. In addition to this "direct" way, some Cuban migrants opt for the possibility of travelling to third countries first, for example Mexico, and enter the United States thereafter. Recent changes in legislation allow Cubans to travel more freely, without going through the lengthy and expensive process of applying for exit visas (BBC News 2012). However, how this newly granted freedom works out in practice remains to be seen.

Another piece of legislation to be kept in mind in this context is the Helms-Burton Act of 1996, also known as the Cuban Liberty and Democratic Solidarity Act. Senator Jesse Helms (Republican) of North Carolina and Representative Dan Burton (Republican) of Indiana originally sponsored the bill. In contrast to what its formal title might suggest, the act was supposed to strengthen and extend the United States' unilateral economic sanctions toward Cuba.[8] Aware of the complexities of the trade embargo and its consequences, informants in the field had very different opinions regarding this type of legislation. While some were convinced of its efficacy, one interviewee criticized it for having "loopholes the size of Texas"; others saw it as harming the Cuban people and at the same time giving the Castro brothers an excuse for the poor economic state of the country.

Cuba is still trapped in Cold War dynamics, and so are parts of the Cuban American community. In the United States, other international issues and national concerns now take center stage, much to the dismay of some segments of the Cuban American community. Even though restrictions regarding travel and remittances have been amended, so far

Introduction

Barack Obama's presidency of the United States has not changed the status quo in any significant way.

Media in Cuba

The Cuban American community is known for its active and vibrant use of, and contributions to, Miami's media scene. The proactive participation in creating media was partly due to experiences the migrants had already had with media on the island. Cubans could choose between 58 daily newspapers in the 1950s. They were pioneers in radio programming. Radio was also an important medium employed by Fidel Castro and his revolutionaries. This lively and diverse media scene slowly changed for the worse after the Cuban revolution. Only 17 daily newspapers were left in 1992. In the same vein, there has been a decrease in the number of television and radio stations, which were slowly brought under state control following the revolution.[9] In some cases, such as that of the magazine *Vanidades*, migrants even brought patents with them and re-established their businesses in the United States after they had their production facilities seized and were forced or thought it their best option to leave the island.

Soon after the Cuban revolution and with the Cold War a stern reality, a propaganda war ensued between the United States and Cuba. The CIA was quick to get involved; it founded (and funded) Radio Swan, which was later to become WQBA 1140. Despite ongoing criticism, examples of this state of affairs can still be found today. Radio and TV Martí, state-funded radio and television stations whose setup is roughly comparable to that of the Voice of America, broadcast programs to Cuba. Even though the following chapters mention and touch upon the activities of the Martís, they are not part of the main focus of this volume.[10] There are three main reasons for this; firstly, programs from the Martís are not easily available to the Cuban American community in the United States and are therefore of minor relevance when considering questions about media in relation to the community. Secondly, because of continuing criticism due to the unknown efficacy of this state-funded undertaking, officials and journalists working for Radio and/or TV Martí were

Introduction

extremely reluctant to answer any questions about their involvement or to assess the output in terms of quality, content, aims, or scope. Thirdly, and perhaps most importantly, the Martís are ultimately controlled by the U.S. government and therefore not outlets that can react freely to events among Miami's Cuban American community.

Migrants, Diasporas and the Exilic Experience

There has been an ongoing discussion in the academic community regarding the theoretical framing of migrant groups. What makes a migrant? What characteristics does he or she have? What exactly do we mean when we speak of a diaspora?[11] Is every ethnic group a diaspora and vice versa? What is the relationship between migrants and nations? And are all migrants cosmopolitans? To gain a deeper understanding of the Cuban American community in Miami, it is helpful to consider notions of migration, diasporic formations, exile and cosmopolitanism.

Analyzing the Cuban American community, Khachig Tölölyan writes:

> The lines separating ethnic behavior from diasporic are not always clear-cut, and they shift in response to a complex dynamic. For example, the Cuban-American "community" contains a few assimilated members, a large number of ethnics, and an even larger group, whose size is fervently debated, that forms an "exile community" committed to an overthrow of Cuban communism and to a physical return to the island; some of the exiles display the full range of diasporic behaviour, engage actively in political and cultural self-representation, and care about maintaining contact with Cuba and Cuban communities in other countries, like Puerto Rico, Mexico and Spain. I emphasize that the boundaries between these groups are not fixed but porous and fluid. They will continue to change as change emerges in Cuba and the United States' attitude toward Cuba. The size and commitment of exiles, ethnics, and diasporics waxes and wanes in response both to internal dynamics of the community and in reaction to the policies, economy, and changing social and cultural allure of the host land and homeland [2007, 653].

Tölölyan (1996, 2007) criticizes the dilution of terms. He argues that the term *diaspora* has been used to refer to larger and larger groups of people in general, such as migrant workers, Muslims living in the

Introduction

West, and Spanish-language speakers in the United States. In a similar vein, Gabriel Sheffer (2003) laments the diffusion of the term and therefore posits a definition that specifically refers to "ethno-national" groups, thereby excluding all-encompassing approaches such as those outlined above. Sheffer states,

> An ethno-national diaspora is a social-political formation, created as a result of either voluntary or forced migration, whose members regard themselves as of the same ethno-national origin and who permanently reside as minorities in one or several host countries. Members of such entities maintain regular or occasional contacts with what they regard as their homelands and with individuals and groups of the same background residing in other host countries. Based on aggregate decisions to settle permanently in host countries, but to maintain a common identity, diasporas identify as such, showing solidarity with their group and their entire nation, and they organize and are active in the cultural, social, economic and political spheres. Among their various activities members of such diasporas establish trans-state networks that reflect complex relationships among the diasporas, their host countries, their homelands, and international actors [2003, 9–10].

One benefit of this definition is Sheffer's emphasis on social and cultural (trans-state) activities of diasporas in their host countries, as opposed to the focus on an intended return. These ethno-national diasporas in fact need to be settled, if not permanently, at least long-term, in order to build and maintain the networks, groups and relations they require for such activities. This of course also includes media, which are significant players in diasporic social and cultural activities.

Despite ongoing debates in the field as to what qualifies as a diaspora, scholars can agree that the circumstances and motivations of departure have a significant part in the organizational structures and emerging features of identity work by the group members themselves and also by outsiders; migrant workers who came on a voluntary basis for economic reasons view themselves differently than do political exiles who were forced to leave in order to save their lives. The first wave of Cubans arriving in the United States have stoically highlighted that they were exiles, not immigrants. So let's unpack the notion of exile.

The original meaning of exile, banishment from one's country over a certain period of time or for life, suggests that exile was and, in some

Introduction

cases, still is seen as a form of punishment. As a consequence, being in exile has been viewed as a painful process, filled with obstacles and disappointments (Krispyn 1973). Other scholars have moved away from this negative viewing of exile, one stating, "Exile must also be defined by its utopian and euphoric possibilities, driven by wanderlust, and a desire for liberation and freedom" (Naficy 1993, 6). A number of authors underline this perception, focusing on the (cultural) productivity of exiles, in most cases relating it to their special state of "in-betweenness," which views exiles as neither belonging nor having a "natural space" in the home nor in the host country.[12]

Edward Said (1984) interprets exile as a means to achieve a privileged insight for intellectuals, while writer Salman Rushdie sees new types of people being created who are rooted in "ideas rather than places, in memories as much as in material things; people who have been obliged to define themselves—because they are so defined by others—by their otherness" (1991, 124–125). These experiences and the overall positive perception of exile, which can lead to a deeper understanding of transnational phenomena and the world at large, might characterize the exilic experience of writers and academics who have managed to live a rather comfortable and successful life in the West. However, the realities of, for example, Burundian exiles in a refugee camp in Tanzania, with their life to a certain extent depending on the support of international NGOs, are very different, as the work of Liisa Malkki (1995) illustrates.

The difficulties of life in exile are further underlined by Ghorashi (2004), who analyzed the experiences of Iranian exiled women now living in the Netherlands and Los Angeles. Ghorashi concludes that a "disrupted sense of time and place prevails. A disrupted sense of life in vacillating between the past and the present creates emptiness and insecurity, feelings that displace their sense of belonging" (2004, 113). Cultivating a feeling of belonging goes beyond an established legal status. Having the correct papers does not serve as an indicator of social integration.[13] Ghorashi's (2004) findings indicate that the continuous emphasis of the migrants' temporary stay can support nostalgic feelings for the home country. As will be shown in the analysis of the Elián González story, this sense of belonging can also dissolve for established migrant

Introduction

groups. Reiterating a point mentioned above, Ghorashi (2004) underlines that the exilic experience is extensively dependent on the host society and generalizations therefore often fall short.

The term *exile* has a strong political connotation and can be seen as an indication of the circumstances of departure. The idea here is not to actually return to the original meaning of "banishment," as exile can also be self-imposed. But, whether made voluntarily or involuntarily, the decision to leave one's country has an obvious connection with policies carried out by the government or the regime in power that the exile suffers and opposes. Exile involves an ongoing process of negotiation: negotiation of identities, negotiation between home and host culture, negotiation of past and present, of "descent" and "consent" (Sollors 1986):

> Exiles attempt to hold on to their descent relations while becoming part of the consensus that forms the new host culture. These impulses fuse to create an uncanny, liminal state and a cultural threshold in which the liminars live in a continual state of otherness and exile from former and new attachments [Nacify 1993, 9].

As a result of its inherent liminality and in-betweenness, the exilic experience is also characterized by the potential of cosmopolitanism (Park 1950, 376), which Naficy sees as accompanied by "a fundamental doubt about the self, reality, home, traditions—in short a doubt about absolutes, ideologies, and taken-for-granted values of one's home or host societies" (1993, 9).

The different angles on exile outlined above resonate to some degree with writings by philosopher Vilém Flusser. In his essay on "Exile and Creativity" (2002, 104–109), Flusser assumes that the exile, or the expelled, is taken out of "his [sic] customary surroundings," which, in combination with the habits associated with that environment, function like a cotton blanket; it "covers up the facts of the case" (Flusser 2002, 104). The expelled, however, is free to see things clearly and from a new perspective. The new situation, with new information, requires creativity in order to survive. This is not necessarily a bad position to be in. Evaluating the state of liminality and in-betweeness, Flusser argues:

> In a situation where one is accustomed to pitying the expelled, this positive assessment is itself unusual, and, according to the hypothesis, it should itself be informative. For it seems—according to the hypothesis—that

Introduction

> those people who want to "help" the expelled to become ordinary again are, in fact, engaged in reeling him [sic] back into their ordinariness. This is an informative assumption, because it forces us to think about what is usual. The assumption does not justify the expellers, but rather it exposes the vulgarity of the expellers: the expelled were bothersome factors who were expelled to make the surroundings even more ordinary than before. Indeed, this assumption leaves the following question to our discretion: Even without intending to do so, have the expellers not done the expelled a service? [2002, 104–5].

Again, these general characterizations and conceptualizations of the exilic experience should be dealt with cautiously, as being in exile might not be a permanent state but rather a subjective, fluid and changing aspect of one's identity. While there might be a sense of liminality and in-betweenness inherent in the circumstances of an exiled individual or an exiled group, it does not necessarily lead to a cosmopolitan view of the world. On the contrary, the pains and hardship associated with an involuntary departure could also translate into rage, anger and a readiness to hit back.

For the majority of Cuban Americans, the term *exile* held strong political connotations.[14] For some it was also defined through notions of banishment and not having the option of returning to Cuba or visiting the island in good conscience. The key to defining oneself as an exile was furthermore associated with the ability to remember life in Cuba. However, in the field, informants would also refer to an "exile mentality" of subsequent generations born outside of Cuba.

Nations, States and Cosmopolitanism

The study of diasporas is strongly linked to work on nationalism, transnationalism, theories of globalization (such as cosmopolitanism and cultural imperialism) and issues surrounding state and citizenship. Diasporas have the potential to challenge the (nation-)state. Together with global economic enterprises and governmental and non-governmental organizations, they are symptoms as well as phenomena of and driving forces for transnational connections that reach across (nation-)states and borders.

Introduction

One of the main points of discussion in the academic field is where to place migrant communities in relation to nations, (nation-)states, transnational activities and processes described under the catch-all term *globalization*. Drawing on Gopinath's (2005) work on queer diasporas in South Asia, Braziel (2008, 26) posits:

> While diasporas may (and undeniably do) contest and disrupt the hegemonic forces of nationalism and globalization, refiguring the dominant discursive framings of nation-state and global capitalism, we must also remain cognizant of the ways that diasporas and diasporic forms of cultural production may also remain complicit and imbricate both with nationalist formation and "with capitalism [and may] shore up the dominance of the latter by making its mechanisms invisible," as Gopinath importantly reminds us [2005, 10].

The past decade produced a considerable amount of scholarship that has argued for the city as a highly useful and relevant unit of analysis.[15] Some argue that the nation even presents a hindering category, interpreting it as a potential "interruption," one representing "a disharmony in the scheme of the diasporic space" (Georgiou 2006, 9).

Among others, Khachig Tölölyan (1996, 4) cautions scholars who see diasporic formations primarily as a potential challenge or even a threat to existing (nation-)states. In his search for reasons for the increased use of the term *diaspora*, Tölölyan (1996) points, among other factors, to the stateless power that parts of the Jewish diaspora (mainly those based in the United States) were able to exert when working toward establishing the state of Israel (see also Sheffer 2003). This success, Tölölyan argues, provided an example for other dispersed groups to assume the traits of and identify themselves as a diaspora. Juxtaposing these dynamics against the previous idea of diasporic communities challenging (nation-)states and their institutions, it becomes apparent that the (nation-)state order, at least in the mid-twentieth century, provided an aim that parts of the Jewish community were keen to work toward and have a share in.[16] In other words, even though diasporic communities might through their mere existence pose a challenge to (nation-)state structures, members of these communities have nevertheless considered partaking in the (nation-)state formation a goal worth striving toward.

On the other hand, there is no doubt that processes of globalization

Introduction

and supra-national structures, such as the European Union, have led to a questioning of the role and function of (nation-)states. German sociologist Ulrich Beck asserts, "The human condition has itself become cosmopolitan" (2006, 2), referring to the international threat of terrorism and the protest against the Iraq War as conditions and events that reach beyond the (nation-)state. Even those protesting the advancement of the processes of globalization taking place today are in fact organized in global networks themselves, as Beck (2006) points out.[17] He also sees great potential for emerging cosmopolitan structures, especially within Europe and the framework of the European Union, and criticizes the limitations of (nation-)states as the main realms of society:

> For in the cosmopolitan outlook, methodologically understood, there resides the latent potential to break out of the self-centered narcissism of the national outlook and the dull incomprehension with which it infects thought and action, and thereby enlighten human beings concerning the real, internal cosmopolitanization of their lifeworlds and institutions [Beck 2006, 2].

Inter- and transnational media have a significant part in the cosmopolitanization of lifeworlds. Television, especially, has the potential to let people take in the world, making global imagery and narratives available in their everyday lives. In her recent study on television news, Alexa Robertson (2010) posits that news programs can have the capacity to further a cosmopolitan understanding of the world. However, this depends on several factors such as the style of reporting, the background information given, and the vocabulary used by journalists.

Schlesinger cautions against Beck's optimistic view of "boundarylessness" by drawing our attention to the "continuing significance of the national dimension" (2007, 415); questions of belonging and of forming a sense of identity are still to a large extent founded within the realms of a nation. Likewise, communication spaces, especially those determined by print media, radio and television (i.e., formerly analogue media) often mirror (nation-)state territories. No doubt there are indications and examples of transnational/trans-state networks as well as media initiatives, such as Arte, Euronews and Telesur. An interesting starting point for this research was to consider the media's position in the binary tension between states and nations on the one hand and

Introduction

transnational structures and networks on the other. The Cuban American community and its media make for a well-suited case study here, as early migration waves in the 1960s started when the Cold War was going into another challenging phase and the importance of (nation-) states was generally unchallenged and unquestioned.

Regardless of where one positions oneself in this debate, the media play a crucial role in the evolution of migrant communities. They are simultaneously indicators and driving forces in the process of identity formation of diasporic communities. How they operate as institutions and media outlets, how media content is produced and consumed, gives researchers empirical clues regarding the dynamics of diasporic communities and their relation to home and host societies. Taking a macro-perspective, this can then also give indications on (global) flows, counterflows, (transnational or trans-state) networks, the position of the state, and the quality and texture of communication spaces. Despite the fact that diasporic media content can often be interpreted as a transnational phenomenon, the significance of place for a migrant group, the importance of being situated in a certain locale, should not be underestimated.[18]

Latinos/as, Hispanics, Cuban Americans, and Miami

Publications on Latino and Hispanic culture have seen an immense rise in the past two to three decades.[19] Recent scholarship bears witness to the media's multifaceted relationship with Latinos/as in the United States, ranging from representation of Latinos/as in music, film and television (think of Jennifer López, Salma Hayek, América Ferrera and Ricky Martin) to questions of transnational belonging and potential threats from undocumented migrants and the U.S.-Mexican border.

For cultural and popular studies scholars as well as for researchers in the field of media and communication, the groups and communities now commonly addressed as Latinos/Latinas (on the West Coast of the United States), Hispanics (on the East Coast) and/or Chicanos/Chicanas (in the Southwest) present a fertile ground for research (Río 2006).[20] The above descriptors indicate that Latino/a identity is not as straight-

Introduction

forward as branding consultants and advertising executives might like to claim.[21] Esteban del Río asserts:

> These complexities call for wider memories and deeper understandings of how different groups are constructed and positioned in relation to each other. However, contemporary expressions of popular and public culture contain few acknowledgments of the historical presence of U.S. Latina/o populations or the ongoing civil rights and political movements that received greater public attention in the 1970s. Instead, general market media texts and mainstream popular culture reconfigure—if not invent—a new Latina/o imaginary for Anglo and capitalist sensibilities and celebrate Latina/o life as an exotic, spicy, and new addition to the multicultural mainstream [2006, 389].

Similar criticism had already been expressed a decade earlier by William V. Flores and Rina Benmayor, who argued that pluralism does not go all that far in U.S. society. Instead, difference is only allowed to be celebrated in confined spaces and at particular times, such as specific holidays, allowing public spaces to remain "culturally neutral" and thereby endorsing "the dominant culture as normative" (1997, 9). Inequalities and power struggles, on the other hand, remain unchallenged and unaddressed.

On a superficial level the above concerns might not apply to the Cuban American community based in Miami. Their visibility and power as a collective in the city make questions about a Hispanic identity and the ability to express *cubanidad* and Hispanic roots within or alongside American mainstream culture seem immaterial. Then again, these issues are still highly relevant to other Hispanics, including Cubans, elsewhere. While Cuban Americans might not face many challenges with regards to expressing their identity in Miami, other so-called minority groups in the U.S. do. While "expressing one's identity" is initially often viewed as a soft topic, it comes down to hard facts when it is time to decide who is allowed to stay in the country and who should be sent back to their country of origin. Who has the power to decide whether someone is considered an illegal immigrant or given a Green Card? Hispanic "belonging" therefore simultaneously tests Cuban Americans on their solidarity and their willingness to stand up for other immigrants.

Introduction

The Structure of This Book

An analysis of the media and the broader media ecology creates the opportunity to disentangle the dynamics between different types of media, in particular the press, radio, television and the internet. It will be shown how these media have been posited in very distinct manners by different segments of the community and what roles are played by the journalists who work for them.

Chapter 1 examines the development of Miami as a place and a social space in relation to incoming migration from Cuba. The first section considers writings on space, place and memory. This is followed by an analysis of the exilic state that emerged as a feature of the Cuban American community in Miami. With the Cuban revolution now over fifty years old, the experience of the first wave of exiles has itself been mythologized, as outlined in the third section. *The Lost City* (2005), a blockbuster directed by and starring Cuban American Andy García, is used as an example of the discourse surrounding those exiles that left in 1959 and the early 1960s. Simultaneously, the family presented in *The Lost City* acts as a trope for the Cuban nation. The chapter closes with a consideration of relations between the Cuban American community and the Anglo and wider Hispanic community. The issue of community relations in Miami will be picked up again in Chapter 5 when reports of and reactions to the Elián González saga, the story of a Cuban boy who safely reached Floridian shores while his mother died at sea, are examined.

The following four chapters go straight to the heart of the matter. They comprise analyses of local, national and potentially transnational media, i.e., press, radio, television and the internet, and their relationship to the Cuban American community. Depending on the nature and terms of engagement between the community and the media in question, some chapters focus on Spanish- and English-language productions, while others concentrate on Spanish-language output exclusively.

Chapter 2 addresses the Miami-based Spanish- and English-language press. Even before the arrival of the exiles after the Cuban revolution in 1959, Miami was home to the first Spanish-language newspaper in the United States, *Diario las Américas*. *Diario* welcomed the exiles;

Introduction

the Nicaraguan American family who run and own the paper have enjoyed a cordial relationship with Cuban migrants, perhaps due in part to the shared experience of exile. The rapport between members of the Cuban American community and the *Miami Herald*, Miami's best-selling newspaper, has taken a very different turn. Sharp criticism of and commentaries on what incoming waves of Cuban migrants mean for the city, South Florida and the local Anglo community have dismayed those exiles whose primary concern was to have their family and friends start a new life with them in the United States. After initial reluctance, Knight-Ridder, Inc., the company that owned the *Miami Herald* until March 2006, made the strategic decision to accommodate Spanish-language migrants by introducing *El Miami Herald*. In 1999, *El Miami Herald* was revamped, including a name change to *El Nuevo Herald*. The latter section of Chapter 2 scrutinizes conflicts between the *Herald*s and the Cuban American National Foundation (CANF). Finally, a case study of the reporting of one particular incident, the Martí moonlighter story, is examined, and wider emerging issues are discussed.

Miami's Spanish-language radio scene is explored in Chapter 3. The first two sections give an overview of the general purpose of foreign-language radio in the United States and then trace the development of Miami's Spanish-language radio stations. Radio has always been "the Cuban medium," and of all the outlets encountered in the field, radio stations and the journalists employed in them are by far the strongest forces in safeguarding and fortifying an exile mentality. The latter parts of the chapter examine two Spanish-language radio stations in greater depth: Radio Mambí and WQBA 1140 AM Radio Mambí is known as the most belligerent station in the Miami area. The station and the way it operates bear witness to the existence of a tightly knit and highly committed network of journalists (and freelancers) with a strong exile mentality whose focus is to "right" the past. As a station, WQBA has a much younger feeling to it, although opinions in the field were split as to how "Cuban" it is.

The subjectivity of perception in regard to a media output having a Cuban or Mexican or Colombian feel is also a theme that runs through Chapter 4 on television, Cuban Americans, and Hispanic audiences. After a brief overview of the development and anticipated growth of

Introduction

Spanish-language television in the U.S. market, sections two and three investigate the history and strategy of the two largest players in the market: Univision and Telemundo. Univision's Mexican roots are still strongly noticeable today, while Telemundo has developed an alternative tactic that includes a significant percentage of in-house production. The following section critiques the notion of a Hispanic television audience and scrutinizes the conceptualization of Hispanics as a "diaspora in reverse" (Sinclair 2005). As the analysis of Univision's and Telemundo's approaches to programming will demonstrate, it is audience figures and advertising revenue that motivate the rationale of television strategists. The same holds true on a local level. The argument that television is not a unifying tool for the wider Hispanic community is further illustrated by and examined through the aforementioned Elián González saga.

The penultimate chapter addresses trends observed in relation to the internet and the treatment of Cuban American and Cuban issues online. The first section provides a comparative analysis of the experiences of two bloggers, both concerned with Miami-based media, the *Miami Herald* and Radio Mambí respectively. The transnational component that the internet has to offer is explored in the following section by focusing on a Cuban American student organization called *Raíces de Esperanza* (Roots of Hope). With younger Cuban Americans making efforts to comprehend and negotiate what the exilic experience means for their (collective) identity and lives, the switch from Spanish to English as the dominant language of second and third generations is considered in the final section of Chapter 5.

Chapter 6 deals with the interplay of media, memory and power. More specifically, this chapter considers how certain segments of the Cuban American community have used memory discourses in order to promote the continuation of the struggle, *la lucha*, and call for violent actions against the Cuban government. Contrasted against this long-time dominant narrative, contained in many mediated memories, is an innovative approach by younger Cuban Americans in their twenties and thirties. These younger members of the community promote a much more reflective style of dealing with historical and present circumstances, memories, power structures of the exile community and thereby develop a more present-centered awareness of the developments on the island.

Introduction

For those readers with an interest in the rich experience of ethnographic research, Appendix A will provide an enjoyable read. Researching Cuban Miami with a European background was a fresh, invigorating, challenging and never-boring experience. Ethnographic work has strong personal dimension that is often lost in the writing-up of research projects and in the publication process of books and articles. Research is then quickly understood as objective and impersonal. However, writers and scholars, especially in the feminist tradition, have criticized and unraveled the pretense that research is completely devoid of personal interests, emotions and the self-image of the researcher. The appendix aims to make the research process more transparent. Finally, all chapters have been written in a way that allows for individual reading.

1

Place and Space
Miami—Havana, USA?

> Places. Strange and common places. Places you visit and places that you can't go. Distant places and places close to home. Mine is a life in places, and a life out of place.
> —Gustavo Pérez Firmat, *Next Year in Cuba*

A well-known joke in South Florida is that Miami is the closest city to the United States. People have certain expectations when visiting or living in an American city, and in a number of ways, Miami does not align with these characteristics. In the course of the twentieth century, Miami experienced a fast-paced evolution in terms of its spatial, cultural, economic, social and political dimensions. In itself, one might argue, this is not a noteworthy phenomenon. What differentiates Miami from other U.S. cities that have undergone considerable growth in the past century are its unique location in relation to the Caribbean and to Central and South America and the role that one group of migrants, the Cubans, have played in shaping the development of the city.[1]

The Choice of Place

Drawing on Harvey's (1989) seminal work on post-modernity and "time-space compression," Urry (1995, 23) points toward the paradox that characterizes choices of place in the post-modern era; due to ready access to electronic media, communication, production and consumption technologies, place—our physical presence in a certain *locus*—becomes less important. On the other hand, the sensitivity to variations of places increases. In varying degrees, it matters to us on a subjective level where we are and what being in that place feels like, the impact the place has on our daily life and our options regarding free-time and professional activities.

For Cuban migrants, the choice of place is simultaneously coined as a demonstration of a political stance. Some purposefully stayed in Miami or the South Florida area to send a statement back to the island. They were waiting on Fidel Castro's doorstep for things to change, peacefully or otherwise. Others, Cuban Americans wanting to express their dismay at the hardliners, their adamant arguments for the trade embargo and the no-dialogue policy, made a point of moving to another city within the United States or elsewhere.

One interviewee who was initially involved with the counter-revolutionary group *Movimiento Contra-Revolucionario del Pueblo* (MRP) in the early 1960s confirmed this notion: "I told them I'm leaving Miami. I think it is a madhouse and we are making it worse and I don't think we are going to do anything good for Cuba here." Similar sentiments are expressed by Román de la Campa:

> As dissidence and a rejection of the 1950s spread throughout American cities and universities, Miami withdrew into a shell, scandalized, embittered, and at times violent. I felt that it had nothing to say to me. At some point I began to refuse to participate in ritualistic Castro-bashing, and when I returned to Miami with my family during the summer, I opted to stay in dinky Miami Beach hotels that were filled with Latin Americans rather than with my Miami relatives. There was only one place to go after that, even if it broke my parents' heart. They had risked everything to take me out of Cuba, but I could think only about going back [2000, 69].

The above quote hints at the fact that the main entity that defined, influenced and inspired Cuban Miami, in particular Little Havana and *Calle Ocho* (8th Street), would always be Cuba itself. This resonates with Doreen Massey's insightful contemplations in *For Space*. She proposes that space is "the product of interrelations; as constituted through interactions, from the immensity of the global to the intimately tiny." She secondly suggests that we "understand space as the sphere of the possibility

1. Place and Space

of the existence of multiplicity in the sense of contemporaneous plurality; [...] as the sphere of coexisting heterogeneity" (2005, 9). Massey's third characteristic of space is that it is "always under construction" (9). These highly interrelated characteristics of space hold true in the case of Miami. In terms of interrelations between places, Havana is of particular significance.

The Cuban capital, paid tribute to in many literary works as well as the blockbuster *The Lost City* (2005), has served as a model and constant inspiration in the creation and negotiation, or continuous "construction" to use Doreen Massey's (2005) term, of Cuban Miami. After all, the area in question is also referred to as Little Havana and not Little Cuba. Even though De la Campa eventually learned to detest the frequent family trips to Miami, they were a way to get closer to Cuba: "In time it felt as if it was Cuba itself" (2000, 62).

Social and Spatial Aspects of Remembering

It has been argued that significant markers within a landscape, a town, or a city are part of the identification process and of identify formation[2]; the negative image of this can be seen in the iconic absence of the World Trade Center in New York City after the 9/11 attacks and the creation of Ground Zero. As Marita Sturken (2004) suggests, absence or emptiness does not stand for a void in terms of meaning, memories and interpretation. On the contrary, it gives room to (new) negotiations and the exploitation of political agendas that are in themselves set in a contingent field or a context.

In the early years after the revolution, Miami developed certain features and landmarks that were inspired by and at the same time served as a constant reminder of what was lost in Cuba. An example of this is *Calle Ocho* with its Máximo Gómez Park, Cuba and José Martí monuments.[3] The *Calle Ocho* area pays tribute to a lost homeland. It also bears witness to the failed attempts to overthrow Fidel Castro and his allies and to those who suffered and died in the process. It holds the memories and unfulfilled dreams of those who were never able to return to the island.

When covering the Cuban American community, reporters make sure to go to the Versailles Restaurant or the Máximo Gómez Park to capture the mood and opinions of members of the community. Little Havana is an essential tessera in the mosaic that feeds the memories of the Cuban community not based on the island, i.e., people of Cuban descent now living in the United States or other parts of the world. It is also renowned for its meeting places for those who want to further delve into the social construction of memory, history and political discourses. Collective remembering as well as collective forgetting is a central aspect of a community's identity. There is a reciprocal relationship between individual remembering and collective memory. On a conceptual as well as on a very concrete level, memory—just like communication—is linked to community and communal sharing. Significantly for the Cuban American community, often times it is through our view of the past that we make sense of the present.

In addition to the social aspect of remembering, Kuhn, drawing on Edward Casey (1987), emphasizes the significance of different locales in remembering and forgetting. Places contextualize memory; they can serve as triggers or mnemonic pointers. Memory itself can be thought of as a place one can journey, an intangible space one can travel to. In addition, and perhaps paradoxically, the process of forgetting is just as significant within a community as remembering (Connerton 2009). What often seems to be forgotten in Miami is remembered in Cuba. And sometimes the same things are remembered but from a different perspective. The writings and poetry of José Martí are brought into play by Cubans on both sides of the Florida Straits, each utilizing Martí's thoughts to support their line of argument. A recent example of this on the Cuban American side is the recitation of a selection from *Simple Verses* (*Versos Sencillos*) during the last scenes of *The Lost City* (2005).

The City—Embedded in National Structures

Exilic and diasporic groups have often been shown to have strong connections to the wider transnational community. Previous studies have demonstrated viable links between diasporic groups based in

1. Place and Space

different places all over the globe.[4] This leads Georgiou (2006, 9) to suggest that the nation-state embodies a "disruption or restriction" for diasporic communities when moving from the local to the global sphere. The city with its cosmopolitan elements is seen to stand outside of or beyond the reach of the (nation-)state. However, this is a somewhat partial and highly contextualized view. Even though Miami with a dominant Hispanic demographic has experienced a constant flow of incoming migrants, the city is still firmly based within the state and federal system of the United States. From a socio-cultural perspective, there are arguably transnational traits, especially when it comes to fine arts, music and literature. Cuban Americans certainly are part of transnational networks with other Cuban exiles based elsewhere. However, politics and policies, for example legislation on immigration, play too vital a role for many migrants based or coming to Miami to overlook or neglect the importance of the (nation-)state. One main reason for many to come in the first place is the political and/or economic failure of the (nation-)state that used to be their home.

Going further along this line of thought, Silvio Waisbord and Nancy Morris make the point that states

> control the processes and mechanisms of formal citizenship and the movement of people across borders. Mobility of capital and goods, ideas and images, does characterize the current global era, but citizenship, contingent on the lottery of birth, continues to be tied to states. Unprecedented numbers of migrants, refugees, and tourists daily cross political boundaries but states still monopolize the privilege of citizenship rights [2001, xii–xiii].

With regard to the specific situation in Miami, several interviewees made the point that Latin American business people like to come to settle deals in Miami because of the legal reliability and the stable political climate the United States can offer. One interviewee phrased it in the following way:

> This is a very international city and its livelihood depends on us being an international city but it is also very important that we geographically belong to the United States. People take pride in coming here and doing business in the United States. There is a certain level of formality here that you do no not necessarily have in other places [interview, June 2006].

The dichotomy between city and state may well exist in certain areas of life, but in the realms of the economic and the political it is not evident in this case.

Almost since the first arrivals from Cuba in 1959, the U.S. government assigned the Cubans a special status and despite unfulfilled promises during (presidential) election runs, local, regional and national politicians have continuously tried to win over the Cuban American community. After it became apparent that there was not going to be a swift return to the island, there was a growing willingness to engage in U.S. politics, get to the power centers and influence decision makers. This process culminated in the formation of the Cuban American National Foundation (CANF).

Guilt and Questions of Cuban Unity

The exilic experience is of course highly complex. But there are two aspects that often became prevalent during more profound conversations in the field. One was the notion of guilt, the other—related to the first—was the concern of how to relate to Cubans on the island. A feeling of guilt sometimes grasps exiles in Miami; this might especially, but not exclusively, hold true for first generation exiles, those who left family members and friends behind. They live (or lived) with the knowledge of being in a better place—at least from a material, civil and human rights point of view. Nevertheless, material comfort and success should not be taken as sole indicators of happiness and contentment. To be aware of the hardship that others have to endure, to receive messages from loved ones who in a worst case scenario are imprisoned, is extremely challenging to cope with on a day to day basis, especially with very little information coming through. Even though the trade embargo still finds a great deal of support within the Cuban American community, the price people pay on a personal level is high. The awareness that Cubans on the island lack basic goods while having such a rich country, and its natural trading partner, as its northern neighbor, is heartbreaking for some exiles.

Fidel Castro has used the trade embargo to blame the struggling

1. Place and Space

state of Cuba's economy on U.S. policies. To assess whether this holds true or not would go beyond the realm of this project.[5] However, it demonstrates the entanglement between guilt and the relation between Cubans on the island and the Cuban American community in Miami. Over the years, the relationship became more and more challenging and multi-faceted. When attending an undergraduate class on Cuba's future at a Florida university, I noted that the lecturer criticized the terminology of "us" and "them," i.e., Cuban Americans in Miami versus Cubans on the island, in the essays that he had marked the night before class. However, my observation was that this kind of rhetoric was also ubiquitous in class, including contributions made by the academic and the guest speaker.

Later, a conversation on this topic was triggered by my own national background. Even though the German Reunification of 1990 was euphorically celebrated by Germans and people all over the world alike, it became apparent that a sense of being *one* country and of forming *one* people takes years, even decades to develop—and for some it might never come.[6] Similar concerns were shared about re-uniting the exile with Cubans on the island by one informant:

> My personal opinion is that there is a large group of Cuban Americans who privately, if the moment comes when these guys [the Castro brothers and their supporters] are no longer in power ... we do not want these people to come here. We don't. Because [...] same music—but to different words, same food—but here at least we have the spices to make it taste good. Same language—yet the way we call each other and interpret things is a bit different. Very different values and attitudes, very, very different values and attitudes.... [There was a study done] a couple of years ago [...] about the values and attitudes of recently arrived Cubans which [showed] that we are almost two countries now in terms of who we are and how we think. Can that be changed overnight? I don't think so [interview, June 2006].

Echoing the above statement by an informant, there is a feeling of resignation among the Cuban American community. The Castro brothers have won merely by hanging onto power for such a long time. Some younger Cuban Americans have realized that exile organizations should take into account that Cuban Americans based in Miami actually know very little about everyday life in Cuba and a connection between Cuba and its exile community might not come as naturally as many would like to think. Cuban Americans look back on a different history than Cubans who remained on the island. The myth of the early exiles is one example of this.

The Myth of the Historic Exiles

At the beginning of the twentieth century Miami hardly resembled the metropolitan area with its strong business ties to the Southern Hemisphere that it is today. The city and the county it forms part of, Miami-Dade, have experienced a major demographic change, particularly in the second half of the last century.[7] Throughout the nineteenth century, there had been a lively exchange between Cuba and the south of Florida in terms of trade, labor, art and education. Cuba's wealthy were welcome tourists in Miami. However, the Cuban revolution under Fidel Castro brought a new dimension to the migration between the Caribbean island and its northern neighbor. What followed Castro's takeover of Havana in 1959 was the exodus of the higher and middle classes (García 1996). The early migrants were mostly well-educated white professionals who initially held the firm belief that they would return to Cuba within the coming two or three years. After the failed Bay of Pigs Invasion in 1961, it became obvious that a swift return might not be realistic after all.

Practical matters of needing something to live on, having to support oneself and the family in the new country, meant that the Cubans had to reconcile themselves to residing in the United States for the time being. They had to create a place for themselves. This led to the accelerated expansion of Miami. Initially, this expansion was mainly spatial; the geographical area of the city grew. Over the years, however, the incoming Cuban migrants also made a very strong contribution to the commercial life of the city.[8] The historic exiles certainly had something to offer: they were well-educated, hard-working, entrepreneurial and used to success. They had left behind a standard of living that they were keen to achieve on a similar scale on the other side of the Florida Straits. The construction of the exodus and the establishment of the first wave

1. Place and Space

of migrants after 1959 have developed into a myth within the Cuban American community and possibly the wider Hispanic community.[9]

In the field, Cuban Americans of the second and third generation often referred to the positive characteristics of their parents and grandparents without a flicker of hesitation. They also repeatedly assumed the same positive qualities for themselves. While in retrospect living their own myth, the historic exiles were in fact living another one simultaneously: the myth of the American Dream, an accelerated one to be precise, going from "rags to riches" within a matter of years. Several interviewees emphasized the hardship and the willingness to succeed and earn a living:

> The Cubans that came [...] from 1959 [onwards], used to come, of course, with a small bag. It was the only thing that they were permitted to bring. They did not permit to bring nothing at that time. If you were a professional you could not bring the diploma with you at all. No! No! No money at all—you could only have a dime to call when you arrive here [for] someone to pick you up at the airport or something like that. And then, it was a very, you know,... All the Cubans that came at the time were really Cuban middle class and also high class. But [they] came with nothing at all. And they had to work whatever, whatever. They used to go to Homestead [a smaller city in Miami-Dade] to work, just lawyers, physicians, all professionals, working whatever. With the *Miami Herald*, just distributing the newspaper [interview, June 2006].

The initial hardship paid off in the long run. Naturally, these kinds of tales make welcome material for Hollywood.

The Lost City—*Fictitious Reality Made in Hollywood*

The myth of the historic exiles is one dominant story line of *The Lost City* (2005), a film which was directed by Andy García and penned by Cuban writer Guillermo Cabrera Infante.[10] Set in Havana in 1958 and 1959, the main character, Fico Fellove (played by Andy García), owner of one of Havana's legendary music nightclubs, *El Tropico*, refuses to play along with the new forces in power after the downfall of the Batista regime. Leaving his parents, his nightclub and the love of his life behind, Fico boards a plane at Havana Airport. Fico goes to New York City, where he starts working as a dishwasher. After some time he gets to play the piano in the bar, and is now working two jobs simultaneously. One night, the infamous Meyer Lansky (played by Dustin Hoffman), former head of the Havana Mob, comes into the bar to meet Fico and once again offers him a deal.[11] Fico had declined to work with Meyer Lansky in Havana but appears to be happy to make a deal with him now, as Fico's *El Tropico*—opens fifteen months after the meeting to a sell-out crowd. In *The Lost City* (2005), Fico has managed to establish himself as a club owner in the U.S. in approximately two years after his arrival.

Fico Fellove's story is fictitious; some might say it is an idealized and forgiving tale—yet it resounds with the biography of many Cuban Americans. The pavilion of the Cuban Heritage Collection at the University of Miami is named after Robert C. Goizueta, who made generous donations to the collection. The commemorative plaque that summarizes his life reads:

Robert C. Goizueta
November 18, 1931–October 18, 1997

Robert C. Goizueta was born in Cuba in 1931. He attended Colegio de Belén and later Cheshire Academy where he learned English. Majoring in chemical engineering he graduated from Yale University in 1953. The following year on July 4th, The Coca-Cola Company in Cuba hired him as a chemist. In 1960, after the Communists assumed power in Cuba and nationalized businesses, he made a fateful decision. Roberto, his wife Olguita and their children left Cuba for Miami. This experience changed his life and his outlook forever.

A Cuban emigrant seeking freedom, Roberto C. Goizueta personified the *classic* American dream. Within 30 years of leaving Cuba, he was leading an American company that symbolized freedom around the world— The Coca-Cola Company. Throughout his career the creation of value for the company's share owners was his passion. During his 16 years as chairman and chief executive officer, the Company's value increased from $4 billion to $145 billion. Upon his death, Fortune Magazine named The Coca-Cola Company "America's Most Admired Corporation" for a second consecutive year.

Robert C. Goizueta was more than a business leader. He was the ideal citizen who believed that every person who enjoys freedom and opportunity has a duty to cherish, protect and nurture it. He strived to make

1. Place and Space

America stronger, not only through his inspirational and exceptional business leadership, but also through his generous educational and philanthropic contributions.

This community, this nation and our world have been deeply influenced by the life, mission and presence of Robert C. Goizueta.

Mr. Goizueta was exceptionally successful, though this type of story on a smaller scale was a familiar one to the historic exiles.

The Lost City attempts to capture the beauty of Havana, a city lost by the exiles, together with the exciting, flamboyant activities, the cultural heritage and the architectural beauty it is remembered for. Havana is likened to a rose: "It has petals and it has thorns. So it depends on how you grab it. But in the end it always grabs you" (Fico in *The Lost City*). Andy García, who was born in Havana but left the country as an infant, is living proof (among many others) of the "very strong sense of Cuban nationalism through combination of nostalgia and refusal" (De la Campa 2000, 9) that is bred in Miami. Another well-known Cuban American of the same ilk is Gloria Estefan: "[Estefan's and García's] Miami is a community built on the premises that Cuba's prerevolutionary memories are all that matter as far as the nation is concerned, and that they are best kept and reproduced in southern Florida" (De la Campa 2000, 9).

The economic success of the Cuban American community stands in stark opposition to the political inertia of the situation. The fact that all the organizations, funds, and lobby groups were in the end not able to change the status quo on the island causes immense frustrations among some segments of the community. There is a sense of having achieved everything—apart from the one thing that is closest to their hearts. The Castro brothers seem to have won merely due to their continuous existence in the places of power. And just when it looked like the Cuban government was finally going to give in due to the downfall of the Soviet Union, new allies in Latin America and the Far East appeared. Seeing Fidel Castro die would be interpreted as a victory in this involuntary waiting game, even though his death might not change much in the end.

Regrettably, the circumstances have in part resulted in alienation between the exile community and Cubans on the island. Much time and effort is spent in Miami in considering the role of Cuban Americans in a free Cuba, while careful thinkers send out reminders that this process is not about claiming back what was taken away by the government decades ago. Neither is it about taking over and setting things right. Even though the willingness to help and support might be there, history and time spent apart have made this a complex relationship.

Community Relations in Miami

In Miami, Cuban migrants formed the nucleus of a growing Hispanic community. With several Latin American countries facing political turbulence over the past decades, more and more people settled in Miami as political and/or economic refugees. It allowed them to work for Spanish-language employers who were rather tolerant with regard to their English-language skills.[12] It is still the case today that recent migrants can get around the city and conduct their everyday business without having to master basic English.

Although the changing demographics meant growth and prosperity for Miami in the economic and cultural realms, communities that had settled in Miami-Dade before the Cuban revolution—the Anglo and the African American communities—found it a challenge to accept their new neighbors, some of whom were living the American dream without even having to learn English. When it came to finding a job, white employers would often prefer (white) Cubans (Portes and Stepick 1993, 12, 14). African Americans faced a form of double discrimination—by the Anglos and by the incoming Cubans—which led to poor community relations. To some extent, these sentiments are still manifesting today. One Cuban American scholar summarized the relationship between the Cuban American and the African American communities:

> There was a lot of resentment among the Black community when the Cubans started arriving because they displaced the Blacks from a lot of jobs. If an owner had a gas station and had a Black pumping gas he preferred a white Cuban who had probably been a lawyer or a physician or somebody like that and gave him the job than a Black. All the bartenders in South Beach.... So the Blacks were replaced and that caused a lot of

1. Place and Space

tension in the community. That has subsided over the years. I think that there is a latent hostility still there that exists [interview, June 2006].

At the early development stages of the Cuban exile, relations between the Anglo and the Cuban communities were promising. Both sides believed that there would be a fast return to the island. It is also worth noting in this context that, unlike other Hispanic groups, the Cubans had a special status in terms of immigration. They were not considered immigrants, but exiles, with Cuba being at an unsettled political stage and the Cuban Missile Crisis of 1962 turning the island into one of the main fronts of the Cold War. However, these initially positive sentiments came to an abrupt hold with the 1980 Mariel Boatlift.[13] Mariel changed the image of the Cuban American community on a local and on a national scale; it had a negative impact on the image of Miami as a place. The arrival of about 124,000 people in the space of only a few months caused upheaval. Due to Fidel Castro's political shrewdness the admission of regular Cuban citizens, most of them with family based in Florida already, also meant the influx of so-called anti-socials. By November of 1980, approximately 1.4 percent of the Mariel migrants had been arrested and were detained (García 1996, 71). Mariel had long-lasting effects on community relations. Members of the Anglo community started to leave the city and to settle in the north of Florida.

A more recent severe fracture in relations between the Anglo and the Cuban American communities was caused by the case of Elián González, a young boy who together with his mother undertook to cross the Florida Straits on a makeshift raft. His mother died in the attempt to reach U.S. shores; however, Elián survived and was awaited by distant paternal relatives based in Miami. The melee surrounding the child received international media attention (see Chapter 4 for an in-depth analysis of television output and the Elián saga), partly because even the U.S. president at the time, Bill Clinton, got involved. For a large segment of the Cuban American community, Elián was more than a boy whom they did not want to grow up in Fidel's Cuba. He was constructed as a religious symbol.[14] And from an atheist point of view, his return to the island would signify yet another victory by Fidel Castro.

Not everyone who wanted Elián to stay is likely to have experienced life in Cuba after 1959. Similar to the development of Cuban long-distance nationalism in Miami, the firsthand experience of what life on the island is like is available only to some. Others understand Cuba by proxy, passed on through collectively mediated memories and further information available in the public sphere. Nevertheless, wanting Elián to stay seemed a uniting goal for large parts of the community. A number of interviewees even went so far as to distinguish community relations in terms of pre- and post–Elián:

> I think that we have to look at it pre–Elián and after Elián. Pre-Elián, there was a significant belief among the Cuban community that they were accepted, that they were part of the community and so on. Elián was a reality check in which they saw that Americans see things very differently than Cuban Americans. The Cubans wanted to keep Elián, the Americans wanted to send him back. There was a disconnect and many people realized that the perception that the media provided of the Cuban community—conservative, wealthy, Mafia [intransigent—there is a stereotype in the media], that alienated the Cuban American community and made them think, "Well, we are really foreigners here. We are not really part of mainstream America." So I think that there is an alienation that has taken place in the past few years among the Cuban American community, from the Anglo American community [interview, June 2006].

In comparison, Cuban American relations to other subgroups coming together under the Hispanic umbrella have been uneventful. The statements received from interviewees when questioned about this issue are (more than in other cases) influenced by their personal experiences and perception, as there is very little public debate on these matters. Nevertheless, one notion that was repeatedly highlighted was that Cubans had a rather high opinion of themselves, their achievements and their heritage. Non-Cuban Hispanic interviewees confirmed that it can be demanding to deal with and interact with the community in Miami:

> In general, many people find that the Cubans… Their numbers are so overwhelming. It's difficult. Not that you want to fight them but you can't melt into it exactly because you are not of that experience. It also creates its challenges [interview, June 2006].

On the other hand, the strong Spanish-language community that grew around the Cuban nucleus can be an exhilarating and liberating experience, as a non–Cuban Hispanic female informant describes regarding her experience of coming to live in Miami:

1. Place and Space

It was the first time that I was really immersed in a Latin community and I embraced it, I mean I loved it. I loved the fact that you come to Miami and everybody speaks Spanish, you know. When I was a child I remember my dad saying, "Keep it down, don't speak in Spanish in public because people look at you" [interview, October 2006].

Despite the decreasing numbers of the early Cuban migrants, the exilic experience is still a decisive factor for a Cuban American collective identity. This is made explicit to other Spanish-speaking groups in the city. It is associated also with a political attitude that is not matched by other Hispanic groups, for example Mexican Americans:

Cubans, for whatever reason... Well, Cubans still have the Cuba-syndrome about Cuba. The Mexican Americans that come, they don't want to be Mexicans, they want to be Americans, they want to make money and so on. So, the Cubans and Mexicans do not mix very well. Not because there is tension but because they have different views of the world. Mexican Americans are probably more Democratic, Cuban Americans are more Republican and conservative. That divides Cubans and Mexicans [interview, June 2006].

Another distinguishing factor between Cubans and other Hispanics is the issue of immigration. Immigration laws are crucial for most Hispanics, a fact well reflected by Spanish-language media, who feature this issue in various forms on a daily basis. Due to their special status, Cubans have had their "own" legislation, the Cuban Adjustment Act of 1966. Even after modification by the Clinton administration in 1995, it is favorable compared to the legislation and procedures that apply to other migrants. Cuban American interviewees in their early twenties confirmed the points made by older interviewees but were also very eager to emphasize the positive points they associated with living in a vibrant Hispanic community:

The question is where do the Cubans lie in solidarity with the rest of the Hispanics, especially in the issue of immigration. One could argue that the reason why we have Cubans in the House and Cubans in the Senate and lots of prosper in Miami is because of the fact that we have laws that somehow favor our prosperity and in that sense allow us to achieve these things. Then again, we are all hard-working, not to discredit the hard work of the many individuals in this community. I would not say that there is any animosity between different Hispanic groups. There might be—like within any heterogeneous society—points of friction. I think one of the great things about Miami is that you can hear so many different Spanish dialects being spoken [interview, June 2006].

Even though there might not be any animosity, neither is there an overwhelming sense of Hispanic belonging or a sense of a Hispanic community in Miami. With one group being so present and strongly represented in the media as well as politically, there is no need to embrace pan–Hispanic sentiments for the majority. At the same time, this could also be read as an indication for the awareness of national belonging; i.e., it does in fact make a significant difference whether someone has Mexican, Cuban, Colombian or Venezuelan roots.

2

Spanish- and English-Language Newspapers in Miami

> We realize that many are put off by the fact that we are constantly talking about Cuba. But what else are we going to talk about? What else are we going to write about if we have a responsibility to the cause?... We realize that many get upset when you talk to them about Cuba. But what do we care? We do not know how to talk about anything else, nor do we want to talk about anything else.
> —Tabloid journalist, quoted in Cristina María García, *Havana USA*

Miami's newspapers are themselves the origin of many good stories. This chapter traces and scrutinizes the development of the Miami-based press in the wake of and after the Cuban revolution in 1959. The aim here is not to give a comprehensive history of the main players involved, but to look at how Miami's local English- and Spanish-language press has dealt with and interacted with incoming migrants and the evolving Cuban American community. Smaller case studies and noteworthy incidents will be utilized to illustrate wider issues at stake. The press, both in individual articles and as an institution, provides an excellent example of the dynamics that characterize Miami's community relations, the influence and power of the Cuban American community, and the complex and at times contradictory interests, agendas and ethical concerns that come into play.

The chapter is narrative-driven and gives ample room to the voices encountered in the field. The first section considers the role of *Diario las Américas* in Miami's media landscape. The market is dominated by the two editions of the *Herald*, the English-language *Miami Herald* and its Spanish-language counterpart, *El Nuevo Herald*, to which the second section is dedicated. The *Miami Herald* especially has had a challenging relationship with parts of the Cuban American community. One recent example of this is the Martí case, which will be examined in more detail. The chapter ends with a consideration of the underlying issues in terms of journalistic ethics, professional identity and reflection on the exile community.

Cuban Writings in the United States

The development of the press in Miami illustrates the changes taking place within the Cuban American community as well as the demographic modifications that Miami has experienced over the past five decades. However, it is worth noting that Fidel Castro's accession to power did not trigger the development of Spanish-language or bilingual publications as such. The United States and the State of Florida in particular have had long-established relations with Cuba, for example in terms of trade, migration and cultural exchanges. Furthermore, relations were also established on an intellectual level, as shown by Rodrigo Lazo in *Writing to Cuba: Filibustering and Cuban Exiles in the United States* (2005). Lazo presents a succinct analysis of mid-nineteenth century Cuban writers who left the island, which was at the time under Spanish rule, to establish themselves in the U.S. and reflect on future options for Cuba from abroad. The result was the establishment of more than seventy newspapers during the nineteenth century. The papers varied significantly in size, duration of publication and the political outlook they promoted for Cuba's future. Nevertheless they bear witness to the increasing relations between the United States and its small neighboring island in the south:

> The development of newspaper publication by Cubans in the United States can be traced back to a long-standing two-way flow of economic, political and cultural exchange between the United States and the island. U.S. travellers and investors made their way to Cuba, and the island's intellectual

2. Spanish- and English-Language Newspapers in Miami

and economic elite reciprocated in kind. In the first half of the nineteenth century, the U.S. became a major buyer of Cuban sugar and coffee as well as provider of imports for the island [Lazo 2005, 7–8].

The *periodiquitos*, as they are referred to in Miami, newspapers of varying sizes, written by members of the Cuban exile community, therefore follow a long tradition of Cuban writing in the United States. A selection of *periodiquitos* can still easily be found in restaurants, cafés and shops in Little Havana today. The Cuban Heritage Collections at the University of Miami hosts the largest collections of *periodiquitos*, among them also publications from Cubans exiled outside of the U.S. In an annotated bibliography, Esperanza de Varona (1987), who serves as chair of the Cuban Heritage Collection, emphatically summarizes the content and importance of the *periodiquitos* in the following words:

> This bibliography is more than a mere listing of periodicals published by an exile group during a specific period of time and collected by a university. It is a chronicle of the hopes and aspirations of the Cuban people in exile, of the struggle to maintain a unity of purpose, of the need to preserve, add to, and transmit cultural heritage. These periodicals are heroic not only in terms of the financial hardships which most of them have had to surmount in order to be published, but also with regard to the very nature of the exile soul striving to be one again, someday, in a free Cuba [xiii].

The *periodiquitos* go beyond the political and polemical realm and cover a great number of topics, including literature, finance and religion, everyday life (in Cuba as well as in host societies) and sporting activities. They are of particular importance for those Cuban Americans who prefer to read and write in Spanish. The fact that the majority of the *periodiquitos* were and are kept afloat through advertising income, as well as the investment of the contributors' own capital, demonstrates the strong conviction of Cuban Americans of the need to make a contribution to the public sphere—even if it is limited in duration and scope (De Varona 1987). An in-depth analysis of the *periodiquitos* would go well beyond the limits of this volume; however, it is worth keeping in mind that these periodicals are easily accessible to Cuban Americans based in Miami and form part of some people's media consumption patterns.

Another distinctive backdrop worth keeping in mind when looking at the interactions between the Cuban American community and the press in Miami is the experience Cubans had with this medium before leaving the island. The press, including newspapers, magazines, bulletins, was well-developed in Cuba:

> During the 1950's [sic], the Cuban people were probably among the most informed in the world, living in an uncharacteristically large media market for such a small country. Cubans had a choice of 58 daily newspapers during the late 1950's [sic], according to the UN statistical yearbook. Despite its small size, this placed Cuba behind only Brazil, Argentina, and Mexico in the region [Cuba Transition Project 2008].

An example of a major success story about a publishing business brought by a Cuban family from the island into exile is told by Cristina Saralegui (1998). Her grandfather, Francisco Saralegui, became known as the Paper Czar, as he supplied paper to all of Cuba's newspapers and presses (Saralegui 1998, 12–13). He also co-owned *Publicaciones Unidades, S.A. (PUSA)* and, together with his sons, the family became more and more involved in the editorial side of the business. The name Saralegui became associated with famous publications such as *Bohemia, Carteles* and *Vanidades*:

> It is important to note that when my family bought *Vanidades*, the magazine had a circulation of 17,000. When we left Cuba in July 1960, circulation had risen to over 170,000 copies per edition.
> *Vanidades* emigrated from Cuba with my family, not as a material possession, since Castro did not allow us to take anything from our country, but merely as a piece of paper registering the name and ownership of the magazine. But there was also the spirit and vision of my father and uncle, who were immediately ready to start over [Saralegui 1998, 21].

The Saraleguis are an example of the affluent and industrious Cuban families coming to Miami in the 1960s. The historic exiles had the resources and know-how to set up new businesses in South Florida. Given the cultural capital and the extraordinary circumstances the exiles found themselves in, demand for local, regional, national and international news was high.

One Miami-based afternoon newspaper, which one could almost suspect had been waiting for the Cubans to arrive, is *Diario las Américas*. Today, *Diario* still makes a significant contribution to the Spanish-language media scene in Miami.

2. Spanish- and English-Language Newspapers in Miami

Diario las Américas

The development of *Diario las Américas*, the first Spanish-language paper in the United States of America, is closely linked with Cuban history and with the Cuban exile. A common misunderstanding in Miami is therefore that *Diario* is Cuban-owned, but it was in fact founded and still is in the hands of the Nicaraguan Aguirre family. Horacio Aguirre and his brother Francisco, started publishing on July 4, 1953, the U.S. Independence Day. Only a few weeks later, on July 26 that same year, Fidel Castro and his guerrillas launched their first attempt to take over Cuba. Alejandro Aguirre, Horacio's son and current deputy editor and publisher, sees this as a significant development for the paper: "Almost from day one, the coverage of Cuba and the Cuban revolution has played an important part in this newspaper" (Alejandro Aguirre, pers. com., June 2006). However, the proximity to Cuba and the stable relations between Cuba and South Florida in the early 1950s were not the main reason for choosing Miami as the location for the paper. When looking for a sensible place to start a Spanish-language paper, the Aguirre brothers chose Miami because they anticipated that, with increasing aviation mobility, its geographical position would make Miami a port of entry for many Latin Americans travelling to the United States. The Aguirres' prediction turned out to be right, but the development of Miami into the Mecca of the Cuban exile has had an even stronger effect. Alejandro Aguirre confirms this:

> Certainly things changed when in 1959 Fidel Castro overthrew the Batista regime in Cuba. You had a mass exodus in Cuba, most of which came to Miami. It changed Miami radically, and it changed us as well because we had to cover very closely what was going on in this community and in Cuba. That was not just for the benefit of the Cubans here in Miami but also because everything that was going on in Cuba has had continental ramifications in other countries—the exporting of the revolution to other countries in the 1970s and the civil wars in Latin America in the 1980s, a lot of these events can be tied back to the situation in Cuba. That was something that changed our paper [pers. com., June 2006].

Diario Las Américas comes out six days a week, Tuesdays to Sundays. It is an afternoon paper with all articles written in Spanish. However, the editorials are translated into English for the online version, which can be found at http://www.diariolasamericas.com.

Diario's brief mission statement under its title reads "*Por la Libertad, la Cultura y la Solidaridad Hemisférica*" (Dedicated to Freedom, Culture and Solidarity in the Americas). According to Alejandro Aguirre the paper aims to promote "solidarity between the different hemispheres and serves as a bridge between people in the United States and in South America." Its focus is "very inter–American and international" (pers. com., June 2006). This purpose is reflected on the title page and in the first section of the paper, with a mix of local, state, U.S. and international news, very often from Latin American countries, Cuba and the Caribbean, including sports. Section A of *Diario* also includes opinion pieces, again with a very international focus. Section B focuses on Miami and Florida and also carries more specialized articles on local events, financial news, health, science, human interests, social happenings, local sports and the like.

In contrast to other news providers in Miami, *Diario las Américas* welcomed the arrival of the Cubans in Miami. The affiliation with members of the Cuban American community hold strong today; older and more conservative Cuban Americans prefer the *Diario* to its Spanish-language opponent, *El Nuevo Herald*. The paper is perceived as the publication of *el exilio histórico*—the historic exiles. To gain and maintain this level of trust and loyalty among its readers, *Diario* has had to tread carefully throughout the years:

> In the highly politicized milieu of the Cuban exiles, objective news was hard to come by; the émigrés trusted the *Diario* to give them just that. While the publishers were clearly anti–Castro, the *Diario* straddled Little Havana's political fence, careful not to side with any particular fraction in the exile community, and it provided a forum for the discussion of opposing political views [García 1996, 104–5].

The strong links between the Aguirre family and the Cuban American community can easily be traced. Horacio and Francisco Aguirre, the founders of *Diario*, were themselves exiled from Nicaragua after the coup d'état of former president Somoza against his successor Leonardo Arguello Barreto in 1947. Therefore, the Aguirre family shares the experience of having to leave one's country with the Cubans in Miami. In

2. Spanish- and English-Language Newspapers in Miami

separate interviews, both Alejandro Aguirre and his sister, Helen Aguirre Ferré, spoke very compassionately of the Cuban American community, the experience of loss and their new life in the United States. When asked if they were tired of talking about Cuban issues, both siblings answered with a firm "no" and expressed their sympathy for the experiences the Cuban people had to go through since 1959. Alejandro Aguirre summarized his thoughts on the Cuban exile in the following words:

> Everything that was once black is now white; everything that was once good is now bad. And everybody has to smile for the camera. All of a sudden [the Cuban exiles] had to go to a place that was willing to accept them but that was totally different. They had to adapt, they had problems with language. But they were highly educated, which was a tremendous help. But all of sudden all that was important to them was literally pulled out from under them. So there is a tremendous sense of loss, there is this tremendous vacuum, there is this tremendous void that they tried to fill here. It only happened mentally. They had to re-create that sense of country and home here. It is natural that they were and are interested in what is going on in Cuba. There was a time in Miami when 80 percent of the Hispanic population was Cuban. As much as I can understand the other 20 percent saying "Enough," did they have any doubt if it was 80 percent Columbians that it was going to be all Columbian news? Be real [pers. com., June 2006].

Sentiments of appreciation are mutual here. During a board meeting of the *Amigos* (Friends) of the Cuban Heritage Collection at the University of Miami in October 2008, it was announced that Horacio Stuart Aguirre, a brother of Alejandro and Helen, was going to take over as chairman of the board. The *Amigos* present at the meeting were pleased to hear this piece of news and one *Amigo* (and former chairman of the Friends of the Cuban Heritage Collection) made a spontaneous statement of how delighted he was to see a member of the Aguirre family, "who has done so much for the Cubans here in Miami," take on this position. Horacio Stuart Aguirre is stepping in the footsteps of his father, Horacio Aguirre, who was a founding member of the Cuban Heritage Collection.

Even though the Aguirre family and *Diario las Américas* have always been strongly associated with news on Cuba and news for the

Cuban American community in Miami, the paper does not want to be limited in this respect. Alejandro Aguirre is not apprehensive about the strong associations with this particular group, but confirms that the community can be very demanding:

> Sometimes you have to remind people that we [as a newspaper] have other things because there is other population in Miami. There always has been, but even more are here now, if you look at the figures. We have to remind people that we have to bring news from other countries as well because that was always the core mission, to be an inter–American newspaper. We do not want to be limited to one area, especially here in Miami, but [Cuba and the Cuban-American community] is just one of the areas we cover [pers. com., June 2006].

In one way Helen Aguirre Ferré agrees with her brother on this. The paper would be misled by putting too great an emphasis on Cuba given Miami's current demographic make-up. As opinion page editor and in her role of overseeing the local news section, she is not tired of discussing and including articles about Cuban issues per se. However, over the years she has changed her way of reporting and selecting news stories about Cuba and Cuban Americans in the States:

> Unless there is something new to tell, we can't afford to do same old, same old. We have to give people reason to buy the newspaper. I do get very tired of the same old, same old from some writers who have gotten too predictable in what they are going to say. I do not even have to read [the article] and I can tell where it's going. I can just tell by the headline [pers. com., June 2006].

However, the Aguirre siblings drew different pictures as to where the real strength and the mission of the paper lie. In contrast to the emphasis on international matters that her brother put forward, Helen Aguirre Ferré portrays local and state news as one of the most important elements of the publication:

> Our audience of *Diario* is Hispanic, the majority is Cuban. To me it is Cuban American today because it is a younger ... you know, time has moved on. Those who read our newspaper and are 50 years old are hyphenated Americans, which is why I try to put a lot of focus on state and local issues whenever possible because even though they will always have a strong interest in their cultural heritage, invariably everything is rooted locally to where they live. Their community is in South Florida, even

2. Spanish- and English-Language Newspapers in Miami

though their curiosity, their passion and their heart might be in Cuba. But when push comes to shove, this is where they live, this is where they vote, this is where their parents are buried, and where their children are going to school [pers. com., June 2006].

These statements by Alejandro Aguirre and Helen Aguirre Ferré shed light on the difficulties faced by their paper. People who could be classified as historic exiles, *Diario*'s prototypical readers, are ageing and dying. Younger members of the community have a hyphenated identity and possibly define themselves as more American than Cuban, with English being their preferred language when reading a newspaper or consuming any type of media.

The image of *Diario las Américas* as the Cuban paper has to some extent become more of a drawback than an advantage when it comes to recruiting new readers—be it in the Cuban American community or among other Hispanic groupings. Decision-makers at *Diario* are aware of this image and of the disadvantages that being labeled as "the Cuban paper" brings. Although according to Alejandro Aguirre there has never been an editorial decision to consciously move away from Cuban topics, *Diario*'s marketing department thinks it necessary to strongly accentuate the "non-Cuban" content of the paper. Furthermore, the paper's online version aims to brighten the slightly stale image of the publication:

I am trying to get the online product to move away from the newspaper. I want it to go through its own natural evolution and forget about the newspaper. And if it means that the website and the newspaper compete against each other—so be it. But it may also mean that the web edition goes into something totally different and evolves into a totally different product. We will utilize common resources where it makes sense but I do not want to tie one to the other because anything that is online needs to take advantage of all of the market forces and technological forces very, very quickly and that is something the print press cannot do [Alejandro Aguirre, pers. com., June 2006].

The inter–American focus on the one hand and the local and regional connection to Miami and Florida on the other are also reflected in the structure of the paper. Apart from the title page, international news and local/regional news, international sports and local/regional sports are not combined in one larger news (or sports) section but kept completely separate. Despite the colored pictures on the title pages of sections A and B, the layout of the articles and impractically long pages give the paper an old-fashioned feel. One informant described the paper as "a dinosaur" and "an anachronism" (interview, June 2006). Another informant commented:

> I wish *Diario Las Américas* had been smart enough to modernize. Because they are Nicaraguans, not Cubans, but the whole family have been so loyal to us, all along. If they were a modern newspaper.... The joke in Miami is [because *Diario* put on tomorrow's date] it is the newspaper that is published today with tomorrow's date and yesterday's news—which is true! [interview, January 2007].[1]

Diario held on to its mission of being a pan–American newspaper and continued to be a paper of Latin America even when its circulation in the U.S., for example in New York City, in some places in New Jersey and on the West Coast, was on the increase. The fact that *Diario* did not take advantage of these emerging markets within the United States has been the ground for endless rumors in Miami. *Diario* is a "mystery to many people and there are all kinds of theories as to why it is the way it is" (interview, January 2007). A common belief is that the two founders and owners, brothers Francisco and Horacio Aguirre, could never agree on what the mission of the paper should be and for that reason the scope of the paper always remained rather limiting and limited, as one interviewee (January 2007) explains:

> Some people say that [*Diario las Américas*] gets money from the federal government, that it is subsidized. I am not sure if that is the case; I would not be surprised if it was. Some people say that the two brothers who own the newspaper have always been at odds as to what the paper's mission should be. One of them [Francisco] lives in Washington, he has always met ... he's always been in some kind of diplomatic mission. That is the crowd he hangs around with. And he is not interested in voter issues, or Miami issues and stuff like that. He's apparently the majority owner of the newspaper. He lives over there, his family live over there. The other brother [Horacio] is the one who lives in Miami. He is now an aging man, probably no longer in direct charge of the newspaper. But I think there has always been this theory that these two brothers have been at odds as to the mission of the newspaper and that has really prevented the paper from growing, developing, becoming a modern paper, competitive and so on. And there are many other theories, including CIA-related theories and stuff like that which I think are rather hard to believe.

2. Spanish- and English-Language Newspapers in Miami

Francisco Aguirre died in September 2008. His obituary confirmed his close relationship to the American intelligence community, though Francisco's son is keen to point out that his father never worked for the CIA (Valdez 2009). So far, no noteworthy changes can be observed with regard to the direction and the mission of *Diario las Américas* since Francisco Aguirre's death. But regardless of whether *Diario* will undergo a significant make-over in the years to come, catching up with the local competition in Miami will not be an easy task.

A further challenge the paper was facing at the time of research was its distribution cost. Not being the dominant Spanish-language newspaper in Miami but having to cover almost the same geographic area as *El Nuevo Herald* to stay in the competition made distribution a more difficult task for *Diario* than for its competitor with higher circulation figures. *El Nuevo* can make use of the same distribution channels and arrangements as its English-language sister paper, while economies of scale do not work in this way for *Diario*. Supermarkets and little shops around the University of Miami campus in Coral Gables, for example, would always have copies of the *Miami Herald* and *El Nuevo Herald*, but *Diario las Américas* was much harder to get hold of. However, several interviewees also commented on the fact that *Diario* could also be found on newsstands in Washington, D.C., and in metropolitan areas of South America. While that confirms the ambitious, pan–American approach, it does not make *Diario* more attractive to local advertisers in Miami, as Diario's publisher Alejandro Aguirre has to acknowledge: "I have advertisers coming up to me, saying 'It is very nice that you sell your newspaper all the way up in Washington but it does not sell me anything in my supermarket'" (pers. com., June 2006).

Despite these difficulties, Alejandro Aguirre remains positive regarding the future of *Diario las Américas*—in print and online: "I am not worried of the newspaper as an agenda-setting editorial type of organization. I think we will always be there if we play our cards right" (pers. com., June 2006). This outlook could prove to be far too optimistic, given the decline in circulation figures of the paper. No reliable circulation figures could be found for *Diario las Américas*, but even at the time of field work it had gone down to 57,000, according to Alejandro Aguirre. It is likely that the current economic climate has led to further decline. In terms of circulation figures, things are looking a bit better for *El Nuevo Herald*, *Diario*'s main Spanish-language competitor.

The Miami Herald—El Miami Herald— El Nuevo Herald

El Nuevo Herald came into existence through an unusual process of transformation. In 1999 the Spanish-language *Herald* was renamed *El Nuevo Herald*. Both the English- and the Spanish-language *Herald*s have had challenging experiences with the Cuban American community and the Cuban American National Foundation (CANF) in particular. The challenges and the difficulty of serving a diverse readership experienced by *Diario las Américas* also resonate with other newspapers in the city. What the *Herald*s had to face, however, was on a different scale.

The *Miami Herald*

While owners and staff at the *Diario* were happy to welcome the exiles as readers (and as reporters joining their newsroom), other groups based in the city of Miami and the county it forms part of, Miami-Dade, had reservations regarding the new arrivals. These were shared and reflected by Miami's largest English-language paper: the *Miami Herald*. Founded in 1903 as the *Miami Evening Record*, the paper was renamed on December 1, 1910 (*Miami Herald* 2009). According to its website, the Miami Herald Media Company (which comprises the *Miami Herald* as well as *El Nuevo Herald*) had 1,165 full-time members of staff and 244 part-timers in 2009. So far, the *Miami Herald* has won 20 Pulitzer Prizes.

The *Miami Herald* took a relatively long time to find ways to accommodate the early exiles and the later arrivals in the 1970s and 1980s. It therefore comes as no surprise that, in contrast to the harmonious relationship the *Diario* has with Hispanic groups in Miami, and the Cubans, in particular, the *Miami Herald* and its Spanish-language counterpart, *El Nuevo Herald*, cannot look back on a cordial connection with the Cuban American community. For a number of reasons, the two publi-

2. Spanish- and English-Language Newspapers in Miami

cations and their former corporate parent, Knight-Ridder, encountered several sites of conflict with the Cuban American community over the past decades. In June 2006 Knight-Ridder was bought by the McClatchy Company, "the third-largest newspaper company in the United States" (The McClatchy Company 2006).

The change of ownership did not bring a significant change to the strained relationship between some members of the Cuban American community and the *Miami Herald* and *El Nuevo Herald*. Despite an acceptance of the early exiles, the *Miami Herald* had not been in favor of a continuing intake of Cubans in the 1960s and 1970s. Like a majority of its prototypical readers, the *Miami Herald* had opposed the freedom flights:

> Editorials in *The Miami Herald* argued that the number of people wanting to leave Cuba was infinite, and the U.S. simply could not accommodate them all. While the editors celebrated the rapid economic adjustment of the Cuban exiles—whom they called the "cream of the nation"—they voiced the widespread concern that Cuba's cream had already been skimmed, and that the continuing influx of lower-class Cubans presented an economic burden to the United States [García 1996, 45].

The *Herald*'s unemotional and Anglo-biased analyses of the situation have been a seed of discontent for members of the Cuban American community throughout the decades. Editorials similar in tone were published once again during the Mariel Boatlift in 1980. With emotions running high on Floridian shores as well as in Cuba, the Cuban Americans based in Miami became fully aware of the opinions the *Herald* was expressing at the time:

> As the voice of the Anglo establishment, it [the *Miami Herald*] considered the Mariel exodus a serious double threat: first, as an economic cataclysm, given the depressed state of local industry and the negative impact of the inflow on Miami's status as a tourist destination; and second, as a direct threat to the establishment power structure, given the addition of many thousands to an already uncomfortably large Cuban population [Portes and Stepick 1993, 27].

The Cuban Americans already based in the city did not regularly get a chance to counter such arguments in the press, as most exile organizations were initially concerned with what was going on in their homeland, not with local politics in Miami-Dade.

Cuban Americans and the Miami Media

El Nuevo Herald

Up to the mid–1980s, the *Miami Herald* was still only published in English and leading figures at the Knight-Ridder Corporation, the owner of the paper at the time, were not very enthusiastic about adding a language, as the following anecdote recounted by an executive of the Knight-Ridder Corporation illustrates:

> So we made a bet in 1960 [about English becoming the dominant language] in Miami as a large number of Cuban refugees came in following Castro's takeover. That didn't happen as fast we thought it would. We belatedly started in our business a Spanish edition called *El Miami Herald*. It's a very expensive proposition for us, but it has helped us gain acceptance and circulation in the Hispanic community. We think it is important to us and important to them that *The Herald* be available in both Spanish and English. We circulate that Spanish section in conjunction with *The Miami Herald*, so that we believe that, by virtue of having the two together, we'll eventually move back toward the ultimate utilization of English as the primary language [interview quoted in Portes and Stepick 1993, 15].

The executive must have lost his bet; Miami is a bilingual city, and several interviewees confirmed that not being able to speak Spanish might be detrimental to one's professional success in the city.

Although the establishment of *El Miami Herald* in 1976 was a noteworthy event, as it was the "first Spanish section in a major American newspaper" (García 1996, 105), it did not bring the *Miami Herald* the increase in subscriptions and sales the management was ultimately looking for. In 1987, *El Miami Herald* was assigned a make-over and was relaunched as *El Nuevo Herald*. Susana Barciela, a Cuban American who now works as an editorial writer for the *Miami Herald*, remembers:

> My first job was in marketing and I worked on the launch of *El Nuevo Herald* because it was completely taken to a different level. That was in 1987.... [The big] business issue was the question whether to rename it and have it as a supplement to the *Herald* or whether it should be a separate paper. They [strategic management] were too afraid that it would minimize the sale of the English-language paper. I think that hampered *El Nuevo* for quite a while [pers. com., June 2006].

From 1987 onwards, the revamped version, which was aptly named *El Nuevo Herald*, was still a supplement of its English language sister paper

2. Spanish- and English-Language Newspapers in Miami

the *Miami Herald*. They began to separate in 1997. Humberto Castelló, executive editor of *El Nuevo Herald*, recounts:

> Essentially, 1999 was the year in which *El Nuevo Herald* became a paper that could stand on its own, with its own personality, independence and everything. It has been a success. Without the Cubans, there would not have been the need to have a publication at that time [pers. com., June 2006].

Knight-Ridder and the *Herald* were arguably slow to react to the demographic changes of Miami and Dade County, partly because—like the Cubans themselves—many Anglos were still under the impression and possibly hoping that the Cubans would return to the island in the near future. And if that was not the case, Cubans were expected to learn English and eventually use it as their first language. As it turned out, nobody was likely to return to the homeland. Quite the contrary: with the *balseros* (rafters) crisis of the early 1990s, more Cubans arrived in South Florida.[2]

But despite a growing Hispanic community and increasing circulation figures of the Spanish-language paper, *El Nuevo Herald* continued to be treated as an "unwanted child." The paper receives fewer resources than its English-language counterpart, and Spanish-language journalists receive a lower salary than those working for the *Miami Herald*. Susana Barciela points out that *El Nuevo* "does an incredible job considering how few resources they have" (June 2006). Despite highly committed reporters at *El Nuevo*, many of them Cuban and Cuban American, the English-language paper remains the better funded one, with more resources and more opportunities for staff. These differences can be explained to some extent by circulation figures, where the *Miami Herald* clearly outpaces *El Nuevo Herald*.[3]

Nevertheless, like Alejandro Aguirre of *Diario las Américas*, the executive editor of *El Nuevo Herald,* Humberto Castelló, is positive regarding the future of his paper. *El Nuevo* is to remain a local paper, targeting readers in Miami, while reflecting the Latin American reality. Castelló confirms: "This is a city run by different people from different countries and most of them were born in those countries. They are interested in what is happening in Miami but also in what is happening in their countries. Talking about events in Bogotá is as natural here as it is in Bogotá. But we are a local newspaper and we cover all the local news for our readers" (pers. com., June 2006). Satisfying such diverse readership continues to be a challenge for *El Nuevo* but Castelló strongly opposes the idea of quotas for news stories:

> I don't believe in that [referring to quotas]. I believe in news and what is interesting for the reader. It is a reality that 50 percent of the readers are of Cuban origin. You have to "take care" of them; they have a particular interest in what is happening in their country. That is the reason we have a Cuba page. But the reason we have a big Latin American section is because of all the others. If you see our front page every day, it looks like a schizophrenic newspaper. The big headline is probably about Bogotá, Caracas, Havana not Miami. That is the reason, and it is very successful [pers. com., June 2006].

Humberto Castelló's concern with "taking care" of Cuban readers stems—at least to some degree—from a series of events that took place in the 1980s and 1990s. During these two decades, the Cuban American community developed into the most influential, resourceful and dynamic group among the Hispanics based in the city. When scrutinizing these events, it becomes apparent that the presence and continuous arrival of Cubans in South Florida impacted hugely the development of the press. After all, the Cuban American community was a market that could not be neglected and was also a political force to reckon with, demanding a forum for themes and issues important to them.

The *Heralds* and the Cuban American National Foundation

The history of the *Miami Herald* in the 1980s and early 1990s is intertwined with the involvement of the Cuban American National Foundation (CANF) and one of its most prominent founding members, Jorge Más Canosa. Más Canosa has been described as "industrious and hardworking" (Bardach 2002, 135), and his achievements certainly prove him worthy of these adjectives. His first job in the U.S. was as a dishwasher in a hotel. By the time of his death, in November 1997, his wealth was estimated to be over $400 million (135). A committed and ingenious anti–Castrista, he realized it could be worthwhile to employ political, i.e., non-paramilitary, means to work against the people in power estab-

2. Spanish- and English-Language Newspapers in Miami

lishment in Havana. In 1981, he therefore set up CANF. The foundation was modeled after AIPAC, the American Israel Public Affairs Committee, a highly influential lobbying group in the United States. Más Canosa, and with him CANF, became powerful players in Miami as well as in Washington, D.C., in the 1980s and early 1990s.[4]

A staff writer for *El Nuevo/Herald* remembers the power of CANF in the following way:

> It was a dominant group of friends, influential people like Jorge Más Canosa who controlled, not only politically, the trends and the attitudes of many Cubans. But also he wanted to control what the media said, about Cubans and about them, so it was a very uncomfortable situation. Even to the point where the vending machines of the newspaper in the streets were vandalized with red ink. They also ran ads on the public buses that said "I don't believe *El Nuevo Herald*." That was a big campaign against us. I think it was a very sour situation and when you wrote about them, you had to be very careful. Anything that set out a problem with them ... sometimes you had to take a copy of an article or column to the in-house attorney and he would recommend this and that [interview, June 2006].[5]

By the time *El Nuevo* was launched in 1987, relations between the *Miami Herald* and CANF were already strained. The difference in funding between the English and the Spanish-language paper is also reflected by the importance assigned to each respectively, as a member of CANF indicates:

> The conflict between the Cuban community and the *Herald* reached its peak when, after the resignation of one of the directors of the Cuban-American National Foundation, the newspaper started speculating, without basis of fact, about internal division of the organization. We decided to write an open letter. Jorge Mas Canosa [...] brought a writer from Washington who wrote the letter in an afternoon, and it was published, as a paid announcement, the following day. The *Herald* never expected that we Cubans would do something like that! There was a meeting in which, in fact we considered organizing a boycott against the newspaper. Richard Capen, the editor, called to complain, but, faced with the threat of a massive boycott, the newspaper relented and has changed course one hundred and eighty degrees in recent months. We've told Capen that it does not matter what the *Nuevo Herald* [...] publishes[...]. Much more important is what is published in English, which is read nationwide. The *Herald* sometimes plays a double game, publishing articles in English that do not appear in Spanish and vice versa [Portes and Stepick 1993, 15].

Cuban Americans and the Miami Media

This criticism of the *Herald* and *El Nuevo Herald* surfaced on several occasion during field work. Readers of both papers do not understand why some articles find their way into the sister paper while others do not. Although some readers might be aware that the papers now work independently and even that *El Miami Herald* was never intended to be a complete translation of its English-language sister paper, a feeling remains that there are "dubious" reasons that some stories never make their way to the other newsroom. One interviewee suggested the role of a liaison editor to solve this issue, which could even have a positive effect on community relations and lead to a greater understanding between English- and Spanish-language readers. Then again, this outlook might be too optimistic. As the following analysis of the Martí moonlighter story will show, more than a liaison officer might be needed to let the two papers cooperate successfully. It is these difficulties that are, at least in part, responsible for certain articles only appearing in one language. I did not encounter any substantiated argument for a coherent strategy of excluding certain information from specific groups.

With the death of Jorge Más Canosa in November 1997, CANF lost much of its influence in Washington and in Miami. As with all organizations of this type, CANF did not (and does not) speak for everyone in the community but was in fact known for a stringent approach regarding all dealings with Fidel Castro, including no leniency regarding the trade embargo imposed by the U.S. administration. Still, the relationship between many Cuban Americans, the *Miami Herald*, and *El Nuevo Herald* remains an uneasy one. Despite sharing the same building and being part of the same company, the divide between *El Nuevo Herald* and the *Miami Herald* runs deep, as the following story of *El Nuevo* journalists working for the Martís illustrates.

The Martí Moonlighter Story

Miami is a great news city. There is always something to report. It can also be a challenging place for a journalist, especially if the news you bring is not appreciated. The Martí moonlighter story includes a series of events surrounding Radio and TV Martí and both of the *Herald* newspapers. Radio and TV Martí is a government-funded broadcaster

2. Spanish- and English-Language Newspapers in Miami

that targets the people of Cuba. The seed of the controversy was an article written by a *Miami Herald* staff writer named Oscar Corral. The case will be examined in detail below, as it is instructive on several levels. It raises questions about journalistic independence and ethics and the role of Miami media organizations and Miami-based journalists in relation to Cuba. It also gives an indication of the split that exist between the *Miami Herald* and *El Nuevo Herald*. It is furthermore insightful regarding how the *Herald*s relate to communities in different manners and at times practice different forms of journalism.

Oscar Corral, a staff reporter for the *Miami Herald*, had been working on a series of stories investigating how taxpayers' money was spent by U.S. government organizations with the aim of promoting democracy in Cuba. What Corral found was that often the success of these programs was very hard to determine because insufficient data could be collected in Cuba to confirm or refute their effectiveness on the ground. Going beyond that, Corral also alleged that some of the programs were purposefully designed to fail, as the U.S. government under President George W. Bush was not wholeheartedly trying to encourage change. A policy change in Cuba could potentially mean another mass exodus from the island to South Florida, which would pose a serious threat to the functioning of welfare systems, such as Medicare and Medicaid, and bring with it a number of social, economic and political challenges. Corral asserts:

> The reality is that these federal programs have been largely unsuccessful and in some cases they have been designed to be unsuccessful by a very clever administration in the White House that does not really want to rock the boat for change in Cuba because that might cause mass migration. That was the point of one of my stories [pers. com., January 2007].

In the course of these investigations, Corral, a second-generation Cuban American, also covered the work of Radio and TV Martí. Comparable to the Voice of America, Radio and TV Martí broadcast programs to Cuba.[6]

On September 8, 2006, an article by Corral was published in the *Miami Herald*, stating that a number of journalists, including two full-time staff reporters and one freelancer of *El Nuevo Herald*, had been receiving payments for their contributions to Radio and TV Martí, which are funded by the U.S. government. Depending on one's own cultural background, this might not even look like a newsworthy story. But it certainly caused a stir not only in Florida, but also on a national level. The fact that journalists who were employed by independent (i.e., non-governmental) media had received money from government funded broadcasters was interpreted as a breach of journalistic ethics by some members of the profession (including Corral and other members of staff at the *Miami Herald*). The two *El Nuevo Herald* staff writers, Wilfredo Cancio Isla and Pablo Alfonso, and the freelance writer, Olga Connor, all of them first-generation Cuban Americans, lost their jobs.

As a reaction to these dismissals, 1,800 readers cancelled their subscription (Reyes 2006). A public debate ignited across local media as to whether this was unethical practice or whether the journalists in question had in fact done their job to the best of their abilities by also serving Cuban viewers and listeners based on the island. Following these reactions, all three *El Nuevo Herald* employees were re-hired, and instead the publisher of the *Miami Herald* and *El Nuevo Herald*, Jesús Díaz, resigned.

While the debate and the allegations were in full flow, Corral was accused of being a Cuban spy, a collaborator of Fidel Castro's regime, who had only run this story to cause distress among the Cuban American community in Miami and to damage the reputation of well-respected journalists. Corral received death threats and his employer had to move him and his family into a house with 24-hour surveillance facilities. Corral remembers the days following the breaking of the story:

> It just created a very tense atmosphere in Miami because even the public who had never read the original story were all of a sudden hearing from their favorite journalists and commentators that the *Miami Herald* was this evil entity and that it was against the Cuban exile community and that it was working for the Castro government [pers. com., January 2007].

What had contributed to the suspicion that Corral might be a Cuban spy were reports that before the story was published in the *Miami Herald*, it had already been discussed on a famous program on Cuban state television called *Mesa Redonda* (Aguirre Ferré 2007). If Corral was not a spy, the fact that the story was being discussed on Cuban television could point toward a mole in the *Herald*'s newsroom. One interviewee was

2. Spanish- and English-Language Newspapers in Miami

convinced of this and could not understand how the *Herald* had not investigated this further:

> So when the *Herald* says, "We don't have any reason to believe that we have a mole in the operation" ... No. 1—Did you investigate? Did you even investigate? They are reporting this on Cuban state television before you even come out with it, the story that you are about to come out with. How does that happen if somebody is not leaking information? [...] Aren't you concerned as a newspaper that your stuff is leaking out, particularly when ... they kind of just slop it off and let it roll off their back.[...] That is your credibility! It is one thing if they said, "Look, we did a six-months investigation and interviewed every single employee. We talked to people and nobody knows anything and we could not find a leak." At least go through the motions of doing an investigation [interview, January 2007].

Another interviewee, a former *Miami Herald* employee, was certain that the "enemy" was much closer to home. He argued that the story had—at least in part—to do with the divide and the rivalry between the two papers:

> Probably when the investigation of the Martís was decided in the newspaper in English, the other people who were ... not only were they excluded, but they were probably targeted. I have no proof of that but I know that is the feeling that some of them have. They were targeted by colleagues from the other paper because of the long-standing, the long-ruling jealousies and differences and discrepancies as to the mission of the two papers and the scope and so on [interview, January 2007].

Several interviewees, among them even one senior *Miami Herald* reporter, acknowledged that the story could have been handled and researched better, as it was no secret that journalists working for various media in the city had also done work for the Martís. One journalist commented:

> I also think that the work itself is very shabby and irresponsible in the way it was done. I think it was very poorly reported. It really ignored the history of how the two Martís came to be. These two Martís were the product of the global influence of the Cuban-American community, including especially commentators, journalists and so on. There was no mystery as to that relationship, you know, even though they portrayed the issue as though some of these people were working surreptitiously for the Martís and mysteriously, maybe illegally, or at least in violation of ethics and so on [interview, January 2007].

Cuban Americans and the Miami Media

The *Miami Herald* arranged for an in-house investigation by Clark Hoyt, a long-time Knight-Ridder employee and now public editor of the *New York Times* (Pérez-Peña 2007). Hoyt's analyses closely focused on the story and its presentation. In essence Hoyt concluded that the *Miami Herald* had rushed to press with this story while failing to acknowledge the wider historical and cultural context. The accusatory tone and the placement of the article on the title page encouraged the assumption that at the heart of the investigation was something much more sinister (Gómez 2006). What angered many readers and journalists most about these events was that despite the outcome of this investigation, the *Miami Herald* never gave an official apology. For that reason, one of the full-time reporters at *El Nuevo* who had been named in the article, Pablo Alfonso, resigned after he had been rehired.

This incident raises several questions regarding journalistic ethics and the role of media in a city that is still to a large extent dominated by an exile community, or to be more precise, a community with an exile mentality. The story and its aftermath demonstrate not only the lengthy and lingering clashes between two papers and two newsrooms; they also indicate a very different understanding of what the role of a journalist, and in particular a journalist in exile, is. Should it matter at all if a journalist had to involuntarily leave their country once they work for a media institution based in the host society? Humberto Castelló, executive editor of *El Nuevo Herald*, who at the time took the stance that *El Nuevo* employees should be allowed to contribute to programs of Radio and TV Martí as long as they did not receive a payment, was aware of this cultural difference:

> For those who have not lived as adults under a socialist regime, understanding the passion exiles harbor for bringing democracy to Cuba can be difficult, Castelló said at an employee meeting three weeks ago. Some exiles see it as their duty to do what they can to overturn the Castro government. "It's very normal and natural for us, for the Cuban journalists," he said [Hoag 2006b].

While some argue that it is strictly unacceptable to receive payments from any institution other than their employer (e.g., an independent media company), others brought forward the recurring notion of the opposition in exile that these journalists form a vital part of. The argument goes that an oppositional movement is established and sustained outside of Cuba as it cannot exist on the island.

2. Spanish- and English-Language Newspapers in Miami

Another argument brought forward was that there had never been any objection to journalists taking payments from other public institutions, such as universities and colleges. Olga Connor, the *El Nuevo* freelance writer who was initially fired, pointed out that she had worked at Florida International University as well and on the paycheck she received it stated that the employer is the State of Florida. During our interview, Connor seemed annoyed and angry about the incident and the way she was treated:

> I signed a contract [to work as a freelance writer for *El Nuevo Herald*] and in no place in the contract does it say that I could not receive money from the government. The government—I'm talking about the state, federal ... State of Florida. It is not like the President is sending you money [pers. com., January 2007].

Then again, for most professional journalists, working for a state university is on a different page than broadcasting to Cuba. Even though both activities are kept alive through public funds, they require very different ideological underpinnings.

A similar story about Olga Connor working for the Martís had been published in *El Nuevo Herald* and the *Miami Herald* in 2002. Connor had received permission for this work from the executive editor at the time, Carlos Castañega. Interestingly, in 2002 the story did not receive wider attention and the management in charge in 2006 made the excuse of not being aware that this had been reported four years earlier. Why was the story not overlooked in 2006? One explanation could be that staff of the *Miami Herald* were aware that another newspaper, the *Chicago Tribune*, was also investigating, and it was decided that it was advantageous to reveal these "open secrets" in the *Miami Herald*, rather than having another newspaper break the story. Nevertheless, loyalty to the sister paper and Spanish-language colleagues was not at the forefront when the decision to go to press with the Martí moonlighter story was made.

The Story Behind the Story—What's at Stake?

The story about journalists working for Radio and TV Martí and the way it was reported by the *Miami Herald* has several interlinking layers and demonstrates the complex relationship between different media organizations and between the media and the Cuban American community. What are the underlying issues at stake here? Broadly, there are three themes: First, there is the question of journalistic ethics and newsroom philosophies. Second, there are questions of allegiance to the Cuban American community, and third, there are matters pertaining to trust and the unity of the community.

Miami's network of media institutions is tightly knit. After the Martí story came out in the *Miami Herald*, the radio stations picked it up immediately, inviting the initially fired *El Nuevo Herald* staff writers for interviews and comments. The story was reported on TV, and discussions online quickly soared. Though there are a significant number of Spanish-language media organizations, they manage to closely scrutinize each other's output. This holds particularly true for talk radio and the popular call-in programs that thrive on stories like these.

In a city like Miami, it is surprising that the management at *El Nuevo Herald* and the *Miami Herald* have been slow to pick up on and honestly assess the relationship between the sister papers and English- and Spanish-language colleagues. To some extent, the story was a story because of the failure to address cultural differences that existed between the two newsrooms. Diverse backgrounds of newsroom staff might, however, be only part of the problem. Another, more deeply rooted concern can be situated with journalistic identity itself and with journalists asking themselves, "What is the purpose of my work?" As the above quotes have shown, some Cuban American journalists might find a very different answer to this than their Anglo colleagues and those trained in U.S. institutions of further and higher education. The dichotomy between personal ambitions and organization requirements can lead to a "professional crisis," as Waisbord (2000, 182–183) points out. The ongoing decline of circulation figures and media companies reducing the number of their newsroom staff adds to the climate of discontent, fear and distrust.

The story about *El Nuevo Herald* reporters working for the Martís raises the question of how attentive a newspaper can or should be to the interests of its readers. In the first instance, this requires that the press can in fact make sense of events and patterns within the community and know who their readers are. For *Diario las Américas* this has always

2. Spanish- and English-Language Newspapers in Miami

been a much more straightforward task than for the *Miami Herald* and *El Nuevo Herald*, although that is not to say that *Diario*'s history of being labeled "the Cuban paper" has not come at a price. How is such a diverse mix of communities best catered to? Furthermore, especially for the Spanish-language papers it is essential to keep the right balance between local and global news. Should a newspaper risk reporting something a significant (and very vocal) proportion of its readers do not want to read—and even find offensive? Oscar Corral commented that he and other reporters at the *Miami Herald* "tried to do what we could. It has been a tough situation because we had to balance up the sentiments in the community with our journalistic principle" (pers. com., January 2007). How is the public best served? Despite having two comprehensive Spanish-language newspapers based in Miami, some informants in the field felt not catered to after all. While *Diario* was considered "behind the times," the *Herald*s were assessed as not being trustworthy. On the other hand, I met dedicated journalists who were trying to balance the needs of their diverse readers and audiences.

In relation to the exile community, the Martí story is a clear indication of the sensitivity certain topics bring out. Still today, fifty years after the Cuban revolution, discussion and information relating to Cuba are sensitive—and at the same time explosive—topics. Debates quickly spiral out of proportion; rumors start mixing with facts. What comes to light through these debates and threats is the underlying concern that "the other" fundamentally does not understand. And the "other" is not only part of the Anglo community or from another cultural background. Oscar Corral, the journalist who investigated the Martí story, was Cuban American. So what gets exposed are the ruptures in the Cuban American community itself and the unsettling questions that the collective as well as each individual has to answer: the question of what it means to be "Cuban American," or a Cuban who lives in America, or an American who has Cuban roots.

The commitment that a lot of first generation Cubans feel for their country is strong, but in their minds this does not cause a discord with their work and their allegiance to values associated with life and work practices in the United States. During interviews and informal chats, several people commented that they simply could not follow the argument, made for example by some English-language journalists, that there could be a conflict of interest by working for an independent as well as a government-funded media organization. Furthermore, the fact that the story was investigated by a Cuban American shows the broad and diverse spectrum of ideals and values that run through the Cuban American community in Miami. Ultimately, every Cuban living outside of the island would like to see a prosperous and democratic Cuba. How to get there is not easily agreed upon. Oscar Corral argued that he was doing the exile community a service by investigating the spending of public money to bring democracy to Cuba. A lot of people would disagree with this stance.

The Martí case also shows that there are still violent elements within the community, and some at least threaten to take serious actions that go beyond any civilized debate. This part of the community has decreased over the past two decades or so, but it is not completely extinct. The threat to Oscar Corral, however, needs to be considered in a wider context of a fear of infiltration by Cuban agents.[7] Cases of Cuban spies that have infiltrated the Cuban American community in Miami are not an everyday occurrence, but they still come into the open from time to time. There is a discourse surrounding the penetration of the community that ultimately leads to the decline of trust: trust in each other, trust in the media and trust in institutions. This causes further fragmentation of the community as well as frustration. Of course this by no means justifies the threat of violent actions, but it allows us to see the wider picture of what is at stake.

One last issue worth considering that was brought to light by the Martí case is that of memory: how history is remembered and forgotten. Radio and TV Martí were established in Miami so that Cuban American and other Spanish-language journalists could make a contribution to these broadcasts. The nature of modern journalistic work patterns, especially those of freelancers or part-timers, includes working for a variety of employers. For that matter, and also keeping in mind the intention of Radio and TV Martí to rely on the input by Cuban American journalists, the way the Martí story was reported shows a lack of understanding of the historical development of the community. For many infuriated members of the Cuban American community, the concern went deeper than the headlines in the *Miami Herald*. They were apprehensive that this was just a glimpse of the many misunderstandings of history and their situations and motivation.

Concluding Remarks

In conclusion, the local English-language press was slow and reluctant in reacting to Cuban migrants as potential readers and a potential market. The loyalties of the *Herald* and the Knight-Ridder Corporation were clearly on the side of the Anglo community. Although *Diario las Américas* nowadays has a reputation of being outdated as a publication, often failing to include the latest news, several of the interviewees aged roughly 50-plus expressed their preference for *Diario*. In contrast to *El Nuevo Herald*, it has been there for them all along. Moreover, *Diario* had readily included Cuban issues.

Knight-Ridder, on the other hand, considered a Spanish-language paper a threat to its existing English-language publication. Thanks to their economic success and their special status as exiles under the Cuban Adjustment Act, the Cuban Americans were able to gain political influence on local, state and national/federal levels. They could hardly be ignored—either by the English- or the Spanish-language press. The evaluation of one member of CANF that *El Nuevo* merely serves to appease Spanish-language speakers in Little Havana does not hold true anymore. The online version of the paper is popular with Spanish-language users abroad, including users in Cuba.

Another key point in relation to the overall themes of this book is that the newspapers analyzed above struggle between transnational and national/local ambitions. For *Diario* this plays out in difficulties regarding advertising revenue. It also shows in the segmentation of the print edition. For *El Nuevo Herald* it means dealing with Cuban issues, but not to such a great extent that other Hispanics would not purchase the paper. Mending this gap has become somewhat easier with the emergence of the internet, though strategic decision on the mission of the printed edition and the paper in general remain. For some exile journalists, a local/national approach is a starting point for their professional identity, but their wish to contribute and provide information for the Cubans on the island potentially clashes with Anglo journalistic ethics and values.

El Nuevo Herald and the *Miami Herald* provide a forum for discussion as well as a source of friction in themselves. Sites of conflict taking place in the media are diverse and complex, very often concerning political issues. Even issues that have a minor political dimension are politicized. The press provides a site of conflict in terms of its content, on the level of individual articles, but also on a higher level, often being criticized as an institution.

An underlying theme these sites of conflict have in common is the notion of "them" and "us." Despite the fact that second and third generation Cuban Americans have actually never lived or visited Cuba, despite Cuba having entered a post-revolutionary stage, and despite a great number of Cuban Americans working in both the Spanish and the English-language *Herald*, a strong sense of *cubanidad* (Cuban-ness) combined with an exile mentality prevails in many Cuban Americans' attitudes and reaction to the press.

In contrast to the press, the establishment of Cuban American radio stations was much more straightforward. Nevertheless, some of the challenges, for example how to deal with changing demographics in the city, are facing radio as well.

3

Miami's Cuban American Radio Scene

In 1960, one year after the Cuban revolution, Miami was home to three radio stations: WFAB, WMIE and WMET (Soruco 1996). With the growing presence of Cuban Americans, the number of Spanish-language radio stations has seen a tremendous increase. Soruco (1996, 36–37) names three main functions of foreign-language radio in the United States:
1. to preserve cultural ties and heritage including language;
2. to provide guidance in the new host country; and
3. to provide entertainment and reduce feelings of isolation.

In addition to these functions, it will be argued here that Spanish-language radio in Miami has had a strong ideological component that emphasized the assumed homogeneity of the political stance of the Cuban exile community. James Carey proposed that communication can be viewed as a ritualistic process that sustains "a presentation of reality that gives life an overall form, order, and tone" (1989, 21). Communication then is more than merely passing on information. It confirms established ways of viewing and understanding what happens in a community. Simultaneously, it can strengthen the sense of belonging to this community. Given the significance of radio for the Cuban American community in Miami, it is helpful to view the output of Spanish-language radio stations from this perspective. Perhaps more so than other media analyzed in this volume, Cuban American radio stations fulfill an important role as agents in memory preservation. A great number of shows broadcast on Radio Mambí, which will be introduced in detail below, are a continuous reminder of the historical circumstances of the Cubans' arrival in Miami. While at times the station is harshly criticized for "being stuck in the past," a notable number of Cuban Americans do not question the existence of this traditional Cuban American station.

New radio stations established in the 1960s and 1970s aimed to provide a valuable service to the Cuban exile. Over time, the increasing buying power of the entrepreneurial Cuban American community also made Cuban American radio stations more attractive for retailers. Businesses began looking for a way to advertise their products, which in turn meant financial viability for the stations (Soruco 1996).

On numerous occasions during field research, radio was described as the number-one Cuban medium in Miami. Even people who are not regular listeners to the Cuban American stations confirmed they tune in if they want to get a feeling for the general mood of the community, which issues are being discussed, and which concerns are prevalent when it comes to the former homeland. Researchers as well as journalists described it as a "great resource."

Since the arrival of the first exiles in Miami, radio stations have experienced a dramatic evolution. From slow beginnings in the 1960s and 1970s, when only three stations served a fairly homogeneous group of people, they diversified along with the growing Spanish-speaking community in Miami-Dade, which encompassed not only Cubans who arrived in different migration waves, but also migrants from other Latin American countries. This diversification in listenership also meant diversification in programming and differing political and ideological approaches. It is not surprising that the majority of stations established in the first decades after the Cuban revolution harbored strong anti-Castro sentiments in their programming, then, and in some cases still today, greeting and figuratively bowing in respect to their *compañeros y compañeras de lucha* (comrades involved in the struggle against communist Cuba and the Castro brothers) in Miami, in Cuba and all over the world during shows. Similar to the situation on the island, radio was soon used for political purposes in Miami as well. In the early 1960s, the U.S. government entered into a propaganda war with Fidel Castro. The CIA was covertly involved in developing a number of radio programs, such as *Voz del Pueblo* (Voice of the People), which were brought

3. Miami's Cuban American Radio Scene

to life with the help of Cuban American journalists based in Miami. Cuba in turn tried to block the signals.

The 1980s and 1990s brought new voices to the spectrum. The exceedingly outspoken camp of the hardliners did everything in their power, legal and illegal, to quiet voices that called for a more liberal stance in regards to Cuban–U.S. relations on a national as well as a local level. However, two or three commentators and hosts that can broadly be described as pro–Castro went on air. Despite numerous attempts to silence them and despite their having to pay a price in regard to their social standing, they are still broadcasting today.[1]

In the past ten years, radio stations have lost some of their influence, but they are still extremely important and popular for Cuban Americans who formed part of the early migration wave. After an overview of the historical development of Spanish-language radio in Miami, two radio stations, Radio Mambí and WQBA 1140 AM shall be examined in detail. The final section of this chapter explores pro–Castro programming in Miami.

Miami's Radio Scene After 1959

Upon their arrival in the United States in 1959 and the 1960s, Cubans were already very familiar with radio as a medium and even widely acknowledged as entrepreneurs in radio production (Soruco 1996). Furthermore, radio was the most important medium for Fidel Castro's rebels. Shortwave emissions were used to establish and strengthen the relationship between the rebels and the wider public. Barlow asserts,

> Rebel radio was the voice of the revolution in the making. Later, in the post-insurrection stages of the two revolutions [Barlow refers here to the Cuban revolution as well as the Sandinista Movement in Nicaragua], the role and scope of radio were transformed to address social needs and priorities [1990, 132].

Given this context, it is no surprise that the early Cuban exiles were keen to use radio for their own purposes. Programs for the historic exile in Miami were started by Cuban Americans buying air time of existing stations, until they were able to set up "their own" Spanish-language-only stations.

The first station, the pioneer of Spanish-language radio in Miami, was La Fabulosa (The Fabulous One). This station no longer exists. The second was La Cubanísima (The Most Cuban), today known as WQBA 1140 AM—La Voz de Miami, a highly successful station that is discussed in more detail below. The third station to join them was La Cadena Azul (The Blue Network). La Cadena Azul was named after a station that exists in Cuba, a rather common practice when it comes to naming not only stations but also individual programs. A journalist, Daniel Morcate, who began his career as a journalist for La Cadena Azul in 1979, described the Cuba coverage in those early years as simplistic and unchallenging. The listenership was a very homogeneous group, with a keen interest in all things Cuban, especially regarding the Cuba–U.S. relationship.

The type of coverage favored by the majority of Spanish-language radio journalists was not, however, unquestioned. Similar to the criticism brought forward by some journalists today, those in charge favored the views of the right wing of the exile community. Whether this stems from true political conviction or from a marketing decision remains hard to judge—then and now. Similar to the balancing act of journalists outlined in the analysis of the Martí moonlighter story, those working in radio had to continuously decide what was appropriate for them to include and to say—and what was not. No doubt personal opinions sometimes clashed with those of radio station owners and mainstream views. As one interviewee pointed out, pro–Castro views were methodically excluded, as those in charge could make a choice of who was allowed to speak in open-microphone talk shows and who was or was not given a job as presenter or reporter. The exclusion of pro–Castro views and any position that would challenge the hardline approach to Cuba was achieved not only through non-recruitment of certain journalists; it was also difficult for listeners with differing political views to get their voices heard on air. Whether knowingly or unconsciously, the enforced creation of ideological homogeneity was a task that the early local radio stations took very seriously. Some stations, especially Radio Mambí, still do so up to this day and are forming a significant part in the cultural expressions that keep the exile mentality alive.

3. Miami's Cuban American Radio Scene

The focus of programming clearly lay on political developments on the island. In the early 1960s, most listeners still believed in a rapid return to the homeland, so every development, every action of Fidel Castro and his supporters, was under intense scrutiny. In addition to providing a close connection to their country of origin, programs were intended to help the exiles, especially the constant stream of new arrivals, to adjust to life in the United States, re-unite families and provide useful information that would ease the transition. By performing these tasks, radio programs furthermore nourished a mainstream understanding and interpretation of history and Cuban American identity. A young Cuban American interviewee underlined this assumed and reinforced homogeneous outlook in the following words: "We were all taught from an early age: 'This is Cuba. This is what happened. Government bad, democracy good.' Instead of learning the ABC you learn that" (interview, October 2008).[2] In spite of a continuous influx of Cubans leaving the island to join members of their families in Miami throughout the 1960s and 1970s, the Cuban American community in Miami had remained relatively uniform in regard to their social capital, their education and their ethnicity. The simplistic approach to programming and reporting on local issues, development on the island, and Cuban American relations remained largely unchallenged until 1980, the year of the Mariel Boatlift.

The arrival of an estimated 124,000 migrants between early April and October caused major disruptions to Miami-Dade County. The Mariel exodus changed not only the Cuba coverage. It also meant a rethinking of the role and function of Miami's Spanish-language stations and the mission of journalists. As Mariel coincided with another migration wave of several thousand Haitians, social challenges and an increasingly diverse community and audience called for each English- and Spanish-language journalist to reassess their position and their work[3]:

> That episode of U.S. and Cuban history really changed the way the coverage was done. Because at that time everybody who was working for the press or radio stations had to develop a mission to try to implore that issue which had brought up all kinds of social challenges to this particular community and for the State of Florida. And we had, we had to be part of that. Our coverage became, I think, a little bit more sophisticated at the time [Daniel Morcate, pers. com., January 2007].

Cuban Americans and the Miami Media

Mariel also led to the first of many conflicts between the *Miami Herald* and the Spanish-language radio stations. The *Herald* displayed very critical coverage of the Mariel Boatlift and the consequences it had for Miami, showing little understanding of the Cuban exiles' wish to bring as many relatives as possible to the United States, even if it meant having to accept so-called anti-socials on board (Portes and Stepick 1993). Coverage by the *Herald* also underlined anti–Cuban sentiments that were prevalent after the full extent of Mariel became apparent. The conflict between the *Herald* and the Spanish-language radio stations was an indication of deteriorating community relations between the Anglos and the Cuban Americans:

> At the beginning, Cubans were welcome, you know, with open arms by government, by the private sector, by all sectors in this particular community. But I think the Mariel Boatlift really changed this dramatically. And everybody who was working in the news had to make a judgment [interview, January 2007].

The diversification of the Spanish-language community has ultimately led to a higher quality of programming and to a more open-minded leadership in most of Miami's radio stations that exist today. A wider approach is taken to news and entertainment, journalists and management being well aware that the times of a homogeneous listenership are past. Apart from Radio Mambí, which markets itself as *the* Cuban radio station, Spanish-language stations make an effort to cater to all Spanish-language listeners, although opinions on this may differ significantly due to individual taste. One interviewee saw no difference between WQBA and Radio Mambí. Others were often not aware of which station they were actually listening to, as they consumed it mostly as a background medium. All informants below the age of 30 emphasized that they were aware of Cuban American stations merely because their parents and grandparents listened to them. Talk radio did not appeal to them, and a number of Cuban American graduates and university students made the point that as a community, they would like to move beyond the belligerent discourse that is associated with programs on some Cuban American radio stations. That is not to say that they necessarily disagreed with the opinions voiced, but they were tired of the way discussions were routinely conducted on some of the radio shows.

3. Miami's Cuban American Radio Scene

In the field, the names of two radio station were mentioned repeatedly: Radio Mambí and WQBA 1180 AM. Both stations were estimated by interviewees to be highly influential and popular. Due to the established power structures, later migration waves did not instigate drastic changes to the way Cuban American radio stations were run. A Cuban American journalist describes today's media scene in the following way:

> The demographics of the community here have changed a lot. The people that have an influence in the media, for example in radio—radio is very strong here—are mainly from the historic generation. With "historic" I mean people who came here in the 1960s and '70s. They dominate the scene [interview, June 2006].

In the long run, new waves of Cuban migrants led to a diversification in Spanish-language stations. The establishment of new networks was made economically viable by Miami's quickly developing into a magnet for other Latin American migrants.

Radio Mambí

While other radio stations evolved, opening up to new, i.e., non–Cuban American, issues, and adjusted to a changing demographics and a listenership with an ideologically heterogeneous outlook on politics, Radio Mambí remained "the Cuban station." In addition, it is the most controversial of all the stations that exist in Miami today. The majority of Radio Mambí journalists belong to the camp of hardliners. The station tends to strongly criticize or condemn every move toward a dialogue with the Cuban government or, for instance, the lifting of the trade embargo.

Radio Mambí went on air for the first time in October 1985. Originally an English-language station, it was bought by a group of Cuban American businessmen to create Radio Mambí—La Grande (The Great One) (Veciana-Suarez 1987). The station now forms part of the Univision Group. All of the journalists and media professionals interviewed in the course of this research argued that Radio Mambí was aimed at the historic exiles, Cuban Americans largely over the age of 60. However, Ninoska Pérez Castellón, a presenter on Radio Mambí, strongly differs on this. She emphasized that it is not only older people who tune in and that the exile community is not in any way losing its momentum in regard to political decisiveness when it comes to combating Fidel Castro's government:

> Radio Mambí is the highest rated station in South Florida, even higher than the English-speaking. They always love to say it's old people that listen to Cuban radio. But it is not true. There are surveys that show there are a lot of younger people that listen to the station. Also, we are a station that has a lot of programs based on callers, call-ins. A lot of young people call too. They always love to picture Miami ... Miami is like a magnet for all these theses [theories]: the old exile is dying. Excuse me!? Are their children or grand-children or nieces ... and all of these people who come from Cuba now will become citizens and politics will change. No, that is not true. All of these people that come from Cuba, even from Mariel, if you listen to them talk now—and I never listen to the people on the radio, I am out on the street, and people know me and talk to me—they have the same concept of putting an end to a system that has caused them their misery, and family division and repression in Cuba [pers. com., June 2006].[4]

As one can probably sense from this statement, Pérez Castellón has very strong feelings about everything relating to Cuba. Before starting as a presenter on Radio Mambí, Pérez Castellón worked for fifteen years as the director of the Voice of the Cuban American National Foundation, which was transmitted on shortwave to Cuba. Radio Mambí still has strong affiliations with members or former members of CANF. Along with Ninoska Pérez Castellón, Armando Pérez-Roura, director of programming and notorious presenter, is one of the best known faces (and voices) of Radio Mambí.

Like Pérez Castellón, Armando Pérez-Roura assumes a confrontational tone when it comes to dealing with Cuban issues, to such an extent that some interviewees expressed concerns about this level of antagonism on air. Does it do more harm than good to the Cuban American community? This question leaves listeners wondering whether Pérez-Roura is in fact fighting *la lucha,* supporting the struggle of the Cuban exile, or whether he is a Cuban government agent: "Radio Mambí goes so much to the extreme right that sometimes we wonder if they are truly to the right or if they are agents of the Cuban government because sometimes they do so much harm—especially Pérez-Roura" (interview, January 2007). Doubts about Pérez-Roura's integrity are fuelled partly by his past and the colorful spectrum of political views he has entertained

3. Miami's Cuban American Radio Scene

over the years; he has switched sides on a few occasions throughout his career. A former collaborator of Fulgencio Batista, he was director of Cuba's National College of Broadcasters under Fidel Castro and took a leading role in "closing down and confiscating the CMQ radio and television station in Havana as part of Cuba's nationalization of all media" (Bardach 2002). However, he then performed yet another ideological U-turn and joined forces with the exiles in Miami: "Then he came over here and said that he was more anti–Castro than anybody else" (interview, January 2007). In addition to his influence through Radio Mambí, Armando Pérez-Roura is also "regarded by many as the power behind the throne at Radio Martí" (Bardach 2002).

Radio Mambí, whose programs were described by one informant as "useless rhetoric" that is "getting people excited about anything and everything dealing with Cuba" (interview, June 2006), is nevertheless taken very seriously—and not only because of its contribution to the public sphere of Miami and South Florida. The station constructs itself as a voice of the opposition. A voice critical of the Cuban government cannot exist on the island. Radio Mambí has a strong signal, which also reaches Cuba. As a station, it has a different remit and self-understanding from other Spanish- and English-language stations.

Radio Mambí—and the journalists and freelancers contributing to its output—speak and think of the station as an alternative or radical media outlet that should be based in Cuba. They argue that because of the Castro brothers' oppressive policies it cannot exist on the island. Furthermore, even very poor people in Cuba are likely to have access to a radio somewhere in their vicinity. With the reach and effectiveness of Radio Martí, the U.S.-government funded station, sitting under a big question mark (see the Martí moonlighter story in Chapter 2), Radio Mambí can only win by giving Cubans on the island either another option or perhaps the only option of listening to a radio station from Miami. This makes their task even more vital. John Downing characterized radical media by stating, "They break somebody's rules, although not all of them in every aspect" (2001, xi). In the case of Radio Mambí, they are aiming at breaking the rules and challenging the status quo in Cuba. For many of those involved, this is much more than something they pursue on a nine-to-five basis: it is a life purpose.

Cuban Americans and the Miami Media

Just to give one example: Nancy Pérez-Crespo is a well known Radio Mambí presenter, and she also contributes to Radio Martí's output. Moreover, she is the founding director of the Nueva Prensa Cubana (NPC), a news agency that publishes stories and reports by independent journalists based in Cuba (Gonzalez 2006; Nueva Prensa website). The engagement with issues relating to Cuba therefore goes far beyond working according to one's professional values for many of these journalists.

Wider questions—some similar to the ones that the Martí moonlighter case in the previous chapter brought to light—arise around this self-assigned role of Cuban American journalists and the work they do. Whose standards apply to journalistic work? Who is to judge and to decide? Is it fair to describe a station such as Radio Mambí as a propaganda tool—even though it is owned by a private company and not government-funded? Or would the term *radical* or *alternative media outlet* suit better? Are these an exile community and exiled journalists at their best or at their worst?

Radio Mambí journalists' understanding of their work has led to practices that do, in part at least, not live up to the standards that the majority of English-language journalists expect from a modern media outlet. This does not mean that standards are necessarily low, but they are "rather different" (interview, January 2007). Information, suspicions, claims and personal opinions are often not clearly distinguished from one another in Radio Mambí's programs. The focus seems to lie instead on adhering to a certain ideology that takes precedence over journalistic standards outlined by colleagues in other Spanish- and English-language media.

Radio Mambí forms part of and informs a segment of the community that is strongly focused on a hands-on approach to removing the Castro brothers. There is a feeling that history needs to be corrected; the record needs to be set straight. Despite Ninoska Pérez Castellón's argument that her station also attracts younger listeners, there is no question that some programs have a very old-fashioned sound and feel to them. An informant who holds a senior role at a Miami-based newspaper agrees: "The major radio stations are still in the hands of people who are completely out of touch with reality. They still belong to those Cold War [years]. It is not valid any more" (interview, June 2006).

3. Miami's Cuban American Radio Scene

A much more pragmatic approach to the existence of Radio Mambí is taken by the editor in chief of *Diario las Américas*. Alejandro Aguirre makes the point that the existence of Radio Mambí is due to market segmentation at Univision Headquarters:

> The bigger question there is ownership which is Univision Radio. If you look at what Univision has, which is four radio stations and a television station, they basically pick one of the four to be the super–Cuban radio station. It is market segmentation. But the other ones go to another audience. There is WQBA, a sister station, which is more aimed at people my age [people in their mid-thirties to mid-fifties] [pers. com., June 2006].

The past years witnessed many stations of a similar nature to Radio Mambí disappear. However, it is certainly a highly lucrative commercial flagship of Univision Radio at the moment and, despite several critical voices, its validity remains unquestioned by great parts of the historic exile and the Cuban American community in general.

WQBA-1140 AM and Radio Wars

WQBA was first set up in June 1966 by the Susquehanna Broadcasting Corporation, which wanted to get a foot into the Spanish-language radio market. In the following twenty years, WQBA—La Cubanísima (The Most Cuban) turned into the most successful Spanish-languish station (Veciana-Suarez 1987). The station was and still is highly news-oriented. Like Radio Mambí, it is now owned by the Univision Group. In contrast to Radio Mambí and despite formerly carrying the alias "La Cubanísima," WQBA employs a more inclusive programming that is not targeted solely toward Cuban Americans. This process of opening up to a wider group of listeners is also reflected in its new descriptor: La Voz de Miami (The Voice of Miami). Based in the same building as Radio Mambí, right in the heart of Little Havana's *Calle Ocho* (Eighth Street), the station has a youthful feel to it. Assistants and presenters are younger in age and easily switch between English and Spanish. Before this renewal, WQBA's predecessor, WMIE, had been selected by the Cuban American community and the U.S. government to play an instrumental part in the propaganda war against Castro (Soruco 1996). In 1985, this role was officially taken over by Radio Martí, which had been set up as part of the aggressive propaganda scheme of the Reagan administration. According to Barlow (1990, 127), the Voice of America also "stepped up its propaganda war against Cuba, particularly in Latin America."

Bernadette Pardo, a host of a popular morning talk and news show, is personally very happy with this development. She tries to avoid talking about Cuban issues, as it sometimes "gets a bit too much to talk about Cuba all the time" (pers. com., June 2006). On the other hand, she does not think that "people are ever bored" (June 2006) of discussing Cuba and U.S.–Cuban relations. Pardo sees WQBA's emphasis as being on serving Spanish-language speakers in Miami and not the Cuban public on the island. WQBA has newer voices, "people who are younger, who have probably studied this profession but at least practiced in the United States or maybe in some modern society" (interview, January 2007). Call-in programs have also been enriched through the advent of car phones and internet radio. Before that, it used to be largely housewives and retirees making contributions to the shows.

Again, it is worth emphasizing here that how WQBA appears to individual listeners is highly subjective. Non-Cubans I met in the field would still characterize it as a Cuban dominant station. While one journalist praised the station's, Bernadette Pardo's and her co-presenter's interesting take on local news, others could not find a strong distinction between WQBA and Radio Mambí. It was partly these similarities that led Univision to give WQBA a make-over in 2012, moving well known hosts to Radio Mambí and stripping away most of the local flavors of WQBA.

Pro-Castro Programming

Even though Miami is the fortress of the Cuban exile, and known for the hardliner attitude that is still aired on Radio Mambí today, the city is also home to two very prominent pro–Castro presenters: Francisco Aruca and Max Lesnik.

Francisco Aruca has completed a U-turn in his political outlook, similar to that of Armando Pérez-Roura—only coming and going in opposite directions. Francisco Aruca was born in 1940, sixty miles west of Havana. A devout Catholic, he thought that communism was "intrin-

3. Miami's Cuban American Radio Scene

sically perverse." According to his own account, he conspired with the Social Democrats against Fidel Castro and spent one and a half years under political protection of the Brazilian embassy in Cuba. When he first came to Miami, Aruca joined the Movimiento Contra-Revolucionario del Pueblo (MRP—Counter-Revolutionary Movement of the People) but in 1962 came to the conclusion that "Cubans with the assistance of the CIA had created a mad house" (Francisco Aruca, pers. com., January 2007) in Miami. Aruca left Miami but in the following decades decided that he had judged the Cuban revolution too quickly. He returned to Miami in the mid-seventies and set up Marazul Tours, a travel agency that—under the new leniency of the Carter administration—organized trips for Cuban Americans to Cuba.

Marazul Tours was highly successful but also highly controversial. Many Cuban Americans had a strong desire to see their homeland and family members they had left behind on the island. However, other members of the community, especially the hardliner camp, were strictly opposed to travels to Cuba. They saw it as indirectly accepting and supporting the Castro government: "We found it immoral because we knew the purpose of Castro to open up the country was to get dollars in. He was in a bad economic situation. So here was the contradiction: his enemies are rescuing him from economic ruin" (interview, January 2007). Due to these opposing views, the local media were not very supportive in explaining to those who had managed to purchase tickets what to expect when they arrived on the island. Francisco Aruca remembers that people were taking a lot of things for friends and family that were already on sale in Cuba. He wanted to inform people on a big scale of how to prepare for the visits and what to expect. In 1988, he happened to come across a community station, 8816FM, which was in financial difficulty. In exchange for acting as a guarantor for a loan, Aruca was given three slots per week to allow him to inform people about conditions of travel and discuss the issue of travel between Cuba and the U.S. He did not have to wait long for reactions to this newest addition to the local radio scene:

> As soon as they heard that I was doing a radio program in Miami, even though it was in an FM station and only three times per week the media [went wild]; "Oh, no, now this guy has a radio program." I was not as con-

troversial as I am now. I wasn't really dealing with other aspects of Miami or other aspects of U.S. society. I was much more really geared to playing fifteen or twenty minutes of Cuban music that was not heard in Miami—because they didn't play Cuban music in Miami. And obviously the market was here. I said "Great. This is good. Let's play Cuban music. It is a good thing because it is also opening up a more normal relationship for the future where we or others can sell Cuban music." And then I participated in the rest of the program basically talking about common issues, what difficulties you have when you travel, what difficulties have been created, what could you do to make things more normal in terms of American government, Congress, approach ... the kind of things that are being talked about constantly out here [Francisco Aruca, pers. com., January 2007].

This comment by Aruca is noteworthy for a number of reasons. First, he clearly envisaged then and still does today a different relationship between the Cuban government and U.S. administrations. From 1959 until recently, the Carter administration was the only U.S. administration that followed a pro-dialogue strategy and showed leniency regarding travel.[5] Second, Aruca also mentions markets and potential commercial interests that might arise through more relaxed relations. Musicians and bands that are considered close to or not opposed to the regime, for example the singer/songwriter Silvio Rodríguez and the band Los Van-Van, will not be played on local Cuban American radio stations. Third, going on air also meant facing the hostility of other media outlets and a group of Cuban Americans with considerable influence.

After nine months of broadcasting, the power and decisiveness of the hardliners had taken its toll on the station. Francisco Aruca was told that the community radio station that broadcast his program was in dire straits once again—this time because of him. Depending on donations, fewer and fewer people were willing to give—apparently because of Aruca's output. As a consequence, he left 8816FM, partly also because he had decided that he wanted more time on air. After a brief spiel on WOCN, he founded Radio Progreso in 1990/1. The station is named after a "sister station" in Havana. Aruca hosts *Ayer in Miami* (Yesterday in Miami). He explains that his aim was "to create [...] a method or an instrument that would answer to all this fanaticism, stupidity that in my opinion is taking place here.... I'm going to be criticizing or commenting things that were said or done yesterday" (pers. com., January 2007).

3. Miami's Cuban American Radio Scene

Right from the start, the program was a success. On the other hand, or maybe because of that, the station was under siege; it was broken into and vandalized and the offices of Aruca's Marazul Tours were bombed twice (Bardach 2002). The wrath of the Cuban hardliners that Radio Progreso was experiencing was even recorded as an issue of concern by Human Rights Watch (Kleinknecht 1999). Further difficulties emerged when local companies started cancelling their commercials due to the pressure they were experiencing from the hardliner camp of the Cuban American community. Nevertheless, Aruca continues with his programs—to the dismay and annoyance of many. Not only does he host *Ayer in Miami*, he also launched an English-language program, *Babel's Guide*, in June 1999.

One issue that irritates Aruca when observing Miami's local media scene is the language divide. He argues that the *Herald* will give certain information to English-language readers and *El Nuevo Herald* will give certain information to Spanish-language readers, with the end result that both sides are not as well informed as they could and should be. As a Cuban American, he aims to explain to English-language listeners of *Babel's Guide* why Cuban Americans react in the way they do because of the lack of or different kind of information: "This is a totally manipulative market" (pers. com., January 2007).

Through his diverse activities as managing director and owner of Marazul Tours and as radio commentator, Aruca developed strong ties to officials of the Cuban government, a fact that makes him even more suspect for some Cuban Americans. Questioned about whether he would describe himself as an exile and whether he would consider a permanent return to the island, he responds that he is not in exile as he can go to Cuba any time. However, he wants to stay in Miami, because his family is in the U.S. and his presence is required in Miami, as he mysteriously put it. Irrespective of his propositions, Aruca's style has been criticized for being not too different from hardliner Cuban American radio shows: "People who called the radio's open line and disagreed with him would be yelled at and ridiculed. Many wondered what alternative he was providing" (De los Angeles Torres 1999, 149).

Despite my tenacious efforts to get in touch with another radio personality known for his pro–Castro views, Max Lesnik, obtaining an interview proved to be impossible. Lesnik, now in his early eighties, is a well known figure in Miami's journalism circles. He was the editor of *Réplica*, a Spanish-language news and entertainment magazine. Similar to Francisco Aruca's experiences, *Réplica*'s offices in Little Havana were bombed several times, and local businesses stopped selling the magazine due to threats and fears of repercussion. Lesnik's proposals to enter into a dialogue with Cuba and lift the trade embargo do not go down well with parts of the community. Citing an FBI agent based in Miami, Bardach (2002, 111) asserts that there have been many attempts to harm Lesnik that could only just in time have been averted. Nevertheless, up to this day Lesnik contributes regularly to a variety of left-wing and anti-imperialist publications such as voltairenet.org and cubadebate.cu.[6]

Concluding Remarks

Cuban American radio stations in Miami can look back on a rich history. The familiarity of the Cubans with this medium and the ease of employing it made radio indispensable for a variety of the purposes and goals of some members of the Cuban American community. A key point is that the involvement of the U.S. government in the evolving radio scene had a significant influence on how Cuban American stations developed and how they are still used and viewed by many today.

The significance of the radio stations can be conceptualized as an indicator of the ideological cohesiveness of the community. All informants were quick to emphasize and continuously reiterate the importance of the Cuban American radio stations in terms of establishing and reaffirming the mood and concerns of great parts of the community. But there was also an awareness that the status quo has changed. Shifts are ongoing and inevitable, as diverse groups of migrants arrive and the second, third and fourth generations of Cuban Americans and other Hispanics are born in the United States. While in the 1960s and 1970s Cuban American stations could be sure to represent the mainstream views of the historic exiles—with disagreeing voices being systematically excluded—other approaches to and perspectives on Cuba and U.S.-Cuban relations could not be silenced from the 1980s onwards.

3. Miami's Cuban American Radio Scene

In the end, many Cuban American radio stations were faced with the choice of adjusting to Miami's changing demographic or being closed down. In itself, this might not be a development particular to these radio stations. What makes the case noteworthy, though, is that younger informants in the field do not necessarily disagree with the political stance held up as a mainstream view. What they disagree with is the way debates are handled on air.

The dislike and disapproval of on-air discussions that have an automatic hierarchy of participants (with the commentator always having the last word and discussions often having a predetermined conclusion of blaming the Castro brothers and communism) is an indicator of a shift not only in media use but also in how younger Cuban Americans view themselves as citizens in relation to the U.S. and the Cuban state. The associations of some Cuban American radio stations with international politics and the early involvement of the CIA seem alienating now. Even more significantly, though, the mere existence of radio stations and the discourse they have perpetuated over the past decades has not meaningfully improved the overall situation. On the contrary, some would argue that it led to violent actions and to isolating parts of the community who did not hear themselves represented on air at all. The power to control and influence the dominant narrative in mainstream Cuban American radio stations stayed in the hands of the historic exiles and their descendants, even when it was challenged by the arrival of later migratory waves.

4

Spanish-Language Television, Cuban Americans and Hispanic Audiences

This chapter focuses on national Spanish-language television as well as on local (English- and Spanish-language) television in Miami. Despite its current popularity, Spanish-language TV in the United States experienced a slow start. While English-language TV stations saw an exponential increase in numbers from the 1960s onwards, Spanish-language audiences were not served to the same extent. Until 1985, Channel 23 (WLTV) was the only station providing Spanish-language programs in Miami (Soruco 1996, 47). One reason for the slow uptake of Spanish-language television was high market entry costs. For migrants, no matter where they were from and why they came to the United States, setting up a TV station, especially in a time before the necessary technology and equipment became widely available, was not an obvious or feasible step to take. In addition, and as expanded on below, rulings by the Federal Communications Commission (FCC) did not allow foreigners or people with unresolved status a straightforward way into television broadcasting. Also, there was still a prevailing hope in Miami that incoming migrants such as the Cubans would learn English, making a Spanish-language network superfluous.

Television is by far the most difficult medium to tackle in terms of the overriding question this book addresses: How does an exilic community use the media to talk to itself and negotiate issues that are of concern to them? Then again, an analysis of Spanish-language television proves very fruitful for the same reason: why is it so difficult to extract

4. Spanish-Language Television

a "Cuban-American connection" when analyzing television networks and programs? And if programs are not concerned with Cuban or Cuban American issues, what are they about?

As indicated by the title of this chapter, national Spanish-language television networks cater to Hispanic audiences. A Hispanic audience is an artificial, and in a sense a transnational, construct that has clear limitations in practice. John Sinclair (2005) has posited the concept of Hispanics forming a "diaspora in reverse." The underlying thought is that a diaspora shares a common home or place of origin. In the case of Spanish-language speakers in the United States, however, what they share is their country of destination, while coming from diverse places.

Generally speaking, there is not a complete absence of a Cuban influence on television stations and the industry. In comparison to other Latin American countries, Cuba was very advanced in terms of broadcasting. In 1957 Cuba had 23 television stations, more than any other country in Latin or South America; Mexico had twelve television stations and ten could be found in Venezuela (Cuba Transition Project December 2008). The expertise therefore existed when the first exiles arrived in Miami. It is no surprise that throughout the evolution of Spanish-language television in the United States, Cuban Americans could be found in front of the cameras and in various decision-making roles behind the scenes. Nevertheless, because of the importance of markets, advertising budgets and a national and often even international approach to audiences, Cuban American influences in television are much more subtle than in radio and the press. Television has never been considered the "Cuban medium" as was the case for radio; it has never been given as much attention as radio, and a particular station or program has never been scrutinized by the CANF as the *Miami Herald* was. Despite a high density of television companies and production sites in Miami, the relationship between the Cuban American community and the national Spanish-language networks has resulted in dispirited disengagement. A major factor in this process was the reporting on the Elián González saga, which is examined in detail below.

However, as Alejandro Aguirre, editor and publisher of *Diario las Américas*, points out: "There is still a lot of interest in Cuban stories on TV. There are several TV stations here and cable has brought some more.... Even in their international news you will always see a lot of coverage from Cuba" (pers. com., June 2006). It is worth noting here that Mr. Aguirre has Nicaraguan roots, because the notion of a channel or a program targeting a specific segment of the Hispanic audience in Miami or in the United States generally is highly subjective and possibly contentious.

Since the slow development of new Spanish-language television stations in the late 1980s, the industry has more than made up for it with an estimated $1.5 billion in Hispanic TV advertising dollars for the 2006–07 season (Hoag 2006a, 1E). Even in the current economic climate, the total Hispanic media advertising spending has increased by 1.8 percent in 2008, while the figure for U.S. media overall was -4.1 percent (Hispanic Fact Pack 2009, 6). Thus, especially in comparison to single-digit growth or decline for English-language television (Hoag 2006a), this demonstrates the popularity and potential scope of Spanish-language TV. This is good news for Univision and Telemundo, the main players in Spanish-language television in the United States.[1]

Univision

The Univision Television Group, together with the TeleFutura Television Group, Galavisión, Univision Radio, Univision Music and Univision Online, forms part of Univision Communication, Inc. At the time of writing, Univision Television Group owns and operates nineteen full-power and eight low-power networks, in addition to two full-power stations in Puerto Rico, one full power station in Bakersfield and two low power stations in Sacramento.[2]

The company's origins lie in San Antonio, Texas, where the first Spanish-language station was founded by Raúl Cortez in 1955. Cortez quickly faced the problem that programming costs were too high and his advertising income was comparatively low (Sinclair 1999, 97). In 1961 he therefore sold the ultra high frequency (UHF) station to the Spanish International Network. This station formed the cornerstone of Univision's predecessor, Spanish International Network (SIN) (Univision 2007a). SIN and its sister network, the Spanish International Commu-

4. Spanish-Language Television

nication Corporation (SICC), were owned by Emilio Azcárraga and five business partners. Azcárraga was a successful Mexican businessman who also owned Telesistema Mexicana, which became Televisa in 1972 (Soruco 1996, 48). Due to complaints about the poor quality of programs and suspicion that ownership regulation might have been violated—foreign nationals are only allowed to hold 25 percent of the stock of a communications company—SIN encountered problems with the Federal Communications Commission (FCC). The problem was temporarily resolved by a new distribution of stocks that resulted in Azcárraga owning only twenty percent of SICC and seventy-five percent of SIN, as there are no limitations on foreign nationals owning a network. In the meantime, SIN had been very successful in selling advertising time to "reluctant Anglo clients" (Soruco 1996, 48). Its programming strategy was built on films from Mexico, Argentina and Spain and Spanish-language *telenovelas*: "the result was an attractive package for advertisers: large audiences at relatively low costs" (Soruco 1996, 48).

The issue of ownership came up once again in 1986 when FCC administrative judge John Conlin denied the stations affiliated with the network the renewal of their licenses, including WLTV in Miami. The argument made was that "while SICC met the FCC's ownership standards, its relations with SIN, which shared the same New York offices and telephone number, opened the stations to foreign control" (Soruco 1996, 49). In addition to the close ties between SICC and SIN, the Spanish Radio Broadcasters Association (SRBA) had filed a claim in protest against SICC's foreign connection, which gave the network an unfair advantage. As Sinclair (1999, 92–120) demonstrates, SICC and SIN were indeed closely entangled, and both organizations were under the patriarchal management of Emilio Azcárraga Vidaureta and from 1972 onwards Emilio Azcárraga Milmo, who took over from his father.

In July 1986, the owners were obliged to sell both SICC and SIN to Hallmark Cards, Inc., and First Chicago Venture Capital (Saralegui 1998, 136). The sale was met with some criticism by the Hispanic community, which would have liked to see both companies in Hispanic hands. As part of the sale agreement, Hallmark "made a commitment to continue the stations' Spanish-language format for two years" (Soruco 1996, 49). With the purchase, the network's name was changed from SIN to Univision and a Chilean, Joaquín Blaya, was named its first president (Saralegui 1998, 136). In 1991, Univision's news department was relocated from Los Angeles to Miami. The move exacerbated the rivalry between Mexican-Americans dominant in California and Cuban Americans based in Florida. Another noteworthy change was that "for the first time in its operating history, local production of programming was emphasized" (Soruco 1996, 50). Blaya signed Cuban American Cristina Saralegui, who with her show *El Show de Cristina* became the Oprah Winfrey of Spanish-language television, and Mario Kreuzberger, a.k.a. Don Francisco, who brought with him the variety show *Sábado Gigante*, one of the longest running and most successful programs on Spanish-language television.

In 1992, the network changed owners once again. Hallmark sold Univision to an investment trio consisting of A. Jerrold Perenchio, Televisa and Venevision. This alliance, with Perenchio serving as chairman and chief executive officer of Univision Communications, Inc., developed Univision into the largest Spanish-language network in the U.S. and the fifth most watched network overall (Univision 2007a). In September 1996, Univision became a publicly traded company on the New York Stock Exchange. However, with the acquisition of the network by Broadcasting Media Partners, Inc. (a consortium including several investors among them Saban Capital Group), in June 2006, Univision's stock ceased trading the following year.

All of Univision's programming is run nationwide. It is also broadcast in Puerto Rico and can be seen in sixteen Latin American countries via cable. Daniel Morcate, news-editor-in-chief at Univision, remembers Univision news teams being recognized on the streets of Panama City and San Salvador. But while the fame of anchors and the brand might be exciting, he also emphasizes the more serious side of the same coin: "That really gives us a major responsibility. We are pretty much aware of that. We are a pretty responsible newscast—sometimes too much so, to my taste" (pers. com., January 2007).

Even though Univision has major production centers in Doral, a smaller town outside of Miami, its strong ties to Televisa, the largest Spanish-language network and the largest producer of Spanish-language programming, clearly shine through in its schedule. According to the

4. Spanish-Language Television

public relations material available on Univision's website, programming is "tailored to meet the tastes, preferences, and informational needs of the U.S. Hispanic audience, providing an unparalleled connection to favorite stars and entertainment" (Univision 2007b). The main program categories emphasized here comprise *telenovelas*, news, sports, entertainment and talk. Despite being based just outside of Miami, Univision was often described as "the Mexican" network during field work.

Even though Univision might employ a relatively high number of Cuban Americans, with talk-show host Cristina Saralegui probably being the most famous among them, Univision does not have strong ties to the Cuban American community as such. There is no special commitment to the Cuban Americans and their cause on the nationwide programming; "I don't like their nationwide operation because the programming is totally focused on the Mexican community. It is not open for other interests" (interview, June 2007). This was a common sentiment among Cuban American informants.

Reporting from Cuba is strongly restricted by the Cuban government and Univision's coverage of Cuba is—according to one informant's assessment—"nothing to write home about" (interview, January 2007). Partly, this is not just a phenomenon that can be observed on Univision's output or Spanish-language newscasts. A few informants in the field shared the view that U.S. television news programs are mostly reactionary in their approach and very little analysis and interpretation of events is offered to viewers. Instead, and despite dwindling sales figures of hardcopies, they ascribed a strong analytical and agenda-setting role to national newspapers. The fast-paced environment of television often does not allow for in-depth reflection. Therefore, to a large extent the lack of analysis is due to time constraints on the production side as well as inherent in the format. As a European viewer, I even found current affairs programs to be densely scheduled, as certain points have to be covered before the next commercial break.

These restrictions apply equally to Univision's approach to covering Cuba and U.S.-Cuban relations. Still, coverage of the Cuban American community is an option, but it is not a significant aspect of Univision's national output strategy. The most important reason for this—and during field research often accompanied with a sigh—is "numbers":

Cuban Americans and the Miami Media

> [There is] very little analysis unlike [the] coverage of other countries that are more accessible to [...] reporters and which frankly are of greater interest to Univision as a company, like Mexico, El Salvador. But I think sometimes sheer numbers dictate these priorities. We have, for example, anywhere between 26 and 30 million Mexicans in the United States, Mexican Americans and Mexicans; whereas we only have a million and half, maximum 1,800,000 Cubans. That is a major difference.... Out of all these [South American and Caribbean] countries, because of the sheer numbers of citizens in the United States, there is a greater priority—not [only] within Univision but any network, television or radio in the United States, including Telemundo, TeleDos, TeleFutura, you name it. So in a nutshell, I think [Univision's] coverage of Cuba is very shallow [interview, January 2007].

On the other hand, another informant noticed a change regarding the coverage of Cuba with the expected, and for many long-awaited, death of Fidel Castro. During my second visit to Miami in January 2007, many rumors were circulating about the failing health of the older Castro brother. The news media were bracing themselves for official confirmation of his death and were already working on reports and features to be printed or broadcast once Castro's end was official:

> I am not saying it represents a major change in the philosophy of Univision as a company because I don't know if it is going to last after the story really dies out or fades away. But hopefully it will be something that we can somehow use as a stepping stone to provide [good] coverage of Cuban affairs in the future. That is only my hope and I am sure that other Cuban-Americans here feel the same way [Daniel Morcate, pers. com., January 2007].

What might have a positive impact on the reporting of Cuba are closer political relations between the island and the United States. This could result in easier access for journalists trying to report on and from Cuba. Still, there is little reason to get carried away by the anticipation of improved news. Televisa, the Mexican network that hugely influenced Univision's early development and to this day is one of its main business partners and sources for content, does not have a great record in bringing quality programs and providing first-class news to its audiences. The media moguls of Mexico, the Azcárragas, have been very clear about whom they consider to be their target audience in Mexico and in the United States respectively during their SIN/SICC involvement. Their programming is targeted not at the educated or the wealthy but at the middle class, the equivalent of Europe's working class. Even in 1997, when taking over the business from his deceased father, the youngest of the Azcárraga clan, Emilio Azcárraga Jean, pointed out, "This is a business. The fundamental thing, the face of this company is the production of entertainment, then information. To educate is the government's job, not Televisa's" (quoted in Sinclair 1999, 50). Univision is not Televisa, but the overriding links in terms of content remain. Others have capitalized on this prime purpose of Televisa and Univision and have made news provision their main selling point: CNN en Español was founded in March 1997 (CNN 2009). The other Spanish-language national network, Telemundo, sees locally produced content as their major advantage over Univision's Mexican-influenced programs.

Telemundo

Telemundo Group, Inc., was formed in 1987, after Reliance Capital Group, L.P., purchased John Blair and Company, a media company that included two Spanish-language stations, WSCV-TV/Channel 51 in Miami and WKAQ-TV/Channel 2 in San Juan, Puerto Rico (Telemundo 2007). At the time, Telemundo Group owned and operated stations in New York, Los Angeles and Miami, allowing it to reach approximately 40 percent of Spanish-speaking households in the U.S. Due to a rights issue, Telemundo became a publicly held company, although Reliance Capital Group continues to be the company's main shareholder. According to Sinclair (2005),

> What was striking about Telemundo [...] was the fact that it was backed by mainstream capital from Wall Street. Small independent Spanish-language stations in all the key markets were acquired and formed into a network. Experienced Hispanic managers were recruited, and programming obtained from a wider variety of sources than the customary fare available on Univisión, given the new network appeal to Hispanics of other than Mexican origin, especially those on the East Coast.

The backing from mainstream capital gives an indication that the purpose of Telemundo was similar to that of Univision in that it was first and primarily a business as opposed to an organization catering to the needs of a specific community or communities.

Three years later, in 1990, Telemundo set out to embark on its most extensive programming launch ever: "16 new programs are introduced and ten others are moved from local to network time slots. The launch brings the tally of shows produced in the U.S. and Puerto Rico to 54 percent, or 43 broadcast hours per week" (Telemundo 2007).

After another change of ownership in 1997, the Telemundo Network was acquired by NBC in October 2001.[3] Having entered into joint ventures with Mexico's Argos Television and Brazil's TV Globo, it was after this acquisition, in 2003, that Telemundo opted for a complete change in programming. The main characteristic that was chosen to set Telemundo apart from its rivals was originally produced content, targeted at Spanish-language audiences in the U.S. In terms of news and current affairs, its journalistic values have been highly influenced by the English-language output of NBC.

At the time of research, developments at Telemundo indicated a widening of its business strategies beyond the Spanish-language television market and the creation of joint ventures online. In conjunction with Grupo Xtra, Telemundo formed two new companies in 2006: Estudios Mexicanos Telemundo and Palmas 26. Estudios Mexicanos Telemundo is working in the production of television content while Palmas 26 has set out to "explore options to participate in the Mexican television market" (Telemundo 2007). With regard to their internet presence, Yahoo!, Inc., NBC Universal Television Group and Telemundo have arranged to "combine their U.S. Hispanic internet properties to form a co-branded internet business to be called Yahoo! Telemundo (http://telemundo.yahoo.com)" (Telemundo 2007). However, this was a short liaison as Yahoo and Telemundo stopped collaborating in November 2008 (Hispanic Online Marketing 2008).

As opposed to Univision, Telemundo is keen to emphasize the importance placed on programs specifically produced for the U.S. Hispanic market. Telemundo's official line is not to target particular groups within the Hispanic market, but to find a middle way that brings in all Hispanics. Alfredo Richard, vice president of corporate communications at Telemundo, explains this goal in the following way:

4. Spanish-Language Television

> We are not trying to create a network for Mexicans that come from Mexico, for Colombians that come from Colombia or Cubans that come from Cuba. We are trying to create a network that appeals to Hispanics that live in the U.S. [...] [E]very immigrant that comes here will, even in the first generation, undergo significant life changes that will impact on the way they see certain issues, the way they dress, the way they... everything they do. We believe that there is a market for Hispanics that are in the U.S. that want to see different content than the Mexicans when they are in Mexico and the Colombians when they are in Colombia or the Chileans when they are in Chile [pers. com., January 2007].

Despite trying to appeal to the "typical" Hispanic immigrant now living in the United States, audience figures remain an essential point of reference. Alfredo Richard points to the challenge of targeting this audience:

> In mass media, you always have this issue: Who do I program for? And it depends ... technology has something to say about it. Now I can program [...] for micro-markets. But overall, traditional media like radio and television, you are casting a very wide net and so you are sending your signal to a lot of people. Internationally, you are able to separate into different feeds and have different programming just to adjust a little bit better to where you are getting. Here in the States of course, you can do it because of the time difference. But at the end of the day, you will always be faced with the challenge of who do I program to [pers. com., January 2007].

The above two statements by Alfredo Richard indicate a predicament for Telemundo. On one hand, it aims to find a middle ground in terms of programming, formats and content that will appeal to as wide an audience as possible within the U.S. Hispanic market. On the other hand, the number of sub-markets within that overall market, i.e., the percentages of Mexicans, Colombians, Venezuelans, Cubans, etc., cannot be completely ignored. Mexicans and Mexican-Americans remain the largest group within the Hispanic market, and a network like Telemundo cannot allow itself the luxury of ignoring them for the sake of an unpopular middle ground or a relatively small number of Cubans and Cuban Americans, for example.

So far, however, the network seems to have been relatively successful in its approach, especially with its hallmark format of U.S.-produced *telenovelas*. *Telenovelas* are one of the most popular and successful formats throughout South America as well as with Hispanics based in the U.S. Tom McGarrity, co-president of Telemundo's network sales, states,

Cuban Americans and the Miami Media

"For many years our novela format was at best misunderstood, at worst made fun of. But now our English-language peers are doing novelas. It's ironic" (quoted in Hoag 2006a). One of the secrets of success for Telemundo's *telenovelas* seems to lie in bringing educational and informational content into the mix. Characters in the show have to deal with "real-life" problems, such as obesity, IBS or immigration difficulties that were identified to be of importance to Hispanics in the States. Audience-specific content is therefore one of the main advantages Telemundo has in comparison to Univision.

Nevertheless, a significant number of interviewees and people in the field commented that they found Telemundo's national output "very Mexican," just like Univision's. Alfredo Richard of Telemundo admits that there are indisputable elements of Mexican-ness:

> Our content will be appealing to Mexicans, it will have Mexican actors, it will have a Mexican feeling. I had lunch with some Cuban people here who hate that. They were saying "It's all Mexican." And in L.A. they say, "Oh, it's all so Cuban." You know, at the end of the day, that is fine. It means that we are not a Cuban network or a Colombian network, or a Mexican network. We try to get content that appeals to all [pers. com., January 2007].

After a promising start, Telemundo has now firmly established itself as the number two Spanish-language network behind Univision. Data provided by Nielsen Media Research on the most popular programs from February 2 to February 8, 2009, in Hispanic households indicate the popularity of Univision's *telenovelas*, as the table below shows.[4]

Rank	Program Name	Net	Hispanic Household Rating (LIVE + SD)	Persons 2+ (000) (LIVE + SD)
1	*Fuego en la Sangre*—Wed., Feb. 4	UNI	24.1	5863
2	*Fuego en la Sangre*—Thur., Feb. 5	UNI	24.0	5718
3	*Fuego en la Sangre*—Tue., Feb. 3	UNI	23.7	5913
4	*Fuego en la Sangre*—Fri., Feb. 6	UNI	22.7	5400
4	*Fuego en la Sangre*—Mon., Feb. 2	UNI	22.7	5426
6	*Cuidado con el Angel*—Wed., Feb. 4	UNI	21.9	4980
7	*Cuidado con el Angel*—Tue., Feb. 3	UNI	21.6	5105
7	*Cuidado con el Angel*—Thur., Feb. 5	UNI	21.6	4995
9	*Cuidado con el Angel*—Mon., Feb. 2	UNI	21.3	4950
10	*Tontas no van Cielo*—Tue., Feb. 3	UNI	20.6	4797

Source: Nielsen Media Research 2009

4. Spanish-Language Television

Fuego en la Sangre is in fact the Mexican, i.e., Televisa, remake of the Columbian soap opera *Las Aguas Mansas*, which had originally been produced by RTI Televisión (IMDB 2009). With *Fuego en la Sangre* nearing its final episode, as well as with *Cuidado con el Angel* (another production of Televisa), Univision even makes the top ten of programs viewed on American television.

Rank	Program	Network	Viewers (P2+)
1	American Idol	FOX	24,941,000
2	Mentalist, The	CBS	19,699,000
3	NCIS	CBS	18,031,00
4	Without a Trace	CBS	14,308,000
5	Dateline NBC	NBC	11,259,000
6	Fringe	FOX	9,828,000
7	Biggest Loser 7	NBC	9,252,000
8	Fuego en la Sangre	UNI	5,746,000
9	Cuidado con el Angel	UNI	4,818,000
10	Charlie Brown Valentine	ABC	4,811,000

Source: Nielsen Wire 2009

This success proves that Spanish-language television is a force to be reckoned with in terms of overall audience share and therefore in terms of advertising income. According to U.S. census figures, Hispanics (excluding the 3.9 million based in Puerto Rico) account for 13.7 percent of the total population (U.S. Census Bureau 2004). Estimates including migrants who entered the U.S. illegally are even higher.[5] Projections of the U.S. Census Bureau see further increases: by 2050 102.6 million Hispanics in the United States could make up 24 percent of the entire population (U.S. Census Bureau 2004).

Despite being runner-up in terms of audience figures, the success of Univision is also advantageous for Telemundo. Spanish-language television can look back on successful years, and this also raises the profile for the second biggest player in the market. But the above tables clearly show that at least for now, Univision's programming strategy draws in more viewers. Is Telemundo right to assume a shared Hispanic identity, or is Univision right to appeal to the largest segment within the Latino and Hispanic community: Mexicans and Mexican Americans?

Cuban Americans and the Miami Media

A Hispanic/Latino Audience and a Diaspora in Reverse?

Understanding (and measuring) Hispanic audiences is further complicated by their use of English-language television: the majority of second-generation Hispanics are bilingual and, even if they are not fluent in English, they might watch English-language television to further their command of the English language. Some viewers also believe that English-language television still has greater resources to provide in-depth coverage, especially when it comes to news and current affairs (Aguilar 2003).

Aside from the difficulty of measuring and predicting Hispanic television audience figures, appealing to Hispanics as a whole is very challenging. During field work it became apparent that the individual communities, such as Mexicans, Venezuelans, Cubans, and especially but not exclusively first generation migrants, predominantly think of themselves in terms of their original nationality, and not in terms of being Hispanic or Latino. This might differ in other locations, but in Miami the Cubans, being still the most influential migrant group, have no need to seek shelter under the Hispanic umbrella.

In light of the data collected for this project, Sinclair's argument that Hispanics "form a diaspora in reverse, since a traditional diaspora is the flow of people from one country into many, but these people have come from many countries into one" (2005) seems doubtful in practice, behind the cameras and on screen. As shown above, decision-makers in television are all too aware that the largest segment of the Spanish-language audience is in fact of Mexican descent. The U.S. Census Bureau American Community Survey of 2006 concluded that of the 44,252,278 Hispanics in the United States, 28,339,354 were of Mexican origin. That accounts for roughly 64 percent. In contrast, there were only 1,520,276 Cubans. They form 3.4 percent of the general Hispanic population (U.S. Census Bureau 2006). Given these figures, Sinclair too acknowledges the constructed nature of Hispanic belonging:

> There has remained a tension between the collective identities which various groups have chosen and asserted for themselves and those which have been chosen for them by media and marketing interests [2005].

4. Spanish-Language Television

How much do an Argentine and a Peruvian have in common, apart from the Spanish language? Admittedly, they potentially share many more everyday life experiences once they are immigrants in the United States, and the common language makes it easy enough to think of them as a combined television audience. However, the main problem with thinking of Hispanics as a diaspora in reverse is that their primary strands of identification are rooted within the framework of nation-states—both their country of origin and the United States. Living in the United States and speaking the same language does not give enough ground for close identification with "the other."[6] This holds especially true in the Cuban American case, as this community was always very careful to see its presence in the United States rooted in the exilic state. One interviewee, the Argentine television journalist Teresa C. Cebrian, summarized this notion in the following way:

> Once I interviewed Jesse Jackson when he was running for president [in 1988]. And he was trying to get me to understand or approach his point of view [...] that he was going to unite Hispanics and Latinos. And I said, "Well, you are very mistaken. It is very, very difficult because culturally, socially, economically, they are very, very different. And it is not going to be that easy." I mean we see it in Latin America, you know. All countries are very different; their customs are very different. And that reverberates here [pers. com., October 2008].

The importance of the "national diaspora" is in fact catered to, to some degree, by local channels. Teresa C. Cebrian also recounted an experience of living on the West Coast, in which a reporter working for the local Univision affiliate in Los Angeles, Channel 34, exaggerated his Mexican accent to appeal to local audiences. Similar stories can be recounted for Puerto Ricans in and around New York City and for local channels in Miami.

Local channels, including GenTV (WGEN, Channel 8), MegaTV (WDLP, Channel 22), Univision's local affiliate (WLTV, Channel 23), América TV (WJAN, Channel 41), Telemundo's local affiliate (WSCV, Channel 51), and Telefutura's local affiliate (WAMI, Channel 69) do cater for the specific needs of the local Hispanic community, or rather the individual national groups.

Cuban Americans and the Miami Media

Local Programming for Cuban Americans

One of the most relevant and respected TV programs for the Cuban American community is *A Mano Limpia*. Broadcasted by América TV, *Mano Limpia* is a political talk show hosted by Dominican-born Oscar Haza that deals with Cuban topics on a regular basis. This one-hour show is scheduled Monday to Friday during prime time between 8 p.m. and 9 p.m. It is usually subdivided by commercial breaks into four segments of roughly twelve minutes. There tends to be either one main topic up for discussion throughout the entire program, or two or three topics are dealt with in the same show, separated by advertising breaks. Depending on the topic itself, Oscar Haza interviews one guest or moderates a discussion between several. According to a producer of *A Mano Limpia*, the show is clearly favored by the conservative segment of the Cuban American community. Much to the interviewee's dismay, the ratings seem to drop when the young and more liberal-thinking production team tries to take things from a different angle:

> There is a very interesting phenomenon, which I am part of, that is that for example our show is for older Cubans but the producers are all young people. The oldest one is 43 and he is a person I would consider open-minded. But our audience is not. We are trying to change the recipe but every time we bring an interviewee that is slightly leftist, you can see the ratings dropping....
> CL: And what do you mean by leftist—a *dialoguero*?
> Yes, for example. This audience is very conservative. Even when we brought Lech Walesa, the former Polish president, the ratings were not good. It is disappointing [interview, June 2006].

Two more local current affairs shows that target a similar audience segment are *María Elvira* on MegaTV, presented by María Elvira Salazar, and *La Última Palabra* on GenTV. Interestingly, *La Última Palabra* (*The Final Word*) is hosted by Ninoska Pérez Castellón, who is a well-known presenter and commentator for Radio Mambí and very active within a number of exile organizations. GenTV's choice of Ninoska Pérez Castellón as host immediately sends out a message as to the direction and the angle the program is going to take, as Pérez Castellón is well known for her outspoken criticism of the Cuban government and those who want to enter into a dialogue.

4. Spanish-Language Television

The above examples indicate clearly that—at least in Miami—grouping Spanish-language speakers in a Hispanic cluster is somewhat artificial, and thinking and identifying oneself along national belongings is still prevalent. The saga of Elián González, a six-year-old boy who came to Miami as a *balsero* (rafter) after his mother had lost her life at sea, is an excellent case study to underline that sharing a language is not enough to form a large Hispanic community.

Memories of Elián

The case of Elián González has garnered substantial attention in the academic community. De la Torre (2003) analyses the religious associations with Elián's survival, while Lauffer, Lancaster and Florentin (2001) scrutinize the framing of the Elián story in three South Florida newspapers. In the opening pages to *This Is Our Land*, Stepick et al. recount Elián's story because "it brought even the most peripheral citizens of the region face-to-face with profound issues of identity, power, and prejudice" (2003, 2). Even a decade after the six-year-old was brought to rescue on Florida shores, recounting the events can quickly add an emotive dimension to a conversation. Elián's story is multi-layered and highly complex. It offers a telling illustration of the divisions between communities.

The events surrounding Elián González are particularly pertinent to the present argument because, to many Cuban Americans' surprise, the nationwide availability of information and the sometimes excessive reporting of the case by local, national and international television news teams did not foster support for the sentiments of the Cuban American community. On the contrary, the Cuban American community's image suffered immensely. Many non–Cubans have problems understanding what it was all about, why this boy was of such immense importance to the Cuban American community and why emotions were running so high. To this day, many Cuban Americans are disappointed by the lack of sympathy for their cause that manifested in other communities.

Before developing this analysis further, let's briefly recount what happened to Elián González. Elián was from Cárdenas, a city in the

Cuban Americans and the Miami Media

Matanzas Province, located in the north west of the island. In November 1999, the five-year-old's mother, Elizabet Brotón, attempted to reach Florida shores by crossing the Straits in a makeshift boat. There were fifteen passengers on the floating device, including Elián and his mother. Only Elián and three others, Nivaldo Fernández, his girlfriend Arianne Horta and her daughter Estefany Herrera Horta, survived. Elián, floating on an inner tube by himself, was found on November 26, 1999. He was quickly brought to Joe DiMaggio's Children's Hospital in Hollywood, Florida. Despite Elián's providing hospital staff with the name and contact details of his Cuba-based father, Juan Miguel González, the child was released into the custody of distant relatives. The Immigration and Naturalization Service (INS)[7] allowed Elián to leave the hospital with Lázaro González. Arguably, this mistake could be considered to be the opening scene of the tragedy that followed. INS officials were understaffed over the Thanksgiving holiday weekend. They later argued that "they acted out of the best of intentions and that it was inconceivable to them that the child's great-uncle would not cooperate in returning him to his father" (Bardach 2002, 72). Elián was forcefully removed from Little Havana and finally reunited with his father in April 2000 after five months in the U.S.

Almost a decade after Elián González was rescued and taken to live with his father's relatives in Miami, just mentioning his name at social events, in casual conversations and in interviews would get people, Cubans and non–Cubans, talking immediately. What is presented here, therefore, are reflections of how different informants remember and make sense of the reporting of the case as well as actual events they witnessed themselves, intermixed with discussion they had at the time of the events and in the years that followed.

Elián's unlikely survival elicited a perception among Cuban Americans that this boy was a symbol of hope. The thought of sending him back to the island was intolerable and was indeed very upsetting for many. The argument recounted again and again by many older exiles in the field is that Elián's mother gave her life so that her son could live in a free country and not be oppressed by Communist, or rather Castrista, ideology. In truth, the story gets more complicated, because one of the reasons Elián's mother is said to have set out to cross the Florida Straits

4. Spanish-Language Television

in the first place was that her fiancé, Lázaro (Rafa) Munero, had imposed an ultimatum on Elizabet Brotón to either come along or accept the end of their relationship. For Elián's mother, there might therefore have been other motives in play, apart from wanting her son to grow up in a democratic society. Nevertheless, the fact remains that she died and Elián survived against the odds.

A further argument recounted by interviewees about why Elián became so important for the community was that he could indeed set a precedent. This issue was not captured by many reporters:

> There were some issues that were probably under-reported..., including what he meant, not as a symbol but as a real thing to many Cuban Americans. If the fight for Elián was lost it meant that the fight for some of their family members who wanted to come over was going to be lost as well. I think that was grossly under-reported, conspicuously absent from most of the coverage [interview, January 2007].

Considering this argument from the other side, it was therefore not only extremely important for the Clinton administration to send Elián back to appease the Castro government and smooth over tense U.S.-Cuban relations; it was also essential to send out the message to the Cuban American community that Elián would not be the first of many children to live in the United States with distant relatives while their parents were still based on the island. Elián's case did not only foreshadow a potentially positive development for the Cuban American community who wanted to encourage more family members on the island to come and live with them. The boy's story also "reopen[ed] the wounds" (De los Angeles Torres 2003, 1) of many Cubans who had arrived with Operation Pedro Pan.

Another issue that was mentioned by several interviewees that did not make it into the wider public debate of the case was the legal argument of Patria Potestas, a term that loosely translates to the paternal right to the child. In Fidel Castro's Cuba, according to the argument of those who fought to keep Elián in the United States, the rights to the child ultimately lie with the state. Elián would therefore technically not be returned to his father, but into the hands of the Cuban state. The Cuban state, i.e., Fidel Castro, would thus have ultimate say over the fate of the boy. Alejandro Aguirre, publisher of *Diario las Américas*,

Cuban Americans and the Miami Media

recounts that this argument was either not mentioned at all by reporters or that it was misunderstood:

> What upset me about the entire coverage, all the 15,000 journalists who were here wrote exactly what everybody else wrote and talked to the same three idiots that everybody else talked to, is that that argument which was the basis of their entire legal argument was never heard by anyone. The American government dealt with it in a footnote in a report that was almost 50 pages long. They had a tremendous interest in that everybody was there but nobody was talking about [the legal argument] because that was the only legitimate argument that was there. But the political theatrics were a lot easier to cover. There is a definite before and after, politically and in the exile community [pers. com., June 2006].

This view was shared by Susana Barciela, a Cuban American editorial writer for the *Miami Herald*. Even local media had difficulties covering the events adequately, as Barciela's following statement underlines:

> We only had one, maybe two Cuban reporters during Elián which I think was also a shame. Because if you are a pro, you are a pro. You are going to be impartial whether you cover Martin Luther King or Gandhi. And if you are not, you should not be working for a newspaper in the first place. What ended up happening—and that is very unfortunate—you end up with people writing about cultures that they do not understand. And then you get really stupid stuff and the newspaper looks really dumb [pers. com., June 2006].

It seems ironic that the largest media event revolving around the Cuban American community in recent years did not manage to capture what was at stake. It saddened and disappointed many Cuban Americans that a large part of the Anglo and the wider Hispanic community showed only mild interest and very little support. There was a sense in the Cuban American community that all the journalists who had come to Miami to report were choosing the easy way out and did not take into account what was at stake. Pulitzer Prize–winning journalist Liz Balmaseda wrote in a front-page commentary of the *Miami Herald* at the time:

> Telling these stories [about human rights violations in Cuba and the hardship of Cubans and Cuban Americans] well may require visas to Cuba and approval from the Castro government. Those are the hard stories to report. The easy ones swell around Elian's great uncle's house, where no visa is required and no government-stamped access is needed. Yes, they may seem colorful and fabulously visual but they only begin to fill out a vast, textured landscape that is very much part of this country [2000, 1].

4. Spanish-Language Television

It is worth noting in this context that the main issue that brings many immigrants from Latin and South American countries to the same table is that of naturalization, and the difficulty of becoming a legal U.S. citizen. Thanks to the Cuban Adjustment Act of 1966, which was moderated slightly by the "wet foot/dry foot policy" in 1995, Cubans do not face this problem. Non-Cuban interviewees and informants very often pointed toward the many privileges that the Cubans had enjoyed throughout the years, mainly because they were initially categorized as political exiles and not as economic migrants. Why should Elián get special treatment? Why should he not be reunited with his father? For many, Hispanics and Anglos, this seemed like the most natural thing in the world.

What angered the Cuban American community even more was that Fidel Castro not only succeeded in bringing Elián back to Cuba, he furthermore managed to successfully use this case to improve his public image. Once Elián was back in Cuba, Castro and the Cuban state media left the family in peace. Dr. Andy Gómez, a senior research fellow at the Institute for Cuban and Cuban American Studies (ICCAS) at the University of Miami, expresses his annoyance over the contrasting treatments of the child:

> To some extent we have put Fidel in a position where he looked good and we looked bad because he was saying: "The father wants his son back. Not me." And Fidel allowed Elián to be totally absorbed by Cuban society. That was clearly contradictory to the way we handled it. Here, every day of the news, it was Elián. There, Elián was whisked off and nobody saw or heard about him for months. Fidel said he wanted to protect the privacy of a family in their moments of sorrow and give the family time for reconciliation. Wait a minute!—Shouldn't we have been saying that over here and not he over there? [pers. com., June 2006].

Tracey Eaton, who worked as a foreign correspondent for the *Dallas Morning News* at the time and covered the Elián saga from Havana, agrees with Gómez's assessment: "Castro took full advantage of the situation for political gain. It was also a big international public relations coup for Castro. The exile community, meantime, came off poorly in the eyes of both ordinary Americans and the international community. Castro clearly won that round" (pers. com., November 2008).

During and after the Elián crisis, the relationship between the

Cuban Americans and the Miami Media

Cuban American community on the one side and the Anglo and the wider Hispanic communities on the other worsened significantly, and participants were adamant that the media coverage, including images of hysterical protestors, had a part to play in this. Cuban American artist Humberto Calzada put it very plainly: "We looked like assholes to the world" (pers. com., January 2007).

Interviewees were split over the importance of Elián to community relations between Cubans and Anglos in Miami. While some interpreted it as a clash that is likely to happen from time to time, with consequences that are maybe not forgotten immediately but definitely no major obstacle, others saw the behavior of the Anglo community as something that Cubans would not be able to wipe from their collective consciousness in the following years. According to the latter group, the Elián case brought to light a deep misunderstanding or unawareness of who the other group was and what they stood for: "They could not understand that we wanted Elián to stay. It was beyond their comprehension. And it was beyond our comprehension that they could not understand what we were about.... But unless you live under a regime like that, you will never understand" (interview, January 2007).

Returning to previous notions about Hispanic audiences, it becomes clear that the over-reporting of the Elián case did not contribute to uniting communities. The opposite was the case: annoyance and hostility grew steadily. Susana Barciela of the *Miami Herald* has somewhat painful memories of the time:

> Elián was a very tough time to live through. I think there was a lot of soul searching. I am not sure if there were any permanent shifts in terms of understanding. In fifty years, you know... It is surprising how it does fade away, the hurts that happened during that time. I mean it was a lot of polarization on all sides....
>
> There was a significant amount of institutional hostility geared against anything Cuban within the immigration offices here. It happened in a lot of other places [too], where it became politically correct to go around and curse Cubans [referring to Cuban Americans based in the United States] [pers. com., June 2006].

Perhaps for the first time in the history of the exile community since the revolution, it became blindingly obvious that the Cuban Americans, including the historic exiles and their descendants, were perhaps

4. Spanish-Language Television

not as welcome and as well understood as they had assumed they were. The community was used to a critical press, especially from left-leaning papers such as the *New York Times*. However, they were not used to these kinds of reactions from their neighbors. Having brought so much prosperity to South Florida, they could not comprehend how people they believed to be their friends would not support their cause and—on the contrary—were even getting annoyed with the ongoing protests.

Teresa C. Cebrian was working for Channel 34, Univision's local affiliate in Los Angeles, at the time. Questioned about her recollection of the events and the reporting, she says:

> People did not understand in Los Angeles why people here were so angry about a boy being reunited with his dad. They thought that that was the most natural thing. Here, with the whole issue of communism, something that is really never been experienced by most of us obviously... And [Elián's] family was portrayed as very emotional, hysterical... What you saw in the English media? You saw these people going on and on and on that they were saving him and they [people on the West Coast] just weren't getting it [pers. com., January 2007].

Aside from the symbolic and religious connotations that many Cuban Americans had attributed to Elián, the case also raised much wider questions about what it means to be a U.S. citizen, and why this particular group of migrants, the Cubans, had and still have the privileges they have. Had a Mexican or a Venezuelan migrant child been given the same kind of media and institutional attention under similar circumstances? Is it more important to grow up with one's closest family around or to trade that for a life in a country that describes itself as the "land of the free and the home of the brave" in its national anthem? Arguably these were much harder questions to tackle in current television formats than showing pictures of a six-year-old riding his bike, or playing with the Labrador puppy that he was given by Republican Congressman Lincoln Diáz-Balart (CNN 2000).

Concluding Remarks

Out of all the media examined in this study, Spanish-language television in the United States tastes least of Cuban American flavors. This is not due to a lack of Cuban Americans working for the TV stations but rather due to the business's dynamics and business models, dominated by audience figures and advertising revenue. With Mexican Americans forming the largest group among Hispanic audiences, the main players in the field, Univision and Telemundo, cannot afford to neglect them.

Spanish-language television, and the Elián Gonzáles story in particular, provide an excellent example of the constructed nature of Hispanic identity. While Hispanic loyalty may be a common feature in other places in the United States, sentiments of pan–Hispanic belonging seemed to be of lesser importance for the Cuban Americans based in Miami. While Cuban Americans were on the one hand pleased with the amount of coverage the case was receiving on a national scale, on English- and Spanish-language national television, there was also a realization that other Spanish-speaking groups in the United States and the American population at large did not comprehend their perspective and their struggle. Moreover, national television coverage did not lead to the kind of understanding, a shared sense of Hispanic or migrant identity and solidarity, that many Cuban Americans were hoping for in this situation. On the contrary, it led to alienation and brought to light misunderstandings that media attention, including the reporting of the case on U.S. television channels including news channels, could not counteract and perhaps even elevated.

The case of Elián Gonzáles underlines the fact that the reporting of another group's concerns alone does not bridge the gap between communities or necessarily lead to a shared outlook and mutual support. On the contrary, the fact that the case was so widely reported, and at the same time immensely underreported, has led members of the Cuban American community to question and re-evaluate their sense of belonging in the United States.

Nevertheless, Hispanic television remains a success story from an economic perspective. Much more than in a European context, it is numbers that count. The next chapter will consider a much more individualized form of consumption and production: how the possibilities of the internet have taken the meaning of an "active audience" to another level and have in fact allowed users to become producers themselves. How this has played with regards to Cuban Americans and their interests, activities and concerns will be examined in the following chapter.

5

The Internet
An Emerging Transnational Sphere?

This chapter examines the use of new media technologies. More specifically, it focuses on the use of internet websites and blogs by selected members and groups of the Cuban American community and others with a strong interest in issues relating to the Cuban American community in Miami and to U.S.–Cuba relations. In comparison to other chapters in this volume, the following pages have a much stronger transnational dimension, especially due to widened access to the internet in Cuba under Raúl Castro, even though this process of opening up is pursued rather reluctantly and indolently. Evolving internet access also does not benefit the Cuban population at large but rather a selected few, while the majority will have to share facilities if they are available to them at all (Voss 2008; Voss 2009).

Recent scholarship has highlighted that internet use is complex and that the purpose, type and frequency of engagement varies greatly between different user groups depending on age, gender and cultural context, to name but a few decisive factors.[1] Murthy (2008) emphasizes the digital divide that runs along lines of age and social capital: people over the age of 55 and the socially disadvantaged are less likely to be found in online discussion forums, posting on blogs or getting involved in other online activities. Field work data showed that some members of the historic exile group used computer and the internet on a regular basis, but perhaps did not make use of the interactive features the internet has to offer. An example of this was a contributor to a *periodiquito*

Cuban Americans and the Miami Media

I met in the University of Miami's Cuban Heritage Collection, who proudly presented to me the online version of their mini-newspaper. However, there was little room for interactivity, such as readers or users posting comments, apart from the "old-fashioned" e-mail or letter to the editor.

On the other hand of the spectrum, there are some very keen bloggers. As can be expected, exile organizations also make great use of online tools. One great example of this is a group called Raíces de Esperanza (Roots of Hope), which will be introduced in detail below.

Blogging to Get It Right

Blogs, or weblogs, have taken the web by storm (McIntosh 2005).[2] As Jill Walker Rettberg points out, "Ten years ago the word 'blog' didn't exist" (2008, 1). Walker Rettberg (2008, 17–22) argues that, like hypertext, blogs can be viewed as a genre as well as a medium. Broadly speaking, a blog can be characterized as "a frequently updated Web site consisting of dated entries arranged in reverse chronological order so the most recent post appears first" (Walker 2005, 45).

Despite the relative novelty of online communication, the positions taken by bloggers are not at all new or unexpected. The two blogs considered here are the *Herald Watch Blog* and *Radio Mambí Watch*. My initial awareness of these blogs grew out of a shared interest: both blogs scrutinize Miami-based media, the *Miami Herald* and Radio Mambí respectively. However, over the course of this research, it became apparent that the blogs, the bloggers themselves and their relationship to the Cuban American community and their motivation deserved further attention. Both bloggers, Henry Gómez of the *Herald Watch Blog* and Paul Benavides of *Mambí Watch*, agreed to be interviewed.[3]

The *Herald Watch Blog*

Before starting the *Herald Watch Blog*, Henry Gómez, an advertising executive in his late thirties, had been a quiet observer of Miami's English- and Spanish-language media for a few years. Having grown up

5. The Internet

in Philadelphia, Pennsylvania, his awareness of issues relating to Cuba was minimal while he was attending school. He became interested in Cuban history only as a young adult; both his parents were born in Cuba. Gómez, who works for an advertising agency, started the *Herald Watch Blog* after a letter he had sent to the *Miami Herald* for publication was edited to an extent that he thought was unacceptable:

> They stripped out all the criticism of the *Herald*. They left the other points in, which I thought, you know… You're the only newspaper in town. You kind of have an obligation, particularly on the opinion page. But look at yourself. Allow people to criticize you. They apparently have a very thin skin over there [pers. com., June 2007].

Over the years, Gómez has become highly critical of the *Miami Herald*, and his blog scrutinizes the *Herald*'s every move, be it editorial or managerial. Initially, I met Gómez to hear his take on the Martí moonlighter story, which he extensively covered in his blog. During the interview, it was obvious that the blog was more than a hobby for Henry Gómez. He was extremely passionate about topics relating to Cuba and the Cuban American community. He had strong feelings about the (in his eyes) misrepresentation of the Cuban American community in the English-language version of the *Herald* and other national English-language newspapers, such as the *New York Times*. Gómez was convinced that the paper was not doing a successful job in serving its readers. Gómez asserts that he writes the blog "for people like me; people that are curious to know what's going on inside the *Herald*. People that really want … that suspect that they are not getting all sides of the story when reading this paper.… You know our newspaper at times has been an embarrassment. It really has done shoddy things" (pers. com., June 2007). Gómez also has and contributes to other blogs and sites; they include *trenblindado.com—Exposing the Truth About Ché Guevara* (http://www.trenblindado.com/), *CubanAmericanPundits-.com—Thought-provoking Essays from a Cuban-American Perspective* (http://cubanamericanpundits.blogspot.com), and *Babalú Blog—An Island on the Net Without a Bearded Dictator* (http://babalublog.com).

A further reason that motivates Gómez to spend so much time and effort in writing about Cuba-related issues on the web is that he would like to see a wider involvement with the Cuban plight. After lamenting the fact that newspapers such as the *New York Times* and the *Washington Post* do not cover or only have very limited coverage of Cuba-related topics, Gómez summarized the impulse for blogging as follows: "The problem is that we are all talking to ourselves and nobody is talking to the general public. That is partly where my other blog and blogs where my colleagues write about Cuba come into play. We are trying to speak to an English-language audience. We are reporting stuff that does not get reported" (pers. com., June 2006).

Over the years, Gómez moved on from being merely an observer to become more and more actively involved in the local exile scene. He has been invited to local radio shows and he is the president of Bloggers United for Cuban Liberty, a group of bloggers that organize campaigns to "generate a lot of awareness about the Cuban reality" (Bloggers United for Cuban Liberty 2009).

On the *Herald Watch Blog*, Gómez runs a small advertisement that encourages people working for the *Heralds* or those who know people employed by the *Heralds* to contact him if they have a story.[4] Gómez confirms, "The interesting thing about blogging is that people start sending you emails and insiders start sending you stuff. They send you loads that you didn't know existed or things to follow up on" (pers. com., January 2007). For Henry Gómez, blogging was a way to take the continued struggle of the Cuban American community online. Blogging helped him—even though he might not have planned this—to strengthen his profile in the exile community online and offline. It is worth noting that within the political spectrum of the Cuban American community, Gómez leans toward the right, toward a hardliner approach and, to some extent, that explains his success outside the world of blogs.

Mambí Watch Blog

Another blogger who started writing due to his critical views on a local media outlet is Paul Benavides. At the time of interviewing, Benavides, a graduate student of conflict analysis and conflict resolution, was in his late twenties; he grew up in the Miami area but was born in Peru. His family received the help and support of a Cuban American family when they first arrived in the United States. Like Gómez, Paul Benavides was a mere observer throughout most of his adult life. He became more

5. The Internet

interested in politics at the start of the second Iraq War. During that time, Paul Benavides listened to many Spanish-language radio stations, in particular Radio Mambí and WQBA. Taking in the arguments and points made by journalists and callers of Radio Mambí, Benavides wondered where "the other side of that debate" was and emphasized that in his view, even national conservative radio allows for a greater number of liberal voices and perspectives to be heard. His concern grew further because in Miami, Miami-Dade County and South Florida more generally, a significant percentage of the population, including Benavides's own parents, prefer Spanish-language stations and consume no or very little English-language news. That limits their sources of information, but in Benavides's view it also means that the kind of information they do receive is extremely biased toward the right.

His blog, *Mambí Watch*, therefore, is an effort to widen the debate:

> What Mambí-Watch tries to do most is talk about the influence of some of the most extreme branch of the Cuban exile community—such like *Unidad Cubana* and they are tied with *Commando F4* and how they talk about or continue to spread messages that if the Cuban government is overthrown, that violence is all right. My personal opinion is that we should be very careful when we support violence and stuff like that. And so I'm very critical of that when you hear it on the radio.... People supporting violence or supporting groups that will support violence or in some cases supporting positions where there is no other resort but violence. I'm really critical of that and I think there should be a voice that counters it so those other voices are not the only ones being heard.... I really had a listen to all the other Spanish radio stations but Radio Mambí and WQBA have such a large audience [Paul Benavides, pers. com., October 2008].

Questioned about whether he considers an English-language blog a serious response to powerful Spanish-language radio stations, Benavides explains that he would like to see his blog translated into Spanish as well; however, English is the language in which he "can get it out faster" (pers. com., October 2008). Contrary to his previous argument that he is concerned about those members of the Hispanic community in Miami who only speak Spanish, he asserts that many people, even people aged over 55, are able to at least read English. However, the point remains that even with the necessary language skills, that segment of the Spanish-language community is highly unlikely to read blogs.

Cuban Americans and the Miami Media

Despite some similarities between the *Herald Watch Blog* and *Mambí Watch* and the bloggers' motivations to start writing, Gómez's and Benavides's experience of how the blog allows them to relate to the Cuban American community could not have been more different. While Gómez became more and more active and involved in the exile community, Benavides has kept a very low profile. Benavides does not speak to his friends about the blog, not even to Cuban American friends who might have a genuine interest in the topics he writes about. Benavides asserts that a discussion about Cuban American issues is best to be had online because it is more suitable for exchanging views about these kinds of issues:

> PB: I think the best way to talk about the U.S.–Cuba issue is in a forum where people know it is going to be discussed. Otherwise it can become an emotional issue, especially with Cubans.... You can run into road blocks and the best way is to have a forum where everyone understands that it is going to be discussed and we are going to have a discussion, a civilized discussion.
> CL: And you think this is better done online than offline?
> PB: Online you have your space, they have their space. Any exchange is kind of regulated by the comments—through [comment regulation features on websites such as blogspot.com] and stuff like that. I think that is a pretty good way. Writing ... when you write you're not too quick to reply to say something wrong. Or maybe you want to ... you take the time to say whatever you want to say correctly or clearly. I think that's a good way to have a discussion online. That's a good way [pers. com., October 2008].

In addition to his reluctance to have an offline discussion about Cuba-related topics, Benavides also takes a more left-leaning political stance. As can be expected, this has led to *Mambí Watch* being ignored by most Cuban American media, including Radio Mambí, the main focus of Benavides' posts. A further point is that Benavides does not have Cuban roots, and despite his extensive knowledge of the issue, he would not easily qualify as a natural candidate for the popular Cuban American current affairs shows on television and on the radio. That said, the host of the very popular Spanish-language current affairs show *A Mano Limpia* (Channel 41), Oscar Haza, is Dominican, so coming from a different background does not automatically exclude one from the debate.

5. The Internet

Local Disconnects and the
Possibility of a Transnational Sphere

While Benavides seemed to be rather indifferent to the lack of overt interest in his blog by the very media outlets and journalists he scrutinizes, another blogger and writer, Emilio Ichikawa, was critical of the lack of attention that the "old media" were giving to online output. Emilio Ichikawa, a writer, commentator and former philosophy lecturer at the University of Havana, has a website (http://ei.eichikawa.com) on which he publishes his own articles and those written by friends and likeminded journalists and commentators. His approach to publishing his thoughts on the internet is based partly on practicalities:

> [The Web, radio, TV], these are a means of transmission and one has to use all of them. I believe that Cuban radio in Miami does not make adequate use of the work we do online. We are "disconnected." Neither do they show much interest in our critiques. Cuban radio in Miami is in a state of stagnation and those who are involved in radio stations do not want to find out more.... For example, they prefer to comment on an article of a national newspaper that is about one week old, instead of reading and referring to our websites [Emilio Ichikawa, pers. com., October 2008; my translation].
>
> [Son medios y hay que usarlos todos. Yo creo que la Radio cubana de Miami no usa adecuadamente el trabajo que hacemos en la WEB. Estamos como desconectados. Tampoco les interesan mucho nuestras críticas. La Radio cubana de Miami está en un momento de estancamiento y quienes lo hacen no se quieren enterar. La radio local es un tema de nuestros blogs y WEBs, pero, como te dije, no quieren enterarse. Prefieren, por ejemplo, comentar una noticia que un periódico nacional haya dado con una semana de retraso, a tomarla y referir nuestras WEBs.]

In contrast to Henry Gómez and Paul Benavides, Emilio Ichikawa publishes and writes in Spanish (although an English translation of certain articles is provided). Furthermore, while Miami's Cuban American community often has a tendency to speak to itself, Ichikawa enjoys the transnational opportunities of connection that the internet can offer. He asserts that he takes comments by former colleagues and by Cuban state media on his work very seriously and tries to enter into a dialogue by seriously responding to articles written on the island.

Emilio Ichikawa's call for transnational exchange and a serious, open and fair debating culture resonates with many younger Cuban Americans. Another interviewee and blogger confirms the need to move away from blackmailing people via accusatory radio announcements and unjustified or personalized comments. However, it would be premature to celebrate the internet as a transnational meeting place in which only civilized discussions take place. Paul Benavides of *Mambí Watch* recounted an incident in which personal details about him and his family were published online. For him, taking an online discussion into an offline environment and involving his family, who knew nothing about his blog, was an absolute breach of etiquette. Observing several blogs and comment sections of various mainstream media over the course of this research also gave a clear indication that posts often go below the belt.

Recent academic work has pointed toward the potential threat blogging could have to a clear definition of journalistic work and to the existence and necessity of professional journalism more generally.[5] However, despite their motivation to widen the debate and at times even discredit mainstream media, the bloggers interviewed clearly understood themselves to be part of the wider media ecology, as opposed to the next generation of journalists who would make mainstream media obsolete. Even though they appreciate blogs as an excellent form of participation, they have no doubt about the necessity and importance of "big journalism" (McIntosh 2005). In a way, this also freed them from adhering to journalistic values, such as impartiality, balance, fairness. Even though there was a great deal of thoroughness and background research, these bloggers' aim was to balance the overall media ecology with regard to the reporting of certain topics.

In summary, the blogs and bloggers introduced here have built very complex and highly varied relationships to each other, to other media aimed at the Cuban American community, and to the existing mainstream media. A strong motivation seems to be the urge to "correct" the debate as it is led by the press, radio and television; to fill a gap that has been identified by the blogger(s). While some use the internet with a strong local focus, others emphasize that the internet gives them the freedom to express their honest views, unrestricted by editorial lines. More so than other media, the internet also has the potential of moving away from old propaganda models and creating a transnational sphere of exchange. This capacity is also made use of by an organization of young Cuban Americans, Raíces de Esperanza (Roots of Hope).

Re-thinking Exile Politics: The Case of Raíces de Esperanza

Raíces de Esperanza (RDE) (Roots of Hope) is a youth organization founded by Cuban American Ivy-League students in the Northeast of the United States. In comparison to other exile organizations, RDE takes a very different approach. Its aim is to connect with people in Cuba on an individual basis. RDE differs from other groupings in explicitly avoiding an official stance on political issues and current U.S. policy, including the trade embargo. One reason why this organization appeals to young Cuban Americans is that its premise is to focus on causes and ideas that unite the exile community, rather than splitting it into fractions. Nathalie Marcos, an undergraduate student at the University of Miami, pointed out that Cuban Americans are extremely opinionated, which has resulted in the existence of many exile organizations. She asserts: "I think we need to focus more on the similarities between those opinions" (pers. com., October 2008). Raíces de Esperanza identified actions that could form a common ground, for example care packages for political prisoners—"nobody has issues with that" (pers. com., October 2008).

Another significant difference between RDE and other exile organizations is their present-centered approach when relating to Cuba. One informant involved with RDE repeatedly emphasized the point that people in Miami do not "know the Cuban reality" and it is the reality of everyday life in Cuba today that needs to inform the approach of an exile organization or any organization concerned with Cuba, not the dominant narrative of collective memories. This type of organization was also called for by Paul Benavides, the blogger who created the *Mambí Watch* blog. Benavides argued that one of the main reasons why the Cuban American community had received relatively little support and sympathy from other Hispanics was that their approach was too "state-based" and not "people-based." Benavides made the case that siding with the U.S. government to overthrow Fidel Castro had never worked in the past[6]; on the contrary, it could be interpreted as a lack of concern for the Cuban people. In addition, most of the initiatives were led by a small group of radical Cuban American hardliners who exploited collective memories of loss to devise violent actions.

While groups such as CANF had a strong focus on big politics, becoming a sizeable player in Washington, D.C., and South Florida, the emphasis of RDE is on a micro-level. RDE's purpose is "bridging the gap between the Florida Straits" as Raúl Moas, a Cuban American student who is a member of the executive committee of Raíces de Esperanza, explains: "Overlooking the embargo and policy, it's about connecting with my fellow friend in Cuba; with someone who is 20 years old, going to University of Havana and has an interest in this, or an interest in anything" (pers. com., January 2008).

In contrast to many other organizations of this kind, RDE does not take an official position on the trade embargo. Overall, this has been a great advantage, because it allows people with differing political views to get involved, and it also allows members to change their views, if they so wish. One interviewee, a graduate who is involved with Raíces de Esperanza and with the Miami-based Cuban American student organization CAUSA: Students United for a Free Cuba, admits that her opinion on the trade embargo and on the United States' Cuba policy was challenged after a visit to the island. Seeing the consequences of the embargo with her own eyes and speaking to people in Cuba made her question the hardline approach that dominates the discourse within the majority of Spanish-language media outlets, especially those targeting the mainstream Cuban American community. Focusing on human rights violations in Cuba instead of U.S. policies allows for broader support from those, Cuban Americans and others, who are tired of discussing politics and would refrain from joining any type of organization with firm political goals.

Transnational Dialogue and Humanitarian Projects

To a far greater extent than radio, television and the press, the internet allows for a transnational dialogue between those based in Miami

5. The Internet

and Cubans based on the island. As an organization, RDE has realized this potential. One of RDE's ongoing campaigns is Cell Phones for Cuba (Cells for Cuba 2010). The idea behind this project is to encourage U.S. students to donate their old mobile phones to Cuban youth or make a donation toward purchasing mobile phones. The aim is to empower young people on the island by allowing them to stay connected and build a stronger communication network as this has shown benefits on a variety of levels in other developing countries.

In addition, Raíces de Esperanza organizes annual conferences that are accompanied by humanitarian actions such as sending aid packages and filming video messages for youths on the island. RDE is keen to establish any form of contact and exchange with young people on the island. However, what might hamper these undertakings are the limited facilities in Cuba.

Even though Raíces de Esperanza has the best of intention to break with the past and promote its campaigns as apolitical, it cannot comply with this ideal completely. Its 2009 annual conference at the University of Miami had actor and director Andy García as a special guest. Their website contains a message from Gloria Estefan (Raíces de Esperanza 2010). Both of these celebrities have made their hardline standpoints in relation to Cuba very clear, and collaborating with them lets RDE to some degree be associated with these views in the Cuban American community.

Internet Access in Cuba

The organization's success is also due to the expanding availability of telecommunication facilities and widening internet access in Cuba. Because of the ease of publishing one's contemplations and observations online, Cuban Americans based in Miami can read and view material from the island that was produced by Cubans who are standing outside of official distribution channels associated with the government.[7] Within this context, one interviewee emphasized in particular the excitement and pleasure he got from reading Yoani Sánchez's award-winning blog *Generación Y* (http://desdecuba.com/generaciony).

After the long years filled with rumors and scarce reports often including unwelcome news, Miami's Cuban American community relishes every piece of information coming from the island that is free from "official spin"—although that is not to say that the internet, in particular blogs and discussion forums, is the place where uncontested information on Cuba can be found. It is, however, an additional and welcome source that was not available before. Since Cuba cautiously widened people's access to the internet, more information comes directly from the island, and this allows Cuban Americans and Cubans to enter into a discussion on a very different level. In return, Cubans based on the island also have the opportunity to receive information from outside the island, although this might dismay the Cuban government.[8] Staff maintaining the website of *El Nuevo Herald* confirmed the site's popularity with users in Cuba.

Within the wider exile community, reactions to the creation and growth of Raíces de Esperanza have been positive. Several young Cuban Americans who are involved with RDE, CAUSA or both point out that the older generation is relieved to see them taking over. As Nathalie Marcos, the executive vice president of CAUSA, phrases it, the question on many aging exiles' mind has been, "Who is going to take the torch?" (pers. com., October 2008). However, even though members of Raíces de Esperanza and CAUSA sounded very committed, there is an awareness that they are facing very demanding tasks:

> It takes a lot to be involved in this cause. It is a frustrating thing. It is a very challenging thing. And I think that the answer or the solution is not only way ahead but it will be a long process as well. It's not something [where] we will find a cure or something so quickly that it will just disseminate. It is going to be a process and it's going to be an issue.... It's almost like a life-long journey and to get someone engaged in that requires a lot of faith and a lot of dedication to that [Nathalie Marcos, pers. com., October 2008].

To conclude this section, it is worth noting that estimating the success of organizations such as Raíces de Esperanza, or any other exile organization for that matter, is extremely difficult. How these organizations and their efforts are perceived in Cuba and how much of a difference they make on the ground would have to be established through research activities on the island. However, that in itself might prove an intricate task, given the nature of state power and citizen surveillance. Interviewees in Miami mentioned video conferences with opposition leaders and "work" with dissidents as part of their engagement, but were—to protect those associates based in Cuba—reluctant to go into great detail.

Apart from taking a different perspective from their parents' and grandparents' generations when it comes to engagement with the island, young Cuban Americans interviewees emphasized their desire to make some form of a contribution to the cause or *la lucha* (the struggle).[9] This desire drives many in the exile community; the waiting—even if it takes a lifetime—has to be filled with some form of activity. From all over the world exiled Cubans send materials such as books, old postcards, and bulletins to the Cuban Heritage Collection or even deliver their treasures in person, because of a desire "to do something" for Cuba.

During some conversations in Miami, the lingering fear that it was all for nothing clearly shone through. Despite organizations such as Raíces de Esperanza, first and second generations of exiles have aged and died in Miami and cultural change is imminent. A great indicator for the slow yet continuous Americanization of the exile is language itself.

The Language Question: Spanish or English?

Miami is a bilingual city. Professional success comes more easily for those who speak both English and Spanish. In relation to the generational shifts in media use and individual as well as collective identities, one has to emphasize the importance of an accompanying shift in the dominant language, from Spanish to English. All informants who were born in the United States preferred English when consuming media, though Spanish was often spoken at home. This is underlined by the U.S. Census Bureau, according to whose statistics, Cuban American households in which Spanish is spoken, although household members speak English very well, amounts to 42.7 percent. In slightly more households, 43.2 percent, Spanish is spoken and household members do not have a very good command of the English language. Only a small percentage, 14.1 percent, speak only English at home (U.S. Census Bureau 2007).

Cuban Americans and the Miami Media

Language is a source for as well as a symptom of a much deeper cultural and generational change. From one generation of Cuban Americans growing up in the United States to the next, something is lost while something else is gained. Those who have completed part or all of their education in the U.S. tend to feel more at home in mainstream America than their parents and grandparents did. This process, and with it the adoption of English as primary and dominant language, is counteracted by the preference for Spanish of incoming migrants; those migrants, who arrive in the U.S. as adults with no interest in undergoing further education in the States are—depending on their professional situation—not urgently required to learn English or improve their English-language skills. With regard to the overall demographic composition of the Cuban American community, the majority (64.8 percent) of Cuban Americans who were born abroad entered the United States before 1990; 24.6 percent arrived between 1990 and 1999; and 11.7 percent arrived in 2000 or after (U.S. Census Bureau 2007). These figures testify to the efforts of the U.S. government to manage incoming migration from Cuba and reduce the number of new arrivals, even though legislation toward Cuban migrants is still more favorable than those aimed at other newcomers, for example, Mexican migrants.

In the field, Hispanics, with impeccable English and native or near-native competency in Spanish, found their language skills and cultural knowledge, which allow them to easily access the mainstream Anglo as well as the Hispanic context, highly enriching. And it is generally the environment that decides whether English or Spanish takes over, as one interviewee, a Cuban American student at the University of Miami, points out:

> For my academic purposes, most of my schooling has been in English. Obviously my analytical thinking works better in English but then there is parts of me that can only be expressed in Spanish. At certain moments I catch myself thinking in Spanish. Catch us during a domino game ... you will not hear a word of English [interview, June 2006].

While the context decides what language is used in face-to-face conversation, media use is a different matter again. Here, English is clearly preferred by younger Cuban Americans who grew up in the United States.

In the field, younger Cuban Americans and Hispanics commented

5. The Internet

on their impression that English-language media seemed to offer a better quality of news and entertainment, which can partly be explained by the comparatively smaller budgets allocated to Spanish-media outlets, as is the case for *El Nuevo Herald*. As the above statistics show, over 43 percent of households have limited English-language skills, and this guarantees the success of Cuban American/Spanish-language media outlets in Miami—a fact that Miami-based media are very aware of.

Online portals, msn, AOL, and Yahoo! cater to the bilingualism of some of their users. They work from the assumption that the online experience of their users is not linear but driven by interests and interrelations between different types and depths of information and entertainment. Hiram Enríquez, news product manager of Yahoo! en Español, explains:

> We work as a network because we think a quarter of the users are bilingual and can read English as well as Spanish.... They can go back and forth from one network to another. For example, a user who is reading a story about the election in Mexico in the English-language site will find a link to our coverage in that story. If you are interested in this story and you read Spanish, then it is not sufficiently covered for you in the English-language Yahoo site. You can go to the Spanish site and you'll find more in-depth coverage on that topic. It is an integration of networks on Yahoo! [pers. com., June 2006].

As with television output, the main news on online portals is meant to draw in as great a number of U.S. Hispanics as possible. But online media have the advantage of being able to provide more detailed information on specific countries in a few clicks: "If you are in the position of trying to work with U.S. Hispanics, you need to understand that what matters in the daily lives is U.S. politics, U.S. Hispanic topics, such as immigration. But they are also paying attention to what is going on in their country of origin" (Hiram Enríquez, pers. com., June 2006).

On the other hand, there is no denying that the observed preference of young Cuban Americans for media in English will have complex long-term consequences. It can lead to a further diversification and fragmentation of audiences and communities; journalistic work in English naturally has a much more diverse audience in comparison to the closely targeted listeners of Miami's Spanish-language radio stations. Unless younger Cuban Americans, who prefer to consume media in the English language, actively seek out journalistic work aimed at the Cuban American community, they are less likely to be surrounded by mediated collective memories once they have left their parents' houses. Then again, transferring journalistic work into the English language gives a wider range of people, including those who do not speak Spanish or prefer to communicate in English, the chance to participate in the debates.

Concluding Remarks

Situating the experiences of two bloggers in relation to other media forms points toward the strong entanglement between traditional Cuban American media and new voices that can be found online. In many ways, what can be observed on the net, in blogs, forums, and sites, is very similar to analogue content. Nevertheless, the Internet offers the option to move away from a certain way of discussing Cuban issues that has been very much associated with some Cuban American radio stations, such as shouting people down on air or calling them names. To some extent this is continued online, depending on which forum one goes to. Ethical guidelines on how to treat fellow bloggers and discussants were called for by several informants. Despite these shortcomings, voices that were unlikely to be heard on traditional Cuban American media are now able to express their views, enter into discussions and create a new sense of how people relate to Cuban issues. The ability to publish one's thoughts online increased not only in Miami but also on the other side of the Florida Straits. More than any other medium, the Internet holds the potential for a much stronger transnational dimension between the Cuban American diaspora and Cubans on the island. Young Cuban Americans see their motivation rise because of their hope for a more vivid exchange with those based on the island.

This chapter also presented some cultural changes that are taking place within the community. Raíces de Esperanza (RDE) is built on the belief that it is time to move away from old ideologies and old fractions within the exile community. That is not to say that RDE is completely independent; there does exist an entanglement with other organizations and more conservative institutions such as the Institute of Cuban and

5. The Internet

Cuban American Studies (ICCAS). However, the idea of founding an organization that does not have an official stance on the trade embargo must have seemed revolutionary. It is telling that RDE was not founded in South Florida.

Even though younger informants preferred to consume their media in English, there is a substantial percentage of Cuban Americans (over 40 percent) who prefer to consume their media in Spanish. Media companies are well aware of this and cater toward the special needs of Hispanics in the U.S. market. In combination with a move to the English language, the increase of digital media has provided a platform for a more inclusive debate. The argument here is not that the debate and the collective remembering of Cuba have completely changed with the arrival of blogs and online discussion forums. Rather, a more varied range of voices can join in, and can potentially challenge the dominant narrative that has for example been sustained by Cuban American radio stations.

6

The Politics of Memory
Pre-Revolutionary Cuba

This chapter examines the role of journalism, in particular radio and online journalism, in reclaiming, negotiating, and maintaining memory. Among other scholars, Kitch (2008), Sturken (2008) and Carey (1989) have underlined the great significance of journalists and journalism in the process of reinforcing and negotiating how we think about and remember the past. Concepts presented by the aforementioned scholars working in the field of media and cultural studies will be enriched by writings of Maurice Halbwachs (1992), whose authoritative and substantial contribution is a cornerstone of today's understanding of collective memory, even though Halbwachs did not address *mediated* memory as such. Scholarship on how we remember and what influences the way we remember is not a new academic field as such (see Yates, 1966). But it was in the past decade or so that the study of collective remembering found a more established place in Western academic disciplines and inter-disciplinary studies.[1]

Questions of collective memory are invariably linked to questions of power. It is suggested here that members of a community who aim to exert control over future actions also aspire to take an active role in how the past is remembered and what aspects of the past are eligible for being remembered. The following paragraphs include a comparison between the media and journalistic practices that are aimed at the first generation of Cuban exiles who arrived in Miami after the Cuban revolution and those aimed at young Cuban Americans in their early twenties, who are influenced by their parents' and grandparents' memories

6. The Politics of Memory

of the island but who are also aware of the static and nostalgic nature of these memories.

Why do we remember? Beyond the positive experience of recounting memories of a beautiful beach we once visited or a childhood friend we used to play with, how is memory useful and what role does it play in current and actual social processes? Maurice Halbwachs (1992, 47) asserts that our memory is a key agent in the continuous process of identity formation, of establishing who we are: "We preserve memories of each epoch in our lives, and these are continually reproduced; through them, as by a continual relationship, a sense of our identity is perpetuated." Halbwachs illustrates that collective memory is socially constructed. We need others to remember with us since collective memory would not exist if it were not for the individual memory and the individual acts of remembering of each group member. There is a reciprocal relationship between the individual's memory and the group's collective memory: "One may say that the individual remembers by placing himself in the perspective of the group, but one may also affirm that the memory of the group realizes and manifests itself in individual memories" (40). Halbwachs argues that we need others to "keep track" of the past, to make sense of it and give it meaning. It is only through getting together with others, our collaborators in memory, so to speak, that collective memory is created and maintained. The discourse of the group provides a framework for the way that a group remembers the past: "No memory is possible outside frameworks used by people living in society to determine and retrieve their recollections" (43).

The past is therefore constructed through the present, and although memories are naturally based within an individual, they are kept alive and relived among other practices through social interaction in the present. The past, therefore, is not a collection of facts in our heads. We have a choice how and what we remember. As Annette Kuhn contends,

> Time is rarely continuous or sequential in memory-stories, which are often narrated as a montage of vignettes, anecdotes, fragments, "snapshots," flashes. Memory texts often display a metaphorical—as opposed to an analogical—quality, and as such have more in common with poetry than with the classical narrative with its linearity, causality and closure [1992, 11].

Cuban Americans and the Miami Media

Drawing on Edward Casey (1987), Kuhn also emphasizes the importance of places in memory work. Places situate memory; they serve as triggers or mnemonic pointers. Memory itself can be seen as "a *topos* in its own right: it is a place we revisit, or to which we are transported" (1992, 16–17).

The dominant narrative of collective memory within the Cuban American community in Miami was for a long time based upon the autobiographical memories of the first generation of exiles who arrived in Miami between 1959 and the mid-seventies. Autobiographical memories of later migration waves, such as those of the Mariel Boatlift in 1980, were a disruption to the dominant narrative, the static memory of the by-then well-established first wave of exiles. Halbwachs (1992) distinguishes between historical and autobiographical memory. Historical memory is gained through what reaches an individual through secondary sources, through written records, pictures or any other form of technology, what Alison Landsberg (2004) argues then forms part of "prosthetic memory." Autobiographical memory, on the other hand, is memory that stems from experiences the individual lived through him- or herself. Unless the individual is in contact with others who went through similar experiences, this kind of memory may fade (Coser 1992, 22–23).

Similar to Halbwachs's view on collective memory as a socially informed process, James Carey (1989) relates to communication as a social ritual that confirms our perception and comprehension of the world. The formation of collective memory and communication, including journalistic work, are both understood as continuous processes. Journalism and memory can be characterized by a symbiotic, if uneven, relationship (Zelizer 2008). Journalistic work and memory work are here not confined to those who consider themselves full- or part-time journalists or freelancers. Especially in the case of digital media, but also in the case of radio call-in shows, the audience can take an active part in this process. Using interactive web technologies ("Web 2.0"), younger generations of Cuban Americans can actively participate in the "making of memory." This inclusive process of "doing memory" links to Carey's (1989) understanding of communication, in which he draws our attention to the original meaning of the term, which entails notions of community and identification. He argues that communication in this sense

6. The Politics of Memory

is not only about sharing important information with others; it is about constructing and reinforcing a shared understanding of the world around us and a sense of ourselves in relation to the world. Communication is about constructing reality, and it is thereby inherently linked to issues of power.

Mediated texts are important agents in the context of memory conservation, feelings of nostalgia and a discourse of current events that is highly informed by the past (Hoskins 2001). As Sturken (2008, 75) suggests, media output feeds into personal memories and influences the individual's understanding of his or her own memories:

> Cultural and individual memory are constantly produced through, and mediated by, the technologies of memory. The question of mediation is thus central to the way in which memory is conceived in the fields of study of visual culture, cultural studies and media studies. This means that concepts of memory in these fields tend to consider it dynamic, contagious and highly unstable.

Our understanding of the past—and therefore of the present and future—is not fixed. Processes of memory formation are permeated by conversations, by information gained at a later stage, for instance, through an informal discussion with friends, books or a media text; historical and autobiographical memory (Halbwachs 1992) intertwine and amalgamate. This is underlined by Carolyn Kitch (2008) in her response to Sturken (2008). Drawing also on Carey (1988), Kitch emphasizes the significant relationship between memory and journalism, which is often overlooked:

> Journalism as a site of memory construction is taken for granted, like air or water—merely the carrier of the thing itself, the memory event or theme of interest. In fact, the relationship between journalism and memory is complex and significant. For much if not most of the public, journalism is a primary source of information about the past and shared understanding of the past. It also is a main site for public anticipation of memory: as "the first draft of history," journalism is also the first draft of memory, a statement about what should be considered, in the future, as having mattered today [2008, 311–12].

In Kitch's model, journalism fulfills several functions. It is in itself a site of memory construction. It simultaneously attracts, engages and interacts with other sites of memory. It causes some players, i.e., journalists and/or pro-active citizens, to initiate counter-perspectives that in turn feed into the collective memory and the collective identity of a community. Journalism, considered as an ongoing dynamic process rather than a finished product, is at the center of collective remembering: "It is not a 'window' through which we can view something else, as many memory scholars have regarded it. Nor does journalism sit at the top of hierarchical truth pile, as many journalism scholars assume. Journalism is *inside* memory; it is at its heart" (Kitch 2008, 3). In accordance with this understanding of journalism as a site of memory, those engaging in journalistic working practices are key agents in the process of remembering.

Remembering Pre-Revolutionary Cuba

Diasporic groups are often characterized by a lively exchange with the home country.[2] Cuba has been a special case, as media coming from the other side of the Florida Straits were largely considered to be propaganda; and opposition groups on the island often did not have the resources or freedom to produce and distribute media texts. Cuban exiles therefore relied extensively on their own media production that catered to the exile community, and still today, very few TV and radio programs made on the island are consumed in Miami.[3] Informants assured me that more Spanish-language programs that are produced in Miami are in fact consumed in Cuba, via hidden satellite dishes, secretly shared videotapes, and digital copies.

Many of the media organizations established in the 1960s and 1970s were created with an awareness of the shared experience of loss and of the collective memory of lives and lifestyles that had been abruptly brought to an end. Despite different formats and ways of transmission, the ritualistic processes inherent in their production and consumption, these media maintained a common purpose: providing a platform for shared remembering, a place where the maintenance and negotiation of collective memory could take place. These media were essential in relation to the frameworks that—as Halbwachs (1992) contends—allow the sharing of individual memories and the formation of a collective memory.

What did the output of these radio stations sound like? How did

6. The Politics of Memory

the journalistic work in Spanish-language radio stations in the 1960s and 1970s contribute to the process of collective remembering? When the first exiles arrived in Miami after the Cuban revolution, they were already sophisticated producers and listeners.

The longing for the lost homeland among the exiles also created a dominant narrative concerning the memory of life in Cuba. Interviewees belonging to the original *exilio histórico* repeatedly constructed Cuba as a lost paradise. This form of discourse and the framework for remembering Cuba was even shared by some journalists who were not of Cuban descent themselves but whose journalistic work catered to the Cuban American community. Even journalists who did not have Cuban roots were sensitive to the history and suffering that the Cuban American community had experienced. The exile mentality of this community was (and is) a well-accepted given.

Luisa Passerini (1983) speaks of two subjectivities coming together when someone is interviewed with regard to their memories. In this context, the interviewer's "place in the construction of memory is essential. Such construction is possible only on the basis of empathy" (Passerini 1983, 195). The same holds true for journalistic work in an environment that is highly informed by collective memories and nostalgia.

Raphael Samuel (1994, 356) characterizes nostalgia, or homesickness, as not missing the past, but as "felt absences" or a "'lack' in the present." Nostalgia often implies a mythologized past that can become frozen in time. The yearning for Cuba was expressed by the majority of Cuban American informants and interviewees in the field, especially those who had a firsthand experience of life on the island and who frequently drew on their autobiographical memory. One Cuban American scholar and journalist put it this way: "[There is] a nostalgia for the island that hasn't disappeared. We love that island. I mean it. It is still alive in my heart" (interview, January 2007).

For the historic exiles, the other side of the "absence of Cuba" was the challenges they were facing in their new home country. The wonderful life left behind in Cuba was contrasted to the hardship of starting all over in the United States, of split families, and of past and ongoing cruelties of the Cuban revolution. Interviewees never tired of pointing out difficulties that the historic exiles of 1959 and the early 1960s had experienced. It was frequently reiterated that even well-educated people such as physicians and lawyers were willing to take any job they could get to make a living and provide for their families.

The hardship of early exiles was in later years incorporated into the dominant discourse and framework of collective memory that still persists in great parts of the exile community today. A Cuban American journalist described the Cuba coverage in those early years as simplistic and unchallenging. The listenership of Spanish-language radio stations was very homogenous, with a keen interest in all things Cuban, and especially Cuba–U.S. relations. This type of coverage, favored by the majority of Spanish-language radio journalists, was, however, not unquestioned. Similar to the criticism voiced by younger interviewees today, journalists and managerial staff at the many Cuban American radio stations contributed to maintaining a dominant narrative that would not allow criticism of hardliners in the exile communities. Expressions of sympathy toward changes Fidel Castro was making on the island were systematically excluded. The idea that anything that developed in the aftermath of the Cuban revolution could have positive aspects was seen to undermine the framework of remembering Cuba prior to 1959. A Cuban American journalist who was working in radio at the time described the frustration some of his colleagues were expressing because they felt pressured to commit to a certain kind of output, a certain view and perspective of political issues that they did not agree with:

> I know that there were some people that wanted to work in radio stations, in Cuban American radio stations, and were kind of frustrated because they thought that they were not free enough to express their views, their opinions, to do the kind of journalism that they wanted to do. [There were some] major injustices committed to some people who probably just wanted to express their views. But I think that used to happen a lot in those days. Especially in talk-shows, the so-called open microphone programs. People call in, sometimes people whose names you could recognize because they were a columnist of a newspaper or maybe a sociologist who probably had some sympathies towards the Cuban government and these people were, I would say, almost systematically excluded at the time [interview, January 2007].

The exclusion of pro–Castro views and any position that would challenge the hardliner approach to Cuba meant the simultaneous affirmation of

6. The Politics of Memory

the static memories of the historic exiles. Perspectives that could potentially challenge these frameworks of collective memory were excluded or met with vehement protest. The maintenance of a dominant narrative was largely sustained through the journalism practiced in Spanish-language radio stations.

Based on this framework of collective remembering, hardliners asserted that there was no option of negotiations or a peaceful solution. Calls for violent action were justified through the discourse of loss and the collective memory of a paradise lost. Another point worth emphasizing here is the enduring link between frameworks of memory and power. The dominant narrative, including the exodus out of Cuba and the resulting hardships, was confirmed again and again, not only to call for violent activism toward the Cuban government, but also to reinforce itself and to completely negate the option for anybody to think differently, let alone voice alternate views.[4]

As outlined above, divergent circumstances and motivations for leaving Cuba made the community highly complex and increasingly diverse. Interviewees and informants in the field who belonged to the first migration wave spoke often about their political motivation that drove them out of the country, which concurrently made them exiles and not immigrants; later groups were often driven by economic motivations, and the historic exiles felt the need to clearly distinguish themselves from later arrivals. Furthermore, their understanding and the subsequent memories of what they had left behind were extremely disparate. The Mariel Boatlift not only challenged Miami's institutions, it questioned the discourse and framework of the historic exiles' collective memory.

It was time to rethink the role and function of Miami's Spanish-language stations and the purpose and mission of journalists and their work. Pressing social challenges—Mariel coincided with the advent of several thousand Haitians—and the increasingly diverse community called for each journalist, whether they were working in an English- or a Spanish-language media outlet, to reassess their position regarding Miami's evolving communities and changing circumstances and to re-evaluate the tenor of their work.

The diversification of the Cuban American community significantly changed the dynamics of community relations. It also caused disruptions to the established framework of memory and the dominant narrative of how Cuban Americans already based in Miami had constructed a very different image of life on the island. The realizations that came with the Mariel Boatlift brought home the fact that the past, which many had believed could be revived in the near future, had in fact slipped away—and perhaps had never even existed in the first place:

> [Mariel] was a culture shock because the Cubans who were already here were like, "Well, this is not really Cuba." Cuba for them froze in time. Cuba for them froze in 1959. But for those who were left behind, the country progressed in a whole different direction and since it was so close, Cuban exiles here were able to see what was happening in Cuba. And they were shocked because, yes indeed, it was a very different Cuba [interview, June 2006].[5]

What was even more shocking for some of the early exiles after the Mariel Boatlift was the fact that many of the new arrivals had no interest in joining into the dominant narrative. For the majority of Mariel migrants, this discourse had little meaning: they had different memories of Cuba and some of them had never seen Cuba in the light in which the historic exiles collectively remembered it.[6] But although Mariel meant a disruption to the frameworks of collective memory of the historic exile, it did not challenge it on the whole. Due to the established power structures, later migration waves did not instigate drastic changes in the frameworks of collective memory of the historic exiles and their descendants.

The power structure of the historic exile therefore allowed for the continuous affirmation of the static memory and left later arrivals little chance to challenge, change or contribute to these collective memories in the existing channels. In the long run, new waves of Cuban migrants led to a diversification in Spanish-language stations. The establishment of new networks was made economically viable by Miami's quickly developing into a magnet for other Latin American migrants.

Rethinking Past and Present

The dominant narrative had been supplemented by other views, though they had to struggle severely to be heard.[7] The hardliners' view

6. The Politics of Memory

of history and the actions against the Cuban government that they called for alienated not only segments of the Cuban American community; they also gave the Cuban American community as a whole a bad reputation on a national scale: Miami Cubans were thought of as rich, conservative power brokers who played according to their own rules and were "worse than the Mujahedin," as one informant (June 2006) put it. Most people in the field, Cuban Americans included, are aware of this image of the Cuban American community, and many informants argued that it is to some extent justified. The dominant narrative of loss, based on collective memories of what has been unjustly taken away and forced them out of their country, has sustained and nourished some radical elements in the community that have arguably had little success in achieving any of their goals. At the time of writing, Fidel Castro is still alive and the Castro brothers and their allies are still—at least nominally—in power.

For younger Cuban Americans in their twenties and thirties, the memories of their parents and grandparents and Spanish-language television and radio in Miami were an important and influential backdrop in shaping their identity and the understanding of their heritage. Media outlets that communicated the collective memories of the historic exiles became part of the archive of historical memory for second and later generations, especially influencing those who did not have firsthand experiences of life in Cuba. Nevertheless, parts of the younger generation have moved forward in a way that allows them to take a much more reflective approach toward the dominant narrative and collective memories of the first wave of exiles.

In-depth interviews with four Cuban Americans in their early twenties brought to light a completely different approach for dealing with Cuban issues.[8] All four informants were grandchildren of early exiles. The memories of their grandparents permeated their childhood and in most cases still dominates conversations around Cuban issues today. I met all of them through their extracurricular activities or work engagements at the University of Miami. These young Cuban Americans agreed on the omnipresence of the dominant narrative that had become second nature within the Cuban American community. A female Cuban American student at the University of Miami summarized her experience of the continuous affirmation of the dominant narrative and the continual construction of a shared interpretation of history in the following way:

In Miami you are surrounded by this, the constant talk, what's going on? Why is it happening? And so you develop this sense of obligation ... this really deep nostalgia for a country you have never been to. You feel like ... I feel as if I was born there, almost, to a certain degree. As much as I do feel American [I also feel] this sense of nostalgia that I share with my parents. And I think it goes back to the roots, and the close links to the culture over there that we develop here. And through that you have the drive and you have the necessity to follow what they [her parents and grandparents] did.... And also for the [Cuban] people [interview, October 2008].

Halbwachs (1992) distinguishes historical memory, experiences learned about through secondary sources, from autobiographical memory; those experiences we have "lived through" ourselves. The above quote asserts that, within this context, historical and autobiographical memories are very much amalgamated. Nevertheless, it is evident that younger Cuban Americans take a much more reflective approach when constructing the past and developing a strategy for future engagement with Cuba. All informants had opinions on and passionate visions for a future Cuba, but there was strong agreement that the politics of memory and the dominant narrative of the hardliners within the Cuban American community had probably done more harm than good: "Some people might just want to step back and not worry too much what the political issues are. And then there are people who try so hard to maybe fix it or help it that they are creating a conflict with it. [Some Cuban Americans] are really trying so hard to fight it when in reality you can't. It is just something that will die down itself" (interview, January 2007). In this sense, these young Cuban Americans strongly differ from the so-called left-wing intellectuals who began to challenge the no-dialogue policy of the hardliners in the mid- to late 1970s. In contrast to them, young Cuban Americans try to avoid further discussions on exile politics and focus their efforts on supporting opposition leaders in Cuba, rather than on opening talks with the Cuban government.

One organization that was founded on the principle of taking a very different approach to politics is Raíces de Esperanza (RDE) (Roots of Hope). The organization's aim is to bridge the gap between the Florida Straits and connect with people in Cuba on an individual basis. RDE

6. The Politics of Memory

differs from other exile groups in explicitly avoiding any official stance on political issues and current U.S. policy, including the trade embargo. Interestingly, RDE was founded not in Miami but by Cuban American Ivy-League students in the Northeast of the United States.

Another significant difference between RDE and other exile organization is the present-centered approach when relating to Cuba. One informant involved with RDE repeatedly emphasized the point that people in Miami do not "know the Cuban reality" and that it is the reality of everyday life in Cuba today that needs to inform approaches of an exile organization or any organization concerned with Cuba, not the dominant narrative of collective memories.[9]

This type of organization was also called for by Peruvian American blogger Paul Benavides. His blog (written in English, not Spanish) was founded to scrutinize and counteract the dominant narrative of one of Miami's Spanish-language radio stations that targets the historic exiles and their descendants. He firmly believed that one of the main reasons why the Cuban American community had received relatively little support and sympathy from other Hispanics was related to the fact that their approach was too "state-based" and not "people-based" (pers. com., October 2008). The blogger argued that siding with the U.S. government to overthrow Fidel Castro had never worked in the past; on the contrary, it was interpreted by some as a lack of concern for the Cuban people. In addition, most of the initiatives were led by a small group of radical Cuban American hardliners who utilized collective memories of loss to devise violent actions.

In relation to the shifts of memory work and the different ways in which collective memory is employed within exile organizations, it is worth emphasizing the importance of an accompanying shift in the dominant language, from Spanish to English. All informants who were born in the United States preferred English when consuming media, though as in the case of the four young Cuban American interviewees, Spanish was often spoken at home (U.S. Census Bureau 2004). A change in the language of remembering implies a change in identity formation. Language is a source for as well as symptom of a much deeper cultural and generational change, as one interviewee underlined: "I'm more American than my parents. And my parents are more American than my grandparents. So you lose a little bit every time" (interview, October 2008).[10]

Journalistic work in English naturally has a much more diverse audience than the closely targeted listeners of Miami's Spanish-language radio stations. Unless younger Cuban Americans, who prefer to consume media in English, actively seek out journalistic work aimed at the Cuban American community, they are less likely to be surrounded by mediated collective memories once they have left their parents' house. On the other hand, transferring journalistic work into the English language gives a wider range of people, including those who do not speak Spanish, the chance to participate in the debates.

In combination with a move to the English language, the increase of digital media has provided a platform for a more inclusive debate. The argument here is not that the debate and the collective remembering of Cuba have completely changed with the arrival of blogs and online discussion forums. Rather, they have allowed a more varied range of voices to join in, and potentially to challenge the dominant narrative. The Peruvian American interviewee who runs a blog scrutinizing Miami's hardliner radio stations was convinced that online discussion forums, blogs, and comment sections in various mainstream media outlets were a more successful way to handle debates as the practicalities of the exchange encourage participants to pause instead of promptly responding in the heat of the moment.

Like journalists, bloggers—and creative audiences more generally speaking—are part of the community. Their memories are personal and at the same time are guided, formed, influenced, inspired and invigorated by frameworks of collective memories. However, as the historic exiles and their children age and die and as the circle of those who can contribute journalistic work widens, the autobiographical memory starts to fade and lose significance—though this is admittedly a very slow process. Moreover, because of the relaxed travel arrangements for U.S. citizens wanting to visit the island, this historical memory, memory gained from secondary sources, is strongly intermixed with newly acquired firsthand experiences and furthermore supplemented by information coming directly from the island. Since Cuba cautiously widened people's access to internet, more information comes directly from the

6. The Politics of Memory

island and allows Cuban Americans and Cubans to enter into a discussion on a very different level (Voss 2008; Voss 2009). The collective memory of young Cuban Americans is therefore informed not only by the media of the exile but also by additional, albeit limited, information from the island. One of the better known examples of this is probably Yoani Sánchez and her blog *Generación Y*.

Many assumptions about the potential changes that digital media can bring have been far too optimistic. It would be unrealistic to see the shift in how younger Cuban Americans deal with the collective memories of earlier generations as a precursor of major disruptions, not least because the discourse of the hardliners can be found online as well. But on the other hand, opinions that would never have been voiced on a radio show in the 1970s are now free to make a contribution to mediated collective memories through digital media.

Concluding Remarks

The findings of the case study support and underline the importance of journalistic work, especially of local journalism consumed on an everyday basis, in creating, maintaining and negotiating collective remembering. Journalistic output was crucial for establishing a sense of community and collective identity for the historic exile, which was largely based on a shared exilic existence and the memories of and nostalgia for a paradise lost. Within this context, some journalists also supported and actively promoted the call for violent actions against the Cuban government. Just like radio, internet forums and blogs are very conversationally driven media and are more inclusive than television and the printed press. However, the way in which different generations relate to media can vary significantly (Slade 2006). The younger informants encountered in Miami were much more aware of the constructed nature of messages and memory and, much more than previous generations, were keen to partake in and negotiate representations of the present and the past in their own way, and at least to some extent on their own terms. For them, this included participating in journalistic practices online and in some cases also offline. Hoskins (2001, 340) theorizes television "as the primary 'subliminal point of reference' where television is the site of the production of the 'original' memory." One could speculate that radio and the internet invite a more active engagement with past, present and future as they are conceived more as a potential site of negotiation than solely a platform for a finished product. The inclusive nature of radio and conversation-driven online spaces therefore encourages active engagement in memory work.

Of course there is not a level playing field, but nonetheless there is a space for discussion that goes beyond personal conversations and is not confined to a specific time and place, nor to a specific group of people. There is a greater transnational pursuit among younger generations, an approach facilitated and enhanced by digital media. While radio as a medium remains for some strongly associated with U.S. propaganda and CIA operations being conducted out of Miami, digital networks allow for the creation of a transnational space that is by no means perfect in terms of equality, access, and freedom of expression—but that comes much closer to the ideal.

The power to control and influence the dominant narrative in mainstream Cuban American radio stations stayed in the hands of the historic exiles and their descendants, even when it was challenged by the autobiographical memory of later waves of incoming migrants. The historic exiles' framework of collective memory proved persistent and extremely resistant to change. The persistence of this perpetual, memory-filled discourse is partly due to its importance in maintaining an exilic identity, but it can also to some extent be explained by the close geographical proximity to the island that provides the backdrop for a mythologized past.[11] Across the world, people meeting for the first time often ask each other what they do for a living. In Cuban American circles, the common question used to start a conversation and learn more about the other person is, "So when did you arrive?" The time of and reason for departure—whether someone can be considered mainly a political exile rather than an economic migrant—provide a way of assessing the merit of their contribution to the dominant discourse and to the process of collective remembering. Memory processes, therefore, do not travel along a smooth trajectory; they are not democratically shared within a group nor do they follow a coherent evolution.

The dominant narrative formed a significant part of the historic

6. The Politics of Memory

memory of later generations. In *Prosthetic Memory*, Alison Landsberg (2004) argues that mass-mediated cultural technologies can create shared social frameworks that go beyond space, cultural background and class. This does not mean, however, that Halbwachs's (1992) concepts are outdated, as he emphasizes parameters such as family and class in the process of constructing frameworks that enable us to relate to the past. Very often, we share mediated forms of collective remembering with people around us; local networks, friends and family, and their memories are still of great significance when it comes to our own remembering, our memory work and identity. The everyday presence and their taken-for-granted existence can make frameworks of remembering extremely powerful yet subtle for those who grow up with them. Stepping outside and going beyond these frameworks challenges the existing politics of memory of "what one chooses to recollect in the presence of others" (Kumar, Hug and Rusch 2006, 211). It takes courage to question the essentials of one's shared identity.

Younger Cuban Americans synthesized the autobiographical memory of their grandparents' and parents' generation with prosthetic memory. However, the local and community dimension of the origin of these collective memories was of great value to them. It formed the basis of their use of digital media to widen the frameworks of remembering and imagining Cuba.

A segment within the younger generation has shifted their focus and has moved away from an agenda that envisions at its center the removal of the two Castro brothers. They aimed to disentangle the close-knit relationship between memory, ideology and calls for violent political activities. These young Cuban Americans concentrate on the humanitarian issues that concern Cuba's population. They take a different route in "righting" the past. Their strategy is strongly focused on including Cuban people in their thoughts and actions on how to approach the future as opposed to removing the Cuban government through violent actions planned from Miami. Within the process of rethinking and reconsidering the dominant narrative of the past, the change from Spanish to English as the preferred language of journalistic work has a significant impact on cultural identity and the engagement with the community.

Conclusion

The previous chapters have traced the evolution of Miami-based media and how they interacted with different segments of the Cuban American community. The findings presented in this volume indicate that some media are strongly linked to particular segments of the community and to different evolutionary stages of the Cuban American exile. There are highly complex structures of interactions between individuals, their choices of consumption, the language they prefer when consuming media, and the role different media play for different groupings of the community. Additional complexities arise through the distinct ways in which different migration waves, different age groups and different segments of the community have reacted to, used and shaped these media.

Imbrications of the Local, the National and the Transnational

The media analyzed in this book can be situated at the crossroads of the local, the national and the transnational. Whether different media do or do not meet the challenge this liminal position brings depends on a number of factors, such as their historic evolution, the audience they are targeting, and where they are trying to situate themselves in relation to their competitors and the wider media ecology. While early migrant media saw one of their main purposes as providing information for the newly arrived, social media and blogs are now employed to organize humanitarian projects for those living in Cuba. The roles media play for the Cuban American community have proven to be tremendously

Conclusion

diverse, with generational and migratory shifts being most noticeable. Over time, the individual as well as the collective relationship to different media outlets has evolved.

The developments of certain media and their consumption are indicators for the evolution of the Cuban American community. During the propaganda war that characterized early transnational relations between Cuba and the United States, Cuban American radio was under the influence of the CIA. The existence of Radio and TV Martí confirm that governmental involvement is still prevalent today. Additionally, the media's potential contribution to a Cuban communicative space is taken very seriously by one Cuban American station, Radio Mambí. Apart from the internet, radio can be seen as one of the most transnational actors in Miami's media scene. The way it is employed and read by many indicates an old-fashioned ideological understanding or struggle that segments of the Cuban American community still engage in. Some radio stations in the field have kept alive a dominant discourse that is characterized by topics such as loss, victimization, belligerence, pain and *la lucha* ("the struggle"). At the opposite end of the spectrum are those suspected of being collaborators with the Cuban government. Pro-Castro programming is in turn targeting the local Miami audience. Still today, voicing views that do not adhere to the dominant narrative can come at a price for the individuals in question.

In contrast to Miami's radio stations, the two main Spanish-language television networks, Telemundo and Univision, see their remit on a U.S.-wide scale. Miami is home to a cluster of television broadcasters, but Cuban American topics are rarely dealt with on national broadcasts. On a superficial level, television strategists would argue they are targeting the Hispanic community as a whole. However, Hispanic identity is not as straightforward as it might seem. The findings presented in this volume challenge the notion of a Hispanic community. At least for a significant number of Cuban American informants, other Spanish-language groups were employed as a means to articulate difference and establish their own special status and collective identity. The early arrivals of the Cuban American community, their cultural capital and their success stories meant that a close association with less successful groups was an unappealing option for many. Furthermore, immigration, an issue that is of high importance for the majority of Hispanics, has a different flavor for Cuban Americans as a result of a special piece of legislation, the Cuban Adjustment Act (1966, modified in 1995). The categorization of "Hispanics" was therefore seen by many informants as an artificial one. However, this is not to say that it therefore becomes irrelevant. As a marketing and branding construct, it has proven successful, especially when comparing the growth figures of Spanish-language television to those of its English-language counterpart. The big players in the Spanish-language television market are influenced by their partners in South America. Their program content often reflects this with films and *telenovelas* coming from Mexico, Venezuela and Brazil, to name but a few. A local dimension is added through affiliate stations that might cater more closely to the taste of audiences in the vicinity.

In contrast to television, Miami's two Spanish-language newspapers have taken a different route in dealing with incoming migrants. *Diario las Américas* embraced the migrants and the accompanying change of demographics. Since its first edition, *Diario* has performed a balancing act between covering the local, the national and the transnational, with varying degrees of success. The English-language *Herald* had a firm sense of its Miami-based Anglo readership. Its Spanish-language sister paper, *El Nuevo Herald*, has no national or transnational ambitions for its print edition. Online editions of all papers have more room to play with communicative spaces on a local, national and global level.

The analysis of Miami's local press furthermore brought to light the diverse interpretations of what good journalistic practice should entail and what kind of role the media should take on in relation to the people. While journalists trained in the U.S. often see objectivity and independence as the highest good of every journalist, some Cuban American and other Hispanic journalists argue that their loyalty is to the community and the reinforcement of democratic processes in Cuba (and in other countries) first. This issue was neither acknowledged nor tackled properly by management and those in charge. The conflicts that resulted from these different priorities and different scales of purpose indicate that it is in the interest of the media organizations and the journalists to address these issues at a much earlier stage. Clashes of professional identities are not unique to the press, however. The differing work

Conclusion

patterns and practices of media organizations, and the way different newspapers collaborate and compete in Miami, have just brought this to the forefront. Similar discrepancies can be found in other media, such as radio and television, as well. The conflict arises out of the transnational ambitions of journalists, which media strategists and executives do not necessarily share.

The internet has brought a new dimension to Miami's media scene through its potential as a global arena. It is used by some to reach as wide and as global an audience as possible. Others use blogs and forums to discuss local issues and engage in local conflicts. As was to be expected, the internet is also employed by the press, radio and television. But beyond that, the internet, and interactive web sites in particular, have given individuals a communicative space that was not available to them before. More significantly, it has also led to great parts of the discussion being held in English, opening up the debate for previously excluded participants. The blogs analyzed for this book had both been started because of the perceived shortcomings of traditional media outlets.

With the internet being available to some segments of Cuban society, youth organizations, such as Raíces de Esperanza, also use it to engage in a transnational dialogue with people on the island. Given the ideological struggle still dominating the approach of some radio stations, this has been a novelty. In contrast to previous studies in which migrants would perhaps engage in a mix of media coming from the host societies as well as their homeland, this has never before been the case for the Cuban American community. Everything coming from the island was interpreted as propaganda and therefore dismissed, unless it was messages from dissidents and political prisoners.

Thanks to social media, groups such as Raíces de Esperanza can operate on a much larger scale. In this case, the perspective of Miami being the center of the Cuban American exile community, the place to be if one plans to "get active" for Cuba, falls short. Younger exile organizations or human rights organizations use social media to disseminate information about their activities and events. Once again, local, national and transnational communicative spaces are imbricate, shape-shifting and fluid.

Cuban Americans and the Miami Media

The Significance of Place and Space

The situation of the Cuban American community clearly points toward the relevance the local and the national dimensions have for a migrant community, perhaps *especially* for a migrant community. Early conceptualizations of diasporas and migrant communities have focused on the relation to the homeland. While this remains a crucial characteristic of diasporic groups, recent scholarship has recognized the importance of transnational activities that comprise hybrid identities.[1] Migrants connect to their homeland, or their parents' and grandparents' country of origin, while simultaneously negotiating their identity in relation to their current locale. The findings of this study suggest an ever-evolving relationship to the country of origin. When analyzing a diasporic community with a longitudinal approach, individual as well as collective understandings of the original home are likely to change. Some Cuban Americans who had the firm intention to return to the island have lost interest over the years, while others have taken the other route and are now planning to rebuild Cuba when their time comes, even though they would probably not choose Cuba as their first place of residence in the foreseeable future.

In relation to theoretical debates, the findings of this study suggest the continuing relevance of the (nation-)state.[2] The United States was clearly recognized by older members of the community as a key player in the struggle against communism and/or Castro's rule in Cuba. For younger Cuban Americans it was a strong point of reference for their identity: They were Cuban American; some even preferred to call themselves American Cuban, as their loyalty to the U.S. was one of the defining features of who they were. As discussed in the introduction, there have been numerous attempts to frame and define what constitutes a diaspora. The empiric data presented in this book suggests a strong relevance of what could be described as diasporic activities, as opposed to automatic forms of belonging and indicators such as mobility or a cosmopolitan outlook on the world. The significance of the homeland does not necessarily diminish for second, third and later generations of the diaspora. However, the option of a permanent "return" is assessed as a very unlikely one.

Conclusion

In addition to shifting and complex loyalties, there is a strong awareness among informants that it was the USA that provided its citizens with the ability to freely express themselves in whichever form they liked—at least from a legal point of view; in contrast to Cubans on the island, Cuban Americans were not being forced to hang on to a certain ideology and—in principle—were free to say what they thought. This freedom was associated with the structure, laws and values of the United States. So here again, the (nation-)state and the framework it provided were of extreme importance to the community.

Perhaps in contrast to what previous studies have suggested, the strong awareness of living in the United States and the advantages this brings with regards to civil rights brought forward a rhetoric that praised the United States. Generally speaking, it did not lead to a cosmopolitan outlook on life. This might also be related to the time and circumstances in which the first exiles arrived in the United States. The exilic state was to some extent very much linked to what the American nation stood for. The early migrants left Cuba to escape a government that threatened their rights as citizens. Due to the historic context of migrants arriving in 1959 and the 1960s, reclaiming their homeland was initially meant to happen with the help of the United States.

The notion of "reclaiming Cuba" interlinks with choosing Miami and South Florida as an adopted home. The choice is a message in itself. Living in Miami, living right on the doorstep of Castro's Cuba, is sending the message that the exiles are not going away or giving up. It was the locale that also had an impact on the evolution of media, especially Cuban American radio in Miami. Some radio stations automatically took on a transnational mission, partly because geographical circumstances had allowed them to do so.

Thoughts of Cuba generated a whole range of emotions for many Cuban Americans. Most poignant for many was a sense of alienation from Cubans on the island. Subsequent migration waves of those who had grown up as *hombres nuevos*, the "new men" of the revolution, brought to light the evolving realities of everyday life on the island. These shifts in Cuban society are likewise reflected in the make-up of Cuban migrants. While early migrants were considered political exiles with high cultural capital, later waves brought a more diverse spectrum of people to the United States. The most powerful and vociferous Cuban Americans are likely to be early exiles or their descendants. However, this is not as simple as it might initially seem. Scholar and writer María de los Angeles Torres (1995, 232) is hopeful that a new kind of understanding will evolve between Cubans on both sides of the Florida Straits.

> Something new may be in the making as a generation that grew up across a divide discovers its other half. Artists, critics, and scholars of the various exile and diaspora generations are sharing experiences with each other in Miami.... There is a common search, a similar disillusionment, a common political vision, and a shared generational experience across borders. This reunion of generations does not necessarily have a happy ending, but is has taken a first step toward gaining an understanding of differences, a necessary requirement of reconciliation.

The decades of waiting have affected the exiles. Time has caused many to rethink their positions and question their perspectives. Whether or not they are willing to say so publicly is a different matter.

Looking Ahead

Diasporic groups have been said to spend considerable time looking back, creating imaginary homelands and reminiscing about times gone by. While this might be the case, their exile mentality also led many informants to constantly look forward. One day, when Fidel Castro dies, when "those guys," i.e., the Castro brothers and their supporters, are no longer in power, they want to be ready to step up to the task of rebuilding Cuba. Perhaps more than other places and narratives, Cuba and her history evoke strongly opposing sentiments and reactions. In a large enough crowd of people, one is likely to find someone wearing a T-shirt, pin or hat that shows the iconic image of Ernesto "Ché" Guevara. For some, the Cuban revolution is a potential trajectory to a better world whose failure can be blamed on imperialist ambition of the United States:

> Old habits are hard to break—none harder than the tendency within the international left to look upon the Cuban revolution as a myth to be cherished forever, from afar. I know intellectuals from the United States, from Europe and Latin America who still travel to Cuba as if it was 1968, and come away reciting official positions as if they had been freshly uttered in 1959 by youthful guerrillas [De la Campa 2000, 124–25].

Conclusion

On the other side of the spectrum are those waiting to dance in the streets when Fidel Castro is declared dead. They point toward the poverty and the devastating economic situation of the country and regard the revolution as a failure.

Assuming the truth to lie somewhere in the middle would be too simplistic. What is at stake is more than an ideological dispute; it leads to the ultimate question of how society can be organized in a way that creates a sense of happiness, belonging and prosperity. It leads us to ask how our institutions should operate and how the individual relates to society and vice versa. In the end, it is these issues that people feel so strongly about. These big concerns, combined with experiences of loss, pain and injustices, bear the danger of hardened hearts and a readiness for violent confrontations that can potentially go on for decades.

In contrast to many other challenges facing the world today, the conflict between Cuba and the United States seems fairly straightforward. Popular discourse would have us believe that the struggles between these two countries very much stem from the settings of the twentieth century; communism vs. democracy, state-owned economies vs. free-market capitalism. The Cuban revolution is largely seen as the point in time when Cuba cut the link of a working association to the United States. Of course many of the strains and tensions that have characterized most of U.S.–Cuba relations do stem from Cold War times. But on closer inspection, things are not so simple. Long before Fidel Castro's rise to power, the United States entertained a fairly unequal power relationship with the island. As it did with other countries in the Southern Hemisphere of the continent, there is no doubt that Washington often pushed for its own interests rather than keeping in mind what would be most beneficial for local populations.

Even though we think of history as a linear process, Cuba's history and evolution teach us that questions we were sure to have satisfactorily answered float to the surface again and again. After the downfall of the Soviet Union, Cuba went through a decade of austerity. Cuba was in search of political allies, and things were looking bleak. But, much to the dismay of many Cuban exiles, Havana managed to find new partners in Asia and South America. Furthermore, the crises of the financial systems, whether stock market and real estate crashes, the question mark currently looming over the Euro zone, the malfunctioning of welfare systems, or the gap between rich and poor in individual countries as well as on a global scale, force us to reconsider if capitalism and contemporary mechanism of governance are truly the best answer we can find.

In an effort to not get stuck with these "big questions," the focus of younger Cuban Americans seems to be less on discussions on a general level and more on approaching the island through grassroots movements. This has come with a shift in awareness and an acknowledgment that the Cubans living outside the island are no longer in charge. It is for people who have stayed on the island to step up and take a leading role. In 2008, Fidel Castro officially passed over the presidency to his younger brother Raúl, who has made a point of putting his military associates in positions of power. Although travel and remittances restrictions have been eased, the U.S. government has made little serious effort to work toward comprehensive change in Cuba.

Searching for a New Equilibrium

Miami would not be what it is today if it were not for the Cuban American community. And the same holds true in reverse: the Cuban American community would not be what it is today if it were not for Miami, its geographical location in relation to Cuba, and the mnemonic triggers it offers for remembering and dwelling upon nostalgic reminiscences. Miami gave home to the historic exiles and provided them with extraordinary opportunities. However, this was supported by the larger framework of the U.S. The early arrivals were classed as exiles in a greater political conflict. The Cold War led the U.S. administration to give Cuban migrants a special status that is often enviously looked upon by others. These positive starting points make the Hispanic community and Hispanic identity an additional layer that has little to offer to Cuban Americans.

The success of the Cuban American community itself became a myth, epitomized in narratives such as the one in *The Lost City* (2005). But accomplishments rooted in the United States came at a price. Feel-

Conclusion

ings of nostalgia are mixed with guilt and with a lingering sense of a duty unfulfilled. Fidel Castro stayed in power, and his longevity has caused ruptures between the exile community and Cubans based on the island. Space and time gave room to interrelations, multiplicities and continuous construction (Massey 2005) in Miami and Havana alike, although these might not necessarily bring a happy reunion of the Cubans on the island and the Cuban diaspora.

In terms of cultural activity, Havana and Miami have a lot in common. But politics and ideologies are holding them apart. The Cuban American community in Miami is struggling to find a balance between looking back, sharing the pains and celebrating the successes of the past; and looking forward to where they want to go as a collective. What is it that holds them together as a group? The media have an essential role to play in these processes of negotiation.

Epilogue
At the Intersections of Socio-Technological Shifts, Social Change and Political Engagement

Years have gone by while researching and writing this book. In retrospect, what is striking and highly instructive about the evolution of the Cuban American community in Miami and their use of different media is the intertwining of technological change, communicative and social spaces and the contested status of individuals and communities in relation to political and institutional actors.

The early years of the Cuban exile in Miami were tainted by a knowing and an acceptance of the strong influence political actors could have on the livelihoods of individuals and communities. Exiles who had to flee their country for fear of being imprisoned by government forces were certain to have an awareness for the institutional and political stake holders. In turn, the significance of nation-states was high, not only in terms of lateral agreements with other states but also in terms of the people's perspectives on how (political and social) change can be brought about. In this process, social change was seen as a consequence of political change, i.e., with a new government in power in Havana was meant to come social change, meaning greater welfare for all, freedom of expression, equality and so on. This understanding of how to initiate change targets the top. It aims at commencing change right at the center of power and initiating all changes to people's material livelihoods from there.

With regard to the historic exiles, this perspective meant setting

Epilogue

up exile organizations whose primary aim was a complete shift of power structures in Cuba. In other words, the Castro brothers had to go—no matter the means employed to reach this goal. It is this attitude which fueled the collaboration with the U.S. government in the 1960s. From this point of view, political change could only be brought about by using extreme force (plans to assassinate Fidel Castro) or through war (the invasion of the Bay of Pigs). Putting aside moral judgments on right or wrong for a moment, this is the *zeitgeist* which can be clearly observed within the early Cuban American community of the 1960s and 1970s.

The top-down approach is also reflected in the way the media are employed during this phase. In line with the technological status quo of the time, mass media are used for propaganda purposes and run by or under the influence of state organizations like the CIA. From a media studies perspective, individuals and communities are best characterized as an active audience. Readers, viewers and listeners can choose what they consume and reflect and discuss what is presented to them. However, the possibilities of participating and producing media content—especially of reaching out on a transnational level—are not yet given at this point in time.

During this time, individual transnational relationships—keeping in touch with friends and family on the island—is done through letter writing and conversations on the telephone. These avenues and ways of transmission are of course vulnerable to state power and perhaps unreliable as well. The options of a group of people who do not form a typical political action group but do want to work toward change are slim. This strongly limits ways of getting involved; a person who does not want to join an exile organization, does not have many possibilities to participate. Of course, people wrote articles for newspapers and *periodiquitos*, but at the time these venues could not allow for mass participation. Plus, there is always the hazard of crossing the editorial line and having the proposed article edited or rejected entirely.

The first ruptures to this state- and power-centered approach can be observed in the 1980s. Left-wing intellectuals and those who had given up on the no-dialogue-policy that still finds support in the exile community today, made efforts to reach out to the Cuban government. In many ways this was an intermediate step toward the more humanitarian and people-to-people based initiatives we can observe today. What it shows, though, is an altered understanding of what individuals can do to work toward change. In this intermediate phase, we see individual actors from the Cuban American community approach Cuban politicians and those in power in order to advocate change and a growing together of the exile and Cubans on the island.

No doubt, for many of the individuals coming into contact with Fidel Castro and his entourage, there is also a fascination of being close to and dealing with a person who is considered a legend by many across the world. In Miami, there is an abundant number of tales about people counting the minutes they were granted to stay in close vicinity to Fidel Castro, the meal they were invited to share with him and so on. It therefore would not be fair to say that all those who crossed the Florida Straits in order to engage in some form of dialogue had social change for the Cuban people and a re-union of the exile and the island at the top of their agenda.

But despite the vanities, the point remains that a shift in the relationship between the individual, political actors and the initiation of social change can be traced. Though debates are still focused on politics and policies, there is a sense that individuals can make a difference. This approach is to some extent mirrored by the Cuban American National Foundation (CANF) in the United States. There too, a limited number of individuals formed a group that tried to influence policies in Washington.

In terms of media, the intermediate phase is characterized by opening up new communicative spaces. In Miami, pro–Castro programing adds a new perspective to the mix with voices and opinions that were previously not heard. The range of thoughts and attitudes becomes more diverse. However, if we suppose that social change ultimately aims at a harmonious communal life as one of its outcomes, then this phase sees more discrepancies and challenges between different segments of the Cuban American community in Miami. Rather than agreeing on the outcome, fights ensue over which route to follow. It is in this phase that it became more and more unrealistic to hope that the political situation on the island was going to change in the near future. This caused disappointment and feelings of defeat.

Epilogue

While many of the older generations of the Cuban American community were at a loss on how to proceed—what more could be done and tried?—it was for the younger generation to develop a new paradigm for *la lucha* (the struggle). The notion of focusing on humanitarian projects on the island and to connect on a personal basis with people of a similar age in Cuba meant that activism or social change was no longer tied to a political stance or even aimed at changing politics. While this was very innovative given the history of activism among the Cuban American community, it is simultaneously indicative of what can be observed in post-industrial countries across the world: Young people tend to get involved in campaigns around specific issues that are close to their heart. They are less likely to join a political party or take a stance in line with a certain ideology.

These kinds of initiatives are strongly linked to digital media technologies, allowing people to participate from different locations and in a variety of ways—from online campaigns and donations to organizing a protest in the streets or putting together an event. It should not come as a surprise, therefore, that Cuban blogger Yoani Sánchez, during a visit to Miami, encouraged Cuban American activist groups to collect mobile phones, USB sticks and other digital devices as donations for people on the island. Social change is not caused by technological affordances alone. It needs people willing to make use of the affordances with certain aims in mind.

These latest developments in the struggle for social and political change in Cuba are also indicative of a shift regarding gender and civil engagement. Early exile organizations were dominated by men. Like the majority of politicians, the majority of individuals highly involved in exile organizations were male. Younger exile organizations which take a humanitarian-focused approach rather than aiming at big politics, have a much larger number of women participating. In general, this way of getting involved seems to appeal to young people, to those who are tired of endless political discussions which have brought little results over the course of the past decades.

The slow but nevertheless notable technological evolution in Cuba has also opened up new communicative spaces between the island and the exile. Communicative spaces—the term sounds rather abstract, but it is in these spheres that a connection between Cuban Americans and Cubans can take place. It is in these social arenas that encounters take place which allow for change from the ground up and thereby simultaneously move away from the old top-down paradigm as the only itinerary on how change can be brought about. It is from this vantage point that each individual who wants to get involved truly has a role to play. Communicative spaces, in addition to allowing for groups to organize themselves, also sustain the individual and the collective imagination through affording a closer connection to a counterpart on the other side of the Florida Straits. Because the truth is that people can find personal solutions in their heads and hearts much more skilfully and with greater ease than states drawing up complicated bilateral agreements.

These technological and social developments, including the shifts that have taken place in exile initiatives, have been painted with a broad brush. No doubt there is a lot more to say about the nature of protest and fights for social and political change among the Cuban American community. For now though, this has provided a meta-perspective on the close ties between individual and collective involvement, social and political change and their interactions with technological evolution. For many people, the most recent developments in the Cuban American community with regards to protest and initiatives for social change on the island have been a cause for excitement. The foundation of novel organizations with a humanitarian focus are indicative of a new dynamic that will hopefully be the grain for an evolved relationship between Cuba and the exile as well.

Appendix A

Going to Miami: Reflections on Methodology and the Research Experience

This appendix outlines the methodology employed for the research underlying this book. Primary data was gathered through ethnographic field work, which included 38 semi-structured face-to-face interviews, several email exchanges and numerous encounters with informants in the field. Other methods utilized were archival and desktop research. In addition, this appendix brings the broader perspective of the researcher in the field, the relationship between the researched and the researcher, and the experience of life as an ethnographic researcher. After all, this project has accompanied me with varying degrees of intensity for the best part of six years.

Journalists, media executives and selected engaged citizens were identified as particularly relevant informants in the field, as their professional identities and their everyday work practices link media institutions, discourses, audiences and the Cuban American community. The informants selected for this study are at the center of negotiation of the role of media for the Cuban American and other communities. While being aware of the transnational aspects of their work, there remained a strong sense of the local dimension and their everyday lives in general. Many of them had worked for different media outlets over the years, or were in fact still doing so at the time of interviewing. They were therefore in a position to compare Miami-based media in terms of working practices, approaches to the Cuban American and other communities, missions, and challenges.

Appendix A

Interviewing journalists and people working in or with the media brought the further advantage of bypassing some of the obstacles associated with the process of mediation (Livingstone 2009; Hepp 2010). Sonia Livingstone (2009) posits that one of the challenges of doing media research today is the mediation of everything. All aspects of social life are shaped by and linked through the omnipresence of media. While this statement generally holds true, there might nevertheless be factors that determine the degree of mediatisation, i.e., age, social and cultural background, and education. The omnipresence of media and mediated life was noticeable in the field by difficulties some informants had in remembering which radio station or TV channel or newspaper they were consuming at a certain time. This never occurred when interviewing journalists.

In response to Livingstone (2009), Andreas Hepp (2010, 45) calls for researching media in a "non-mediacentric way." This approach includes going beyond researching individual media and focusing on the broader media ecology or "media ensembles," as Hepp (2010, 46) calls them. He furthermore argues for approaching research in a dialectic way by not assuming media to be the central force in social life and processes of change. Thirdly, Hepp (2010, 46) argues that "cultural sensitivity" is needed to assess the role media play in a certain contexts.

My experience of ethnographic work has been that it can meet these criteria. It allows one to view the collective and the individual in a wider context that goes beyond media consumption. It allows the researcher to become aware of phenomena that are perhaps not immediately related to media production, policies and audiences. Cultural sensitivity is a must in an etic approach to field work. However, I would also encourage emic researchers to be more reflective of underlying dynamics when they are in the field or engaging in data analysis. An exploratory ethnographic approach, as selected for this thesis, proved successful for researching a diasporic community that is well-established in a certain locale

In contrast to other parts of this publication, the "I," the persona of the researcher, is much more prevalent here. Arguably to a greater extent than other research methods, field work is a method, or rather a mix of methods—including interviews, participant observation, casual

Appendix A

conversations, reading, and experiencing primary and secondary sources—that has a significant embodied and personal dimension. I follow Amanda Coffey's line of thought in considering field work as "personal, emotional and identity work" (1999, 1).

The methodology evolved out of a post-positivist and explorative approach to research. From the start it was assumed that notions of identity and community are in constant negotiation, fluid, ever-changing and hybrid (Georgiou 2006). Feelings of belonging and the notion of being a part of a particular group or a particular segment of a community are not rigid but in motion. What is captured here, therefore, is a deep and detailed reflection of the Cuban American community and Spanish-language media in Miami at a specific point in time.

The Choice of Methods

Absorbing and monitoring the output of different media organizations in Miami was highly enriching for the general understanding of the local, national and transnational media scene. However, discourse and textual analysis of a sample of media texts are not best suited to fully answer the questions that guided this project. The main reason for this was that thoughts, sentiments and reactions of members of the community, journalists and non-journalists, were to be the focus of this project, as opposed to the researcher's interpretation of selected texts. All research questions aimed at how members of the community perceived, thought of, made sense of and reacted to media, (fellow) journalists and their output, and what role this had to play in the dynamics of the community. To answer these questions, it was necessary to be aware of current issues discussed in the media. However, the analysis of media organizations and the interpretation of their output by members of the community and by people working in the media were deemed the best approach to answer these research questions.

In order to observe the routes of communication, the negotiation of issues and interests taking place between different media and the Cuban American community, particular emphasis was placed on the role of the journalist as a key agent in this process. Journalists are seen

Appendix A

to fulfill multiple roles; throughout the research process—in and outside of the field—they were constructed as gatekeepers, as analysts, as politically active community members, as significant players in the fight for democracy in Cuba, and as a critical audience for the output of their colleagues. This is not to say that these roles are exclusively filled by journalists, or that every single journalist saw him- or herself in one or several of these parts. But all interviewees, Cuban Americans and people of different descent, were very aware of and sensitive to the needs of this particular community and the media's contribution in this respect.

Field Work in Miami

"Research is hard work, it's always a bit suffering. Therefore, on the other side, research should be fun," asserts the sociologist Anselm Strauss (2004). His brief summary gives a first glimpse of the encompassing experience that is field work. This section provides an overview of my experiences during periods of field research in Miami, Florida. I visited Miami in July 2006 (for approximately four weeks), in January 2007 (for approximately four weeks) and again in October 2008 (for two weeks). The main reason for all the research trips was to carry out interviews with journalists, media executives, public relations professionals and people I had identified as active members of the community. Moreover, I was keen to experience life in Miami and to get a firsthand impression of a city I had previously only studied from a distance. Also, I was eager to get a closer look at the media scene of Miami and gather data, mainly from various newspapers, radio programs and TV, to get a sense of the output on offer from various providers.

In total, I carried out 38 in-depth, semi-structured, open-ended interviews, twenty-four with men and fourteen with women. Apart from one, all interviews took place on a one-to-one basis and all interviews were face-to-face. Three further interviews were conducted via e-mail. I met some interviewees more than once, sometimes in a more social context or at events they also attended as guests. In addition to "official" interviewees, there were many individuals who provided most helpful information that I included in field notes.

Appendix A

Debates in the social sciences point toward the ambiguity of how to deal with details of research participants and places (Nespor 2000; Shulman 1990; Wiles et al. 2008). While methods textbooks and guidelines disseminated by research associations generally emphasize the importance of confidentiality, which is assumed to be best accomplished by anonymizing participants' identities, there are few instructions on how *exactly* this is to be achieved in the context of qualitative research.[1] Moreover, if anonymization has taken place, there is rarely an account given of how this was done. It is the researcher's call to judge that the process necessary to maintain promises of confidentiality made to interviewees is balanced with the validity of data for primary and secondary use. These concerns are especially prevalent when dealing with so-called vulnerable research participants. On the other hand, there have been calls for viewing participants as "empowered" individuals who, in many cases, might be in favor of seeing their name next to a statement they had made. Anonymization as a default procedure can therefore silence individuals who would prefer their voices to be clearly heard and identified.

As I experienced research participants as eloquent, educated and responsible individuals, who were often familiar with the practices of academic research, I decided to include interviewees' real names in this volume. However, for a number of quotes, the source is kept anonymous. This was done for one or more of three reasons; firstly, to reflect a general sentiment noted in the field. Assigning the quote to one particular interviewee would counteract the way in which it is used in the text and misrepresent the frequency with which a particular sentiment was encountered in the field. Secondly, no source is given when agreements toward this end were made between the interviewee and me. Finally, if my judgment is that a quote could be problematic for the interviewee and/or for his or her family and friends, I made a choice to anonymize the quote by not including the research participant's name.

First Encounters

My first point of contact in Miami, Donn Tilson, is an alumnus of Stirling University (where I first started my PhD). Donn is an associate

Appendix A

professor at the University of Miami. Without him and his support, this research project would probably not have taken the same route and I would have found it much more challenging to find suitable interview partners. Donn was able to accommodate me at the libraries of the University of Miami—a private institution with facilities that are generally not open to the public. The University of Miami also hosts the Cuban Heritage Collection (CHC), home to the greatest collection of Cuban exile newspapers. With Esperanza de Varona, the chair of the CHC, I found another invaluable source of knowledge about Cuban exile publications as well as the history and people of Miami's Cuban American community.

Despite a rather good start and plenty of help from the people I met during my first week of field work, I was wary of my sample of interviewees. On the one hand, following people's advice on who would be "good for me to talk to" could ensure that I would speak to people who were considered to be important and well known players or personalities within the local and sometimes national media scene. Here it was also helpful to specifically ask the advice of Hispanic (but non–Cuban) interviewees, as they turned out to be more likely to suggest a diverse mix of future interviewees, as opposed to a "best friend" who worked in the office next door. The snowballing method to locate interviewees proved to be very successful. On the other hand, I was afraid of being passed around a circle of friends with a similar political outlook on Cuban issues and local matters in Miami and Miami's media. I therefore tried to get in touch with a number of people whose contact details had not been given to me by previous interviewees. My efforts were rewarded in a few cases, although it turned out to be much easier when I could drop the name of a person whom I had already interviewed, someone who had recommended the person I was "cold-calling" as a potential interviewee. Having a contact name when approaching a potential interviewee might be advantageous in any case, but I suspect that there is a further dimension to this in the case of Cuban Americans.

A profound reluctance to talk to someone who is not part of the community and is doing some form of investigation—be it in an academic or in a journalistic context—has grown among some members of the community. This goes hand in hand with what is perceived as an

Appendix A

unfavorable treatment of Miami Cubans in English-language mainstream media, for example the *New York Times*. The Cuban American community traditionally leans toward the political right and always had an ambiguous relationship with left-leaning, liberal journalists and the media they worked for. My feeling is that even academics might sometimes be seen in the same light. One interviewee also confirmed this to some extent by exclaiming: "They always love to picture Miami … Miami is like a magnet for all these theses: the old exile is dying. Excuse me?" At a later stage in the interview the same research participant also asserted: "I have come to realize that a lot of journalists have lost their integrity when covering Cuba." Therefore, the Cuba coverage of these media very often put a further nail into the coffin.

Sensationalism, Romanticized Coverage and Reflexivity

These sentiments, the periodic disinclination to agree to an interview, also ties in with how easily the people in the field and their actions can be sensationalized and, at the same time, how easily the historic context can be romanticized. It is challenging to put my finger on precisely why I was worried about being culpable of one or the other (or possibly both) when doing research, thinking and writing about this particular field and the people that "inhabit" it. Dealing with the Cuban exile by default means dealing with Cuba and the Cuban revolution. And the most famous faces of the revolution are without a doubt Fidel Castro and Ernesto "Ché" Guevara; the iconic depiction of Ché's face has especially left its mark on popular culture. Apart from being viewed as charismatic leaders, Ché's and Fidel's fight against the Batista regime for many proves that they stood up against a corrupt establishment, formed a guerrilla movement in the Oriente Province and turned the power structures in Cuba upside down. Combined with a latent dose of anti–Americanism and/or anti-capitalism, one can imagine that these men, their ideas and ideology and the images they took on in the public eye helped them to achieve a legendary and maybe even mythical status. What is much less frequently referred to in popular culture is that the success of the Cuban revolution came at a cost. Part of that cost is the

Appendix A

uprooting of a significant fraction of the population and the division of families, friends and ultimately a nation. With the Cold War over and Cuba being a country that is severely suffering economically, the exiles' attempts to assassinate Fidel Castro can be viewed as somewhat bizarre if taken out of context: poisonous cigars make for a good story—but many times they do not let the exiles appear in the light that they would want to be seen in, and this kind of story certainly does not convey the main points a lot of exiles would want to bring across. Can I as a researcher stand outside of this discourse? Certainly not! Even reflexivity does not provide a smooth escape route:

> Reflexivity may seem comfortably neutral for some. That depends how it is interpreted. In its fullest sense, reflexivity forces us to think through the consequences of our relations with others, whether it be conditions of reciprocity, asymmetry, or potential exploitation. There are choices to be made in the field, within relationships and in the final text. If we insert the ethnographer's self as positioned subject into the text, we are obliged to confront the moral and political responsibility of our actions [Okely 1992, 24].

For better or for worse, it is impossible for this research to not be political or at least be interpreted as a piece with a political dimension. Interviewees were as aware of this as I was, if not more so. The occasional reluctance to meet me and talk to me was therefore no surprise.

Researching Beyond the Media

In addition to pursuing selected members of the community for interviews, it was also highly beneficial to attend a number of different events, such as book presentations and exhibition openings that allowed me to meet and observe people who were not necessarily directly involved with the media on a professional level.

An observation that I made regularly was that deep splits run between different fragments of the community. People know each other, and they are aware of who is a friend of whom, who works for whom and who is involved in certain professional, political and social networks. As I became more and more aware of this, I tried to keep my options open, hoping not to be drawn in by any particular section of the Cuban

Appendix A

community. However, my base at the Cuban Heritage Collection might already have been taken as an indication of my supposed ideological stance by some. During my third visit to the field in October 2008, it became apparent that the staff of the Cuban Heritage Collection try very hard to maintain a neutral stand and to not side with any particular segment of the community. This takes a balancing act extraordinaire.

To my dismay, I found myself drawn into the divisions of the community, as the following incident illustrates. Once interviews were finished, some interviewees would ask whom I had interviewed previously—maybe just out of interest, maybe to go on and suggest future interviewees. I had never considered in detail what kind of reactions interviewees might have to my naming of previous contacts. Firstly, reactions were mostly positive. Secondly, all interviewees had some understanding of what research entails and that I would naturally want to speak to as many people and as many "sides" as possible.[2] In one particular case, though, the interviewee showed clear disapproval of my talking to a journalist at the *Miami Herald*. At the time, I did not take this minor condemnation very seriously, but in retrospect it turned out that this interviewee could have been a valuable source for further information and contacts. After this first interview, he did not respond to any further attempts to contact him. It taught me that it is wise to hold my cards closer to my chest in such a sensitive environment.

Interviewing Academics

A professional group that turned out to be in some cases even more elusive than journalists were academics. Generally speaking, people were very generous with their time and the information they shared. The staff of the Cuban Heritage Collection invited me to come along to several events and were very helpful in drawing my attention to upcoming lectures, receptions and so on. The same holds true for several researchers working in the Institute for Cuban and Cuban American Studies, where I was kindly invited to observe summer school classes on the future of Cuba. However, I also had a couple of bemusing exchanges with academics.

One professor at the University of Miami whom I had emailed to

Appendix A

ask for an interview following a recommendation from a previous interviewee e-mailed back, asking whether he would be assisting me in a research project; if so he would need an e-mail from my supervisor regarding the project to "avoid misunderstandings and professional conflicts." After I explained that I would like to interview him and that I would not require academic advice I never heard from him again.

Another scholar, a Cuba expert and widely published author, told me that he did not want to comment on the situation in Miami. The main reason for this was that he was not an expert and not Cuban American. Nevertheless he works at a research institute of a Miami-based university. Time constraints could be a straightforward explanation here, but the sensitivity of the issues, knowing the ropes of academic research and the danger of potentially being misquoted or quoted out of context, would be something that most academics would have buzzing around in the back of their minds when approached by a researcher.

The Cuban Heritage Collection

Despite minor hiccups, it was ideal for me to be placed at the Cuban Heritage Collection (CHC). During my second visit, it turned out that the staff had made plans for me too. I was asked to attend a conference the CHC was hosting and speak about my research. In the end, I could not attend this conference, as I would already be back in the United Kingdom. However, I did accompany Gladys Gómez-Rossié, the community relations coordinator of the Cuban Heritage Collection, to a meeting of the Cuban American student group, the Federación de Estudiantes Cubanos (FEC), based at the University of Miami. At the meeting, I was asked to introduce my project, which the students seemed to meet with a mixture of curiosity and bewilderment. I suspect that they were surprised by someone coming such a long way to study something that they paid very little attention to, mainly because of its everyday omnipresence. A couple of weeks later, the president of the FEC at the time agreed to talk to me in more depth about the aims of the group and her personal views of Cuba- and Cuban American–related issues.

Besides being places to go to in the mornings, to have a chat, to ask questions and to have internet access, the University of Miami and the

Appendix A

CHC were also good places for me to hang out, meet and chat with people informally, and observe. Arguably one of the main drawbacks when it came to being in the field were my looks, my hair color and complexion. I do not look Cuban or Hispanic. While in the University of Miami, and more generally in the Coral Gables setting, I could practice life as what Philip Schlesinger (1980, 348) calls "an experienced shrinker." Blending in was impossible in *Calle Ocho* (8th Street) and Little Havana. People probably perceived me as a tourist there—and I always drew attention to myself. This was also the case because *Calle Ocho* has much more of a "street culture." People, mostly men, stand outside cafés, sit on benches, and stand in front of shops, and I was frequently approached with comments and remarks when I was walking by. No hope of "shrinking" there. And also it was not an environment that made me feel particularly safe or at ease.

During my second visit it became apparent that some members of the Cuban American community had heard about me and the study. On a couple of occasions I was presented with business cards accompanied by the comment that the person would be happy to be interviewed. Although these people were usually not very high up on my own "wish list," it was a good opportunity to get a new perspective on some matters and see others confirmed or rejected. Quite in contrast to that, I also encountered interviewees who did not actually show much of an interest in me or what exactly I was doing. Neither did they pay much attention to the questions I was asking. The interview was treated as an opportunity to put forward a political message; I was introduced to an agenda and presented with issues that bore little if any relation to my research topic.

Field Dynamics

Thinking along the lines of Wooffitt and Widdicombe (2006), interviews are a form of social interaction and like any other form of human social encounter are governed by certain unspoken rules and dynamics. In my case, these dynamics were characterized by issues revolving around age, gender, my personal background and my personality. Given the complex nature of social interaction in general, and the added inter-

Appendix A

cultural dimension in this case, it is doubtful whether the dynamics of formal and informal interviews and dealings in the field can be pinned down and analyzed in their entirety. Nevertheless, in an effort at self-reflexivity, I will explore these issues in more depth.

The majority of my interviewees were male and roughly between eight and forty years older than me. At times, this age gap was even verbalized in the interview. I was clearly constructed as a young female research student who "needed to be told" certain things because it was assumed that I would not know otherwise. Drawing on Easterday et al. (1982), a number of interviews and encounters especially during the first phase of field work would fall into the "father-daughter" category. In certain ways, this might have made the interaction less awkward for the interviewee—and possibly for myself as the researcher who, in the field for the first time, had to come to terms with lingering concerns about the value, relevance and feasibility of the project and about myself as the one to carry it out: "Given the legitimacy of traditional sex role relationships, the father-daughter relationship offers older males—threatened by young women or unable to interact with young women as peers—a safe, predefined interactional context" (Easterday et al. 1982, 65).

During the first phase of field research I was not too concerned about this particular dynamic during some of the interviews, as it did indeed sometimes provide me with useful information and the way the interviewee told "his-story" was at the same time an indication of a point of view, a certain take on events. On the other hand, after a number of interviews I felt information was being repeated to me, and I noticed that it was time to dig deeper, interrupt people if necessary and ask more refined questions that would demonstrate my existing knowledge and understanding of the issues discussed. To some extent, this meant falling out of the role that I had been given in the interviewee's mind and led to a subtle shift in the dynamics of the interview.

Despite my best efforts, I felt that the construction of myself as a "student researcher" was also aided by the fact that I found it challenging to look professional and actively work on "impression management" as for example Hammersley and Atkinson (1983, 78–88) advise in the context of doing ethnographic research or conducting interviews. Being

Appendix A

accustomed to the climate of Central Scotland, I am not convinced I managed to fully acclimatize to high humidity, subtropical thunder storms and temperatures of 40 degrees Celsius (104 degrees F) and above. I found it extremely difficult to keep up the construction of myself as a "professional" and present myself in the way I usually do in colder climates. What made me even more conscious of this fact is that Cuban Americans tend to be very elegant. Chronically underdressed, I frequently found myself sitting at an event, wondering if some Florida or Washington VIP was coming to join us, say for instance Jeb Bush, because everyone was looking so smart, men in suits and women showing off their pearls and gold. I mentioned this to a non–Cuban and was told that this is just "the Cuban way." Of course this does not hold true for the entire exile community, but merely for some of the historic exiles. It would also be fair to assume that many people who attend these kinds of events not only enjoy the "Cuban American content" (book presentation; lecture; exhibition) that they entail but see it as an opportunity for a social get-together. With respect to image management, it is also worth noting that most people who can afford it will travel by car in Miami and, at least during the hot months in the summer, spend most of the day in air-conditioned rooms. The fact that I used public transport garnered me a few puzzled, bemused and at times concerned looks from interviewees and other people I met in the field.

Another aspect of the ongoing process of identity construction in the field was my nationality. As a significant number of people, especially among the older exiles and many Cubans who arrived after 1980, speak English as a second language, they were aware of the fact that I obviously do not have an American accent, but not everyone realized that I am a German national with German being my native tongue. Some of the interviewees left with the idea that I was a British citizen. If they only mentioned this in passing, maybe to illustrate a point, or draw a comparison for example between their heritage and mine, I did not correct them, as I did not think it an issue, as long as it was clear that I was European. The fact that I was a foreigner was important because it gave contacts and interviewees a clear indication that I was not inherently leaning toward or sympathizing with any particular segment of the Cuban American community.

Appendix A

A further characteristic of interviews and interactions in the field concerned language. Miami is a bilingual city. As one of my interviewees pointed out, insufficient Spanish-language skills can be disadvantageous to one's professional career. I had a strong preference for conducting interviews in English. With German being my mother tongue, I did not want to end up in a situation where I would have to translate hour-long conversations from one foreign language into another. Apart from three interviewees, all participants were more or less happy to talk in English. For a few interviewees, this meant a true effort, with words not coming easily to them and a notable feeling of uneasiness overshadowing parts of the interview because, being well-educated and eloquent in Spanish, conversing in English was a minor struggle.

Despite feeling slightly uncomfortable and possibly too self-conscious at times, I enjoyed field work immensely. The majority of interviewees were happy to share their thoughts with me and patiently answer my questions. But like Amanda Coffey (1999, 45), I was uneasy when it came to talking about myself. While I defined the majority of my relations as mostly, though not entirely, professional, some interviewees did have a different take on this. In particular, I felt that one interviewee who after the interview started asking me personal questions about my choice as a German national to study in Scotland (hinting that it might have been for romantic reasons) clearly overstepped an invisible line, although it would have been perfectly all right from my perspective to ask him similar questions, though different in tone, within the context of the interview.

Evolving Relations in and to the Field

A distinction between the first and second visit to Miami was the average length of interviews. In June 2006, interviews lasted around thirty minutes on average, while during my second visit half an hour never seemed enough time. This might be due to a number of reasons: for one thing, I was more familiar with the material and was able to ask more in-depth questions about the issues discussed. This in turn might have led interviewees to go into more detail and be willing to give more of their time to me. Secondly, I had probably further developed and

Appendix A

refined my skills as an interviewer. It was also helpful that the study I was undertaking had caught some people's attention. Through word of mouth, because they had seen me working in the Cuban Heritage Collection or noticed my attendance at events with a specific Cuban American focus, some people knew who I was and additionally were aware of friends and/or colleagues I had interviewed previously and therefore felt being one of my interviewees would give them a chance to either underline some points or "set the record straight."

Interviews and more generally interpersonal dynamics were similar between my first and second visit. During my third visit in October 2008 I observed a clear shift. One of the main reasons for that was probably my increased confidence about the feasibility of the project; I saw light at the end of the tunnel. Due to secondary sources that I had consulted and desktop research I had completed in the meantime, I felt much more certain of the historic context of the field, the exile, the main players and issues in relation to my research. As an interviewer, I was much harder to impress this time. During one interview, for instance, an interviewee (male and about 60 years old) made a point of letting me in on "a little-known secret"—namely that the two Republican congressmen and brothers Lincoln and Mario Díaz-Balart are distant relatives of Fidel Castro. If it is a secret, it is a very open one; I had heard and read this several times before and therefore did not show the reaction the interviewee was aiming for.

While the gap between the second and third visits was too long to uphold occasional communication with most people in the field, my relations to the staff in the Cuban Heritage Collection was more open and intensive in October 2008 than they had been before. To visitors I was jokingly introduced to as "part of the family." I also had many more informal and open chats with CHC employees. For the first time I felt comfortable enough to bring up more sensitive issues, questions about race, for instance, that I had wondered about but not verbalized during my previous stays.

In comparison to previous field work, I also had a much clearer understanding of what the final thesis should look like and had written drafts of a few chapters. The development of the thesis and the ongoing research and writing process brought a significant change to the way I

Appendix A

approached the field. It made me realize the very diverse nature that field work as a multi-method approach in itself can have. In June 2006 and January 2007 I had the exploratory mindset that "just being in the field" would give me the information I needed to construct my argument, or an argument rather. In October 2008 I was much more pro-active, seeking specific information to fill gaps and find the missing pieces. During interview situations I caught myself on several occasions going back and forth between what was being said and how it would fit in with what I had written so far. The memory of mind-numbing transcription of hour-long interviews led me to be more assertive in bringing interviewees back on track if I felt they had gone off on a tangent. After all, I was finally able to tell the difference between track and tangent.

Despite my increased focus, I did not manage to speak to everyone I had approached for an interview. October 2008 was characterized by the presidential election campaign of Barack Obama for the Democrats and John McCain for the Republicans. Florida's swing state status made it a major battle ground between the two sides and kept journalists very busy. Observing the presidential campaign and chatting to people in the field were insightful in other ways. Nevertheless, going to Miami shortly before Election Day on November 4 might have been one reason why it was difficult to get hold of television journalists especially. Even so, I left the field in good spirits. More than before I could see the direction in which the data and my experiences in the field were pointing.

Data Analysis

The experience of anthropological material is, like fieldwork, a continuing and creative experience. The research has combined action and contemplation. Scrutiny of the notes offers both empirical certainty and intuitive reminders. Insights emerge also from the subconscious and from bodily memories, never penned on paper. There are serendipitous connections to be made, if the writer is open to them. Writing and analysis comprise a movement between the tangible and intangible, between the cerebral and sensual, between the visible and invisible. Interpretation moves from evidence to ideas and theory, then back again. There can be no set formulae, only broad guidelines, sensitive to specific cases. The researcher is freed from a division of labour which splits fieldwork from analysis. The author

Appendix A

is not alienated from the experience of participant observation, but draws upon it both precisely and amorphously for the resolution of the completed text [Okely 1994, 32].

My life not only revolved around field work when I was physically in Miami, it also took over my life in Scotland. As the above quotation from Okely encapsulates, the topic and the method I had chosen stayed with me for the best part of six years. When reading the section titles of this chapter, one might get the impression that there was a clear distinction between the collection of data and the analysis and interpretation; this was not the case, however. The three stages were highly intertwined, one triggering the other, and despite an ocean between myself and the field, it was in some sense always very close. Daily e-mail feeds from the *Miami Herald* and weekly specials on news from the Americas allowed me to keep a virtual finger on the pulse. One might think that the three-odd months I spent in Miami over a considerable space of time should not have had such a strong impact on my life. But through reading, online searches and research, writing, and thinking, Miami and the Cuban American community stayed with me, whether I was there or not. My physical presence in one or the other place also interlinked with my thoughts: some things seemed perfectly clear to me when I was in the field. Yet, sitting at my desk in Scotland I could not make sense of it at all—and vice versa.

One of the most ambivalent characteristics of field research is the wealth of data that it produces. As a novice to this method, I was thrilled with the amount of material I could gather when in Miami, the vast amounts of interview material and general and participant observations I made on a daily basis. The downside became apparent when I had made my way back to Scotland and was trying to find a sensible way to proceed.

After my first time in the field in June 2006, I transcribed in full all fifteen interviews I had conducted and also copied all the field notes I had taken. I then went through these roughly 70 single-spaced pages of data, labeled, categorized and looked for recurring themes; issues that were mentioned again and again by interviewees. Naturally these themes may have come up because of my questioning during the interview. But, as already indicated above, I had made a point of conducting these semi-

Appendix A

structured interviews in a very open manner, allowing plenty of time for interviewees to expand on their views, even if I felt at the time of the interview that this was more of a sidetrack than relevant data in regard to my research questions. This also ties in with the role of the student researcher I felt I was ascribed by a number of interviewees during my first visit to the field.

In total, I identified seven themes that deserved further scrutiny in future field, archival and desktop research. The themes were:

- The development of a Spanish-language media scene
- Diversity of the Cuban American community and the notion of exile
- The Cuban Americans within the Hispanic community
- The development of Miami as an urban, prospering center
- The relationship between the Cuban American and the local (white) Anglo community and the case of Elián
- The misuse of Cuban issues and raising false hopes
- Academics, intellectuals and the question of succession in Cuba

Some of these early themes materialized in one or several chapters later on. Some formed background issues that went beyond the scope of this work but were still highly useful for my general understanding of the history and the concerns of the Cuban American community.

Concluding Remarks

In his ambitiously titled *Getting the Most out of the Research Experience: What Every Researcher Needs to Know*, Brian Roberts (2007, 72) characterizes good research in the following way:

> Good research is a thinking person's game. It is a creative and strategic process that involves constantly assessing, reassessing, and making decisions about the best possible means for obtaining trustworthy information, carrying out appropriate analysis, and drawing credible conclusions.

Field work as a multi-method approach produces a lot of data to take in, analyze and interpret. What it does not give the researcher is a clear-cut story. What one observes firsthand in the field might be poles apart from

Appendix A

what interviewees say. Once I understood how some things "worked" within the community and the relationship between the media and community, new questions arose, new developments were to be taken into account. The engagement with the field on so many levels makes it challenging to draw the line and especially in the beginning to tell apart the essential and the useful from the interesting but less relevant information.

A further constraint was that the field I was trying to research was not as clearly defined for the outside world as it was in my mind. This relates to a previous point about Cuban and Cuban American identity and constructions and negotiation thereof being intertwined with other loyalties, groups, and communities that an individual forms a part of. I was especially aware of this when talking to younger people in their twenties and thirties and people who had come to the U.S. at a relatively young age, for example the Pedro Pan children, who had received a significant amount of their education in the United States. How prevalent were Cuban issues and topics in their everyday life if it were not for some researcher asking them about it? My presence in the field simultaneously changed it. No matter how I phrased questions, it influenced the interviewee. This made the combination of methods even more important.

A major drawback of conducting field work is that it is time- and cost-intensive. Compared to many European and other American cities, Miami is not a cheap place to live, and my work as a teaching fellow did not allow me to stay as long as I would have liked. But even longer periods of time in the field would not have been a guarantee to get interviews with all the people I would have liked to talk to and to observe everything I would have liked to see. This rings especially true in relation to Radio and TV Martí, on which I was trying to gather more data. Even though I did interview several people working for the Martís, some were reluctant to answer questions in relation to their work or their personal opinions in any depth. After the *Miami Herald* ran several stories claiming that journalists working for independent (i.e., commercial) media were receiving government funds through their work for the Martís that would ultimately hamper their impartiality, the topic became too sensitive for most people to comment on. Notwithstanding my efforts, I never got an interview or even heard back from Radio and TV Martí, despite handing in my questions in advance.

Appendix A

Physical disengagement with the field was in many ways straightforward. The end of my relationship to individuals in the field was determined in most cases by my departure. I remained in sporadic contact with Donn Tilson of the University of Miami and Esperanza de Varona of the Cuban Heritage Collection. Considerable geographical distance and cultural differences have had an influence on the entire research and writing process that should not be underestimated. When explaining about the research project and the fact that it is based at a British institution, some interviewees seemed relieved and more at ease. As outlined above, though, mental disengagement with the field was much more difficult and the engagement itself varied in intensity depending on other things going on in my life.

Something that I had in common with the exiles was that my interest did not just stay within the realms of Miami and South Florida but also moved across the Straits to Cuba. If Fidel Castro or anything Cuba-related was on the news, I was glued to the television. My family and friends made an effort to pass on articles they saw about Cuba and Miami. Funnily enough, some people even assumed given the research topic that I would have a strong interest and be an expert on *Scarface* and *CSI Miami*.

I quoted Amanda Coffey earlier, and I would like to end with another citation from her monograph *The Ethnographic Self*:

> The construction and production of self and identity occurs both during and after fieldwork. In writing, remembering and representing our fieldwork experiences we are involved in processes of self presentation and identity construction. In considering and exploring the intimate relations between the field, significant others and the private self, we are able to understand the processes of fieldwork as practical, intellectual and emotional accomplishments [1999, 1].

Owing to its time-extensive dimension, field work and the preparation of data, analysis, reliving memories and so on goes through ups and downs. However, one of the most positive side-effects of doing ethnographic work is that it gives the researcher not only the opportunity to get to know a new context with new people but also the chance to get to know oneself better—and hopefully come out at the other end with a sense of achievement.

Appendix B

Persons of Hispanic Origin by Country of Origin, Miami-Dade County, Florida, 1990 to 2007

	1990	2000	2001	2002	2003	2004	2005	2006	2007	Annual Average Change 1990–2000	Annual Average Change 2000–2007
Total	953,407	1,291,737	1,333,462	1,374,106	1,398,974	1,403,983	1,423,697	1,471,709	1,479,530	33,833	26,828
Mexican	23,112	38,095	54,558	38,124	58,966	58,643	43,361	41,942	45,776	1,498	1,097
Puerto Rican	72,827	80,327	70,043	85,362	93,373	92,972	80,854	88,579	94,264	750	1,991
Cuban	563,979	650,601	704,423	695,122	710,937	735,327	736,073	767,349	794,883	8,662	20,612
Dominican	23,475	36,454	49,023	50,349	52,872	65,421	58,372	49,430	48,635	1,298	1,740
Central American	119,534	128,903	190,286	200,443	184,374	170,974	195,914	210,821	201,428	937	10,361
• Costa Rican	4,743	4,706	6,622	6,997	1,814	8,732	4,727	7,944	7,045	-4	334
• Guatemalan	8,242	9,676	9,183	7,197	12,046	15,234	12,018	24,292	17,843	143	1,167
• Honduran	18,102	26,829	43,395	35,172	57,076	44,065	51,588	47,927	49,137	873	3,187
• Nicaraguan	74,244	69,257	104,776	124,198	88,588	79,896	95,745	100,258	105,415	-499	5,165
• Panamanian	6,729	5,863	7,955	10,224	7,044	5,243	9,844	9,881	7,346	-87	212
• Salvadoran	7,339	9,115	17,041	14,421	14,448	16,642	19,914	17,556	12,615	178	500
• Other Central American	135	3,457	1,314	2,234	3,358	1,162	2,078	2,963	2,027	332	-204

	1990	2000	2001	2002	2003	2004	2005	2006	2007	Annual Average Change 1990–2000	Annual Average Change 2000–2007
South American	108,768	154,348	198,965	222,456	243,526	220,602	237,760	242,196	232,248	4,558	11,129
• Argentinean	8,585	13,341	18,870	38,032	25,071	27,545	30,973	25,134	21,120	476	1,111
• Bolivian	2,309	2,418	3,347	1,288	2,503	4,458	3,220	1,387	4,847	11	347
• Chilean	7,929	7,910	16,214	9,354	17,101	8,956	11,925	13,363	8,228	-2	45
• Colombian	53,852	70,066	94,254	95,441	96,936	85,588	90,303	102,118	94,511	1,621	3,492
• Ecuadorian	7,986	10,560	7,408	8,522	24,460	19,834	12,705	16,336	19,124	257	1,223
• Paraguayan	166	434	723	2,622	1,401	237	857	506	191	27	-35
• Peruvian	16,452	23,327	27,048	32,201	30,237	29,916	37,361	34,106	36,258	688	1,847
• Uruguayan	1,482	1,829	872	2,118	9,595	6,314	5,277	5,371	6,824	35	714
• Venezuelan	9,846	21,593	28,952	29,540	33,147	31,602	42,849	40,981	37,865	1,175	2,325
• Other South American	161	2,870	1,277	3,338	3,075	6,152	2,290	2,894	3,280	271	59
• Other Hispanic	44,498	203,009	66,164	82,250	54,926	60,044	71,363	71,392	62,296	15,851	-20,102

U.S. Census Bureau. 1990. Census of Population, Summary Tape File 1A & Summary Tape File 4A. 2000. Census 2000, Summary File 1. 2001–2003. American Community Survey, Table PCT006. 2004—2007. American Community Survey, Table PCT011.http://factfinder.census.gov/. Miami-Dade County Dept. of Planning and Zoning, Research Section, 2001, 2005 and 2009. Source: Miami-Dade County Facts 2009, 19.

Appendix C

Format: *Fuego en la Sangre*, Weds., Feb. 4

Rank	Program Name	Net	Hispanic Household Rating (Live + SD)	Persons 2+ (in thousands) (Live + SD)
1	*Fuego en la Sangre*, Wed., Feb. 4	UNI	24.1	5863
2	*Fuego en la Sangre*, Thur., Feb. 5	UNI	24.0	5718
3	*Fuego en la Sangre*, Tue., Feb. 3	UNI	23.7	5913
4	*Fuego en la Sangre*, Fri., Feb. 6	UNI	22.7	5400
4	*Fuego en la Sangre*, Mon., Feb. 2	UNI	22.7	5426
6	*Cuidado con el Angel*, Wed., Feb. 4	UNI	21.9	4980
7	*Cuidado con el Angel*, Tue., Feb. 3	UNI	21.6	5105
7	*Cuidado con el Angel*, Thur., Feb. 5	UNI	21.6	4995
9	*Cuidado con el Angel*, Mon., Feb. 2	UNI	21.3	4950
10	*Tontas no van Cielo*, Tue., Feb. 3	UNI	20.6	4797

Source: Nielsen Media Research 2009

Rank	Program	Network	Viewers (P2+)
1	American Idol	FOX	24,941,000
2	Mentalist, The	CBS	19,699,000
3	NCIS	CBS	18,031,00
4	Without a Trace	CBS	14,308,000
5	Dateline NBC	NBC	11,259,000
6	Fringe	FOX	9,828,000
7	Biggest Loser 7	NBC	9,252,000
8	Fuego en la Sangre	UNI	5,746,000
9	Cuidado con el Angel	UNI	4,818,000
10	Charlie Brown Valentine	ABC	4,811,000

Source: Nielsen Wire 2009. P2+: person aged 2 years and older. Live+SD: refers to watching while the show is aired and viewers recording the program and watching it on the same day. Net: Network. Hispanic Household Rating: percentage of Hispanic households that were tuned into a program. Nielsen makes the household percentage the prime indicator for its ranking, not the absolute number of viewers.

Chapter Notes

Introduction

1. Information from named informants is referred to in citations as a "personal communication" ("pers. com."). Information from anonymous informants is cited as being from an "interview."
2. I will follow Baym and Markham's (2009) suggestion in referring to the "internet" as opposed to the "Internet." In their insightful anthology *Internet Inquiry*, they convincingly argue for spelling "internet" in lower case, as it is neither a place you can go to nor a coherent communicative space or entity in itself. Accordingly, Baym and Markham see power and agency with the creators and users of the internet, rather than with the medium.
3. A thorough and authoritative account of Cuban history is offered by Hugh Thomas (1971) in *Cuba, or The Pursuit of Freedom*.
4. I attempt to spell Spanish names with accents when appropriate. However, some authors and informants have altered the spelling, i.e., lost the accent, of their names, and I aim to respect that. Depending on the original, I therefore included González as well as Gonzalez. In the case of Elián González, I have adopted the spelling with an accent.
5. This argument is for example put forward by Brian Latell (2005) in *After Fidel*.
6. In this context, Nancy Raquel Mirabal (2003, 368) argues for "a more expansive framework, one that links the history of pre–1959 Cuban diaspora with that of the post–1959 diaspora." Mirabal (2003) criticizes the fact that research has focused extensively on Cubans who migrated after the revolution. As a result, she sees "the over-emphasis on the 1959 exile model" resulting "in a fragmented Cuban–United States historiography; one that has not weathered recent political and economic developments well" (379). While Mirabal is right to call for a greater awareness of pre-revolutionary Cuban history and U.S.–Cuban relations, Fidel Castro's takeover of Havana did signify an unprecedented shift in the 200-year-long history of these two countries (Thomas 1984, 9). It marked the start of the migration of about one million Cubans to the United States.
7. All figures refer to 2007. See Appendix B.
8. For an in-depth analysis of national and international powers in play when negotiating, passing and putting into practice the Helms-Burton Act, see Perl (2006).
9. All figures were quoted from *Cuba Facts* (issue 43, December 2008) offered by the Institute of Cuban and Cuban American Studies at the University of Miami. It is available at http://ctp.iccas.miami.edu/FACTS_Web/Cuba%20Facts%20Issue%2043%20December.htm, and is based on statistics provided by the United Nations Statistical Yearbook.
10. Daniel C. Walsh offers an in-depth account of the history of Radio and TV Martí in *An Air War with Cuba* (2012).

Notes—Chapter 1

11. Theoretical as well as empirical research on diasporic and ethnic formations has generated a high amount of scholarship over the past two decades; some classic examples of such literature are Cohen (1997), Hall (1991, 1992 and 1997), Peters (1999), Tölölyan (1991), Robbins (1995), Karim (2003), Tsagarousianou (2004), Naficy (1999 and 1993) and Van Hear (1998). Among others, Sinclair and Cunningham (2000), Morley (1999, 2000 and 1991) and Naficy (1999, 1993, 2001) have provided essential reading on diasporas and their media use.

12. This positive connotation of exile can be found for example in the work of Naficy (1993 and 2001), Agha (1997), Hartenstein (1999), Elsaesser (1999), Trommler (1995), Becker (1995), and Strack (1995).

13. Reoccurring public debates (see for example Gessler [2010] and *The Economist* [Nov. 13, 2010]) in Germany about insufficiently integrated Turkish and Arab migrants (the majority of them with German passports) demonstrate the irrelevance of legal status when it comes to feelings of belonging and acceptance by the host society.

14. In contrast to the term *exile* or the Spanish *el exilio*, employed in the field to refer to those parts of the Cuban American community who arrived shortly after the revolution in 1959 and in the 1960s and early 1970s, terms such as *diaspora* or *diasporic community* seldom came up in everyday conversation.

15. See, for example, Robins (2001), Georgiou (2006), and Sassen (2001, 2002 and 2006).

16. In addition, diasporas are also often characterized by their engagement with what Benedict Anderson (1992) coined "long-distance nationalism."

17. Resistance to globalization is often misrepresented in public discourse. Organizations such as Attac (Association pour la Taxation des Transactions pour l'Aide aux Citoyens) are not against globalization per se, but are concerned about the neo-liberal expansionist thinking and profit of global companies as the main beneficiaries of current structures (http://www.france.attac.org/; http://attac.de/).

18. An in-depth examination of the significance of place for diasporic communities can be found in Lohmeier (2013).

19. See for example Valdivia (2008 and 2010), Vargas (2009), Chavez (2008), García Bedolla (2009), and Albarran (2009), to name but a few works dealing with Hispanics more generally. In addition, there has been a large amount of writing on the Cuban American community and Miami as a space and place: Calvo Ospina and Declerq (2001), Castro Ruz (2009), Levine (2001), Levine and Asís (2000), Pérez-Firmat (1994), O'Reilley Herrera (2001), Cornillot (2009), Gjelten (2009), Grenier and Stepick III (1992), and Medina (2002). In this context, Joan Didion's *Miami* (1987) is still a seminal work when considering non-academic writing.

20. In the following chapters I will use the term *Hispanic* to refer to all people with roots in countries south of the United States and the Caribbean. This term was used by informants in the field.

21. The constructed nature of Hispanic identity and its inherent diversity has also caused methodological concerns. Who is considered Latino/a or Hispanic in U.S. censuses has changed over the past decades. Furthermore, whether general statistics on Hispanics apply to the same degrees to all sub-groups is more than doubtful. For a detailed exposé of this issue see for example Soruco (1996, chapter 2) and Valdivia (2010, 14–21).

Chapter 1

1. The majority of Cubans arriving in the United States were and still are eligible to apply for U.S. citizenship. They therefore technically become "Cuban Americans," although how they interpret and identify with this legal status is a highly subjective matter.

Notes—Chapter 2

2. See, for example, the work of Urry (1995), Smith (1986), Carter et al. (1993) and Ballinger (2003).

3. The significance of these places for older Cuban Americans is captured in a humorous yet heart-rending short story by Miami-based author Ana Menéndez (2001) entitled *In Cuba I Was a German Shepherd*.

4. Kolar-Panov (1997) examines links between Croatian and Macedonian migrants to their countries of origin. Drawing on Silverstone (1994) and Ang (1989), Georgiou (2006) looks at Greek Cypriots now based in London while Naficy (1993) analyzes the collective identity and media use of the Iranian diaspora in Los Angeles. Ogan (2001) considers identities and media use of Turkish guest workers in the Netherlands.

5. For recent discussions of the trade embargo see, for example, *The Cuban Embargo* by Haney and Vanderbush (2005) and *Cuban Exiles on the Trade Embargo: Interviews* by Edward J. González (2007).

6. Even in 2010, twenty years after the reunion, the categories of "Ossis" (people from the former German Democratic Republic) and "Wessis" (those from the Federal Republic of Germany) are still existent in popular discourse and some German minds and hearts.

7. For an extensive analysis of the city's transformation in relation to migration waves and demographic changes, see Portes and Stepick (1993).

8. Between 1950 and 1987 the size of the "economically active population" in the Metropolitan Miami area rose from 157,321 to 712,568. The number of business establishments went up from 14,894 to 58, 036 (Portes and Stepick 1993, 209).

9. The term *myth* is here used as set out by Segal (2004). Myths are broadly defined as stories with a significant function.

10. Infante was initially a supporter of Fidel Castro and his reforms but then fell out with him. He eventually went into exile in London. Infante is most famous for the highly acclaimed *Tres Tristes Tigres* (first published in 1967; translated as *Three Trapped Tigers* [2008]).

11. For an in-depth account of Havana's night life and its underground scene in the 1950s see, for example, T.J. English's (2007) *The Havana Mob*.

12. Difficulties with the English language are still common today, indicating that later migration waves also lived or live with a language barrier. According to a survey conducted by Jessica Lavariega Monforti and Lisa García Bedolla (2006) entitled "Social context and exile politics: A look at Cuban and Cuban American political attitudes," only twenty-eight percent out of a random sample of 600 adult Cubans and Cuban Americans say they speak English "very well."

13. The Mariel Boatlift is named after the Port of Mariel, west of Havana. Due to turbulences in Havana (see Portes and Stepick [1993, 18–37], García [1996, 46–80], Bardach [2002, 118 and 129] for detailed description and analysis), Castro invited Cuban exiles in Miami to come and collect members of their families who wanted to leave the country.

14. A fascinating examination of the symbolic and religious interpretation of the Elián Gonzalez saga is offered by Miguel de la Torre (2003) in *La Lucha for Cuba*.

Chapter 2

1. *Diario* is delivered in the afternoon. The paper carries the date of the next day. However, the stories included have already been reported by other news outlets on the previous day.

2. A detailed overview of incoming migration is provided in Appendix B.

3. Average circulation figures for the *Miami Herald* and *El Nuevo Herald* (stated

Notes—Chapter 3

in parentheses) for the period of March to September 2010 were as follows: weekdays 151,612 (57,749), Saturdays 127,230 (54,056) and Sundays 214, 891 (73,616) (http://abcas3.accessabc.com/ecirc/newstitlesearchus.asp; accessed November 27, 2010).

4. As can be expected with such a powerful figure, Jorge Más Canosa was also extremely controversial and divided the already polarized Cuban American community, as David Rieff (1993, 52) points out: "People might disagree about what a post–Castro Cuba should look like. They most certainly did disagree about political strategy, since exile politics was, predictably enough, riven by faction and divided into any number of competing, often mutually antagonistic groupings. One could divide Miami into those who supported the Cuban American National Foundation and those who did not, and further, into those who had once supported it but couldn't stomach Jorge Mas Canosa's leadership and those who did not support it ever but who viewed it as a useful tool for pressuring the U.S. government."

5. The staff writer of *El Nuevo Herald* (interview, June 2006) also emphasized that despite the practice of having articles looked over by an attorney, he never had to self-censor his articles.

6. During field work it became apparent that it was extremely difficult to gain access or detailed information about the Martís. After Oscar Corral's story had been published in the *Miami Herald*, even people who were happy to be interviewed per se were not willing to talk about their work for the Martís.

7. When I first arrived in Miami, I was slightly uncomfortable with notions surrounding secret missions, agents, and the infiltration of the Cuban American community by Castro-loyal spies; I was afraid that in academic circles this might not be taken seriously and make my work resemble a bad replica of a Graham Greene novel. However, in the course of the project I realized that this is a true concern of some members of the Cuban American community. It is impossible for me judge what is fact and what is fiction and paranoia. But cases such as the ones of the "Cuban Five" (BBC World Service 2007) and Ana Belén Montes (see Carmichael 2007) bear witness to something boiling beneath the surface.

Chapter 3

1. During my last visit I learned that one of these radio hosts, Max Lesnik, has in fact withdrawn his programs from the air. However, they were still available as downloads (podcasts) online (Radio Miami website).

2. Interview with the author, October 2008. Similar sentiments are mirrored by Miguel de la Torre (2003, xv) when he reflects on his childhood and his feelings toward Cuba, Fidel Castro and the exilic state: "My hatred for Fidel Castro has been ingrained in me since childhood. From a very young age, I have considered Castro the earthly personification of Satan. My earliest memories are of extreme poverty in New York City, where I recall my parents personally blaming Castro for our plight."

3. Alex Stepick III (1992) provides a thorough analysis of the situation of Haitian migrants. In many aspects, the challenges of Haitians wanting to enter the United States stand in stark contrast to the fortunes many Cuban migrants have experienced. This is partly due to a legislative bias against Haitians as well as the misconceptions of those communities already based in Miami.

4. It is worth noting that the surveys referred to by the interviewee are probably paid for by Radio Mambí or its umbrella organization Univision Radio. They are not in the public domain and it is difficult to assess claims that a significant percentage of younger people are among the listeners of Radio Mambí.

5. The Obama administration has introduced new legislation that allows Cuban

Americans to travel to Cuba more easily. Moreover, restrictions on remittances have been reviewed too (Silva and Wilkinson 2009; BBC News 2011).

    6. Recent work by Lesnik (2010) includes for example a sarcastic commentary on a protest march carried out in March 2010 in Little Havana. The demonstration had been co-organized by singer/songwriter Gloria Estefan and her husband Emilio to demand respect for human rights in Cuba. Lesnik regularly contributes opinion pieces to cubadebate.cu (see http://www.cubadebate.cu/categoria/autores/max-lesnik/; accessed October 3, 2010), a Cuban website that also includes articles and reflections by Fidel and Raúl Castro. Cubadebate.cu aims to counteract the claims made by the United States about the island and Cuban politicians while also bringing to light the various attacks by the United States on Cuba (http://www.cubadebate.cu/editores/; accessed October 5, 2010).

Chapter 4

    1. The particularities and challenge of Spanish-language television are discussed for example by Sinclair (1999 and 2005).

    2. Since 1982 the FCC has allowed the set-up of low power television (LPTV) service. The aim was to encourage stations and networks providing locally oriented television for smaller communities. They can be operated by a diverse range of actors including religious groups, educational institutions and even individual citizens (Federal Communication Commission 2008).

    3. The acquisition was approved by the FCC in 2002.

    4. For a detailed description of terms and abbreviation used in these tables, please see Appendix C.

    5. The Center for Immigration Studies, a non-profit think tank, estimates that the number of migrants without necessary documents was 11.3 million in 2007. This agrees with figures that were regularly quoted in the field. Of these 11.3 million, 57 percent are believed to be from Mexico and a further 11 percent from Central America, adding to potential audiences of Spanish-language media (Center for Immigration 2004).

    6. This argument is underlined by Alvarez Borland and Bosch in their analysis of Cuban American literature. In comparison to other Spanish-language writing, Cuban American literature "seems to be less concerned with issues of political advocacy than its Chicano or Puerto Rican counterparts" (2009, 5).

    7. In 2003 the INS underwent a restructuring, and matters of immigration are now dealt with by the United States Citizenship and Immigration Services (USCIS) (Library Index, n.d.).

Chapter 5

    1. For more in-depth information on different internet user groups, see for example Lee (1999), Livingstone (2003), Singh (2001), Sooryamoorthy, Miller and Shrum (2008), and Cheong (2008).

    2. Estimates as to the number of existing blogs range widely between 2.8 million and 100 million worldwide, with up to 50 million in the United States (Hookway 2008, 93). However, McIntosh (2005) reminds us that a very high percentage of these are infrequently updated or altogether abandoned.

    3. I interviewed Henry Gómez in January 2007 and Paul Benavides in October 2008.

    4. The advertising on the *Herald Watch Blog* read: "HELP WANTED: Watch the watchdog. Do you work for the Heralds? Do you know someone who does? If you have a story Herald Watch can tell it. Your anonymity will be guaranteed. Send your tip via email to

Notes—Chapter 6

this address: … Don't delay, do it today" (Herald Watch Blog—Help Wanted!—no date stated).

5. Among others, McIntosh (2005), Thurman (2008), Matheson (2004), and Deuze, Bruns and Neuberger (2007) examined the relationship between traditional forms of journalism and blogging.

6. This is to a large extent also credited to shortcomings of the CIA. For a recent summary of CIA failures, see Cornwell (2009).

7. Examples of official government channels are Granma (http://www.granma.cu), Juventud Rebelde (http://www.juventudrebelde.cu), and El Caimán Barbudo (http://www.caimanbarbudo.cu); these are the digital editions of newspapers that are available in hardcopy in Cuba.

8. Information on what kind of behavior will not have any serious consequences, even though it might not conform to the ideology of the Cuban government, varies. See Sujatha Fernandes' (2006) *Cuba Represent!* for an account of criticism of the status quo that is acknowledged and simultaneously "overlooked" by the Cuban government.

9. Younger informants are familiar with terms such as *la lucha*. However, my observation in the field was that, if they use it all, it is to a much lesser degree than older Cuban Americans. Furthermore, this is not terminology to be found in official communiqués from Raíces de Esperanza, which contain a discourse coming from a humanitarian aid perspective.

Chapter 6

1. Karen E. Till (2006) provides a useful and comprehensive overview of the evolution and developments in the field.

2. The relationship of migrants to their country of origin is complex and manifold, as can be seen in the work of Kolar-Panov (1997), Georgiou (2006), Gillespie (1995), Naficy (1993) and Kosnik (2007).

3. In contrast to this, other diasporas have been located as viable markets for media production in the home country; see for example Mishra (2001) for the case of Bollywood and the Indian diaspora.

4. Miami's Spanish-language radio scene has diversified in the last ten to fifteen years. However, traditional radio stations still enjoy very high popularity. One radio presenter, Francisco Aruca (interviewed in January 2007), had in fact set up a station that repeatedly challenged the hardliner views and the dominant narrative of collective memory. However, he found the station very difficult to maintain due to a lack of businesses buying advertising time for fear of being associated with pro–Castro views. No doubt this kind of journalistic work comes at a high social cost and made Aruca an extremely controversial figure within the community.

5. García (1996, 6) underlines this arguments when she states, "[Mariel émigrés] came of age or lived most of their adult lives in Cuba's new revolutionary society. They were the so-called *hombres nuevos*, the New Man, or New Cubans, produced by the revolution. Many of them had no experience to which they could compare their lives under Castro; thus, their migration was prompted by a different reality."

6. For an in-depth analysis of Mariel and the challenges it brought home in terms of Cuban and Cuban American identity, see Sandoval (1986).

7. Román de la Campa (2000) bears witness to this in *Cuba on My Mind*.

8. These interviews were conducted in January 2007 and October 2008.

9. Then again, it is not possible to erase memories as we wish; see José van Dijk's (2009) illuminating and pop-culture-informed opening to "Mediated memories as amal-

gamations of mind, matter, and culture." We can, however, make a conscious choice to not found present and future actions on memories and beliefs of the past.
 10. In this context, the oral dimension of memory and passing on stories from the island is of significance as well.
 11. Casey (1987, 213) points out that "places are as much in us as we are in them." Climatic and scenic similarities between south Florida and Cuba may account for embodied memories that provide another form of mnemonic trigger in remembering Cuba.

Conclusion

 1. See for example Georgiou (2006), Kosnick (2007), and Portes, Escobar and Arana (2009).
 2. See for example Safran (1991), Clifford (1997), Bhabha (1994), Tölölyan (2007), Appadurai (2003), Beck (2006), Schlesinger (2007), and Braziel and Mannur (2003).

Appendix A

 1. Thomson et al. (2005) offer an insightful account on their experiences of anonymizing personal details of interviewees. One of the main challenges is to disguise identities to an extent that even insiders would not be able to recognize the research participant while not losing relevant contextual details.
 2. In addition to navigating a polarized field in an offline environment, researchers are also faced with the challenges of online encounters. See Lohmeier (2009) for a detailed account of impression management on- and offline.

References

Agha, Tahereh. 1997. *Lebensentwürfe im Exil: Biographische Verarbeitung der Fluchtmigration iranischer Frauen in Deutschland*. Frankfurt: Campus Verlag.
Aguilar, Louis. 2003. "Telemundo, NBC stations pool resources to deliver news to Colorado Hispanics." http://www.hispanicbusiness.com/news/2003/2/18/telemundo_nbc_stations_pool_resources_to.htm. Accessed January 27, 2009.
Aguirre Ferré, Helen. 2007. "Codes of ethics in journalism: The case of Radio and TV Martí." http://helenaguirre.blogspot.com/2007/08/codes-of-ethics-in-journalism-case-of.html. Accessed January 12, 2009.
Albarran, Alan B., ed. 2009. *The Handbook of Spanish Language Media*. New York and London: Routledge.
Alvarez Borland, Isabel, and Lynette M.F. Bosch. 2009. "Introduction." In *Cuban-American Literature and Art: Negotiating Identities*, ed. Isabel Alvarez Borland and Lynette M.F. Bosch, 1–11. Albany: State University of New York Press.
Anderson, Benedict. 1992. "The New World disorder." *New Left Review* 193: 3–13.
Ang, Ien. 1989. "Wanted: Audiences. On the politics of empirical audience studies." In *Remote Control: Television, Audiences and Cultural Power*, ed. Ellen Seiter, Hans Borchers, Gabriele Kreutzner, and Eva-Maria Warth, 96–105. London and New York: Routledge.
Appadurai, Arjun. 2003. "Disjuncture and difference in the global cultural economy." In *Theorizing Diaspora: A Reader*, ed. Jana Evans Braziel and Anita Mannur, 25–48. Malden, MA: Blackwell.
Attac. 2009. http://www.france.attac.org and http://attac.de.
Babalú: ... an Island on the Net Without a Bearded Dictator. http://babalublog.com. Accessed January 30, 2011.
Ballinger, Pamela. 2003. *History in Exile: Memory and Identity at the Border of the Balkans*. Princeton, NJ: Princeton University Press.
Balmaseda, Liz. 2000. "Exiles' struggles lost in sound bites." *The Miami Herald*, April 6, 1.
Bardach, Ann Louise. 2002. *Cuba Confidential: Love and Vengeance in Miami and Havana*. New York: Random House.
Barlow, William. 1990. "Rebel airways: Radio and revolution in Latin America." *Howard Journal of Communication* 2.2: 123–34.
Baym, Nancy K., and Annette N. Markham. 2009. "Introduction: Marking smart choices on shifting ground." In *Internet Inquiry*, ed. Annette N. Markham, and Nancy K. Baym, vii–xix. London: Sage.
BBC News. 2011. "Barack Obama eases rules on U.S. travel to Cuba." http://www.bbc.co.uk/news/world-latin-america-12197939. Accessed April 14, 2013.
———. 2012. "Cuba to end exit permits for foreign travel." http://www.bbc.co.uk/news/world-latin-america-19958577. Accessed February 8, 2013.

References

BBC World Service. 2007. "The case of the Cuban Five." http://www.bbc.co.uk/worldser vice/programmes/newshour/news/story/2007/07/070702_cuban_five.shtml. Accessed January 20, 2011.
Beck, Ulrich. 2006. *The Cosmopolitan Vision*. Cambridge: Polity Press.
Becker, Sabina. 1995. "Zwischen Akkulturation und Enkulturation: Anmerkungen zu einem vernachlässigten Autorinnentypus: Jenny Aloni und Ilse Losa." In *Kulturtransfer im Exil*, ed. Claus-Dieter Krohn, Erwin Rotermund, Lutz Winckler, and Wulf Koepke, 114–36. Munich: edition text + kritik.
Benjamin, Jules R. 1990. *The United States and the Origins of the Cuban Revolution: An Empire of Liberty in an Age of Liberation*. Princeton, NJ: Princeton University Press.
Bhabha, Homi K. 1994. *The Location of Culture*. London: Routledge.
Bloggers United for Cuban Liberty. 2009. "Welcome to Bloggers United for Cuban Liberty." http://bloggersforcubanliberty.blogspot.com/search?updated-max=2007-04-26T23%3A11%3A00-04%3A00&max-results=4. Accessed June 17, 2009.
Braziel, Jana Evans. 2008. *Diaspora: An Introduction*. Malden, MA: Blackwell.
_____, and Anita Mannur. 2003. "Nation, migration, globalization: Points of contention in diaspora studies." In *Theorizing Diaspora: A Reader*, ed. Jana Evans Braziel, and Anita Mannur, 1–22. Malden, MA: Blackwell.
El Caimán Barbudo: La revista cultural de la juventud de Cuba. http://www.caimanbar budo.cu. Accessed January 29, 2011.
Calvo Ospina, Hernando, and Katlijn Declerq, eds. 2001. *Originalton Miami: Die USA, Kuba und die Menschenrechte*. Köln: PapyRossa Verlag.
Carey, James W. 1988. *Media, Myths and Narratives*. Newbury Park, CA: Sage.
_____. 1989. *Communication as Culture: Essays on Media and Society*. Boston: Unwin Hyman.
Carmichael, Scott W. 2007. *True Believer: Inside the Investigation and Capture of Ana Montes, Cuba's Master Spy*. Annapolis, MD: Naval Institute Press.
Carter, Erica, James Donald, and Judith Squires, eds. 1993. *Space and Place: Theories of Identity and Location*. London: Lawrence and Wishart.
Casey, Edward S. 1987. *Remembering: A Phenomenological Study*. Bloomington: Indiana University Press.
Castro Ruz, Juanita. 2009. *Fidel y Raúl, mis hermanos: La Historia Secreta. Memorias de Juanita Castro contadas a María Antonieta Collins*. Doral, FL: Aguilar.
Cells for Cuba. [2010]. http://cells4cuba.org. Accessed December 2, 2010.
Center for Immigration. 2004. "Illegal immigration." http://www.cis.org/illegal. Accessed August 18, 2009.
Chavez, Leo R. 2008. *The Latino Threat: Constructing Immigrants, Citizens, and the Nation*. Stanford: Stanford University Press.
Cheong, Pauline Hope. 2008. "The young and techless? Investigating internet use and problem-solving behaviors among young adults in Singapore." *New Media and Society* 10.5: 771–91.
Clifford, James. 1997. *Routes: Travel and Translation in the Late Twentieth Century*. Cambridge, MA: Harvard University Press.
CNN. 2000. Transcript: "Crossfire: Are lawmakers playing politics with the future of Elian Gonzalez?" http://transcripts.cnn.com/TRANSCRIPTS/0001/11/cf.00.html. Accessed March 11, 2009.
_____. [2009]. "Executives: Christopher Crommett." http://edition.cnn.com/CNN/ anchors_reporters/crommett.christopher.html. Accessed February 12, 2009.
Coffey, Amanda. 1999. *The Ethnographic Self: Fieldwork and the Representation of Identity*. London: Sage.
Cohen, Robin. 1997. *Global Diasporas: An Introduction*. London: University College London Press.

References

Connerton, Paul. 2009. *How Modernity Forgets.* Cambridge: Cambridge University Press.

Cornillot, Jeanine. 2009. *Family Sentence: The Search for My Cuban-Revolutionary, Prison-yard, Mythic-Hero, Deadbeat Dad.* Boston, MA: Beacon.

Cornwell, Rupert. 2009. "The big question: What's gone wrong at the CIA, and should it be abolished?" http://www.independent.co.uk/news/world/americas/the-big-question-whats-gone-wrong-at-the-cia—and-should-it-be-abolished-1744983.html. Accessed July 14, 2009.

Coser, Lewis A. 1992. "Introduction: Maurice Halbwachs 1877–1945." In *On Collective Memory. Edited, Translated and with an Introduction by Lewis A. Coser,* by Maurice Halbwachs. Chicago and London: University of Chicago Press.

Cuba Debate: Contra El Terrorismo Mediático. http://www.cubadebate.cu/. Accessed October 5, 2010.

Cuba Transition Project. 2008. "Cuba facts—Issue 43." http://ctp.iccas.miami.edu/FACTS_Web/Cuba%20Facts%20Issue%2043%20December.htm. Accessed October 6, 2009.

CubanAmericanPundits.com: Thought-provoking Essays from a Cuban-American Perspective. Accessed January 30, 2011. http://cubanamericanpundits.com.

De la Campa, Román. 2000. *Cuba on My Mind: Journeys to a Severed Nation.* London: Verso.

De la Torre, Miguel A. 2003. *La Lucha for Cuba: Religion and Politics on the Streets of Miami.* Berkeley: University of California Press.

De los Angeles Torres, María. 1995. "Encuentros y Encontronazos: Homeland in the Politics and Identity of the Cuban Diaspora." *Diaspora* 4.2: 211–38.

_____. 1999. *In the Land of Mirrors: Cuban Exile Politics in the United States.* Ann Arbor: University of Michigan Press.

_____. 2003. *The Lost Apple: Operation Pedro Pan, Cuban Children in the U.S., and the Promise of a Better Future.* Boston: Beacon.

Deuze, Mark, Axel Bruns, and Christoph Neuberger. 2007. "Preparing for an age of participatory news." *Journalism Practice* 1.3: 322–28.

De Varona, Esperanza B. 1987. *Cuban Exile Periodicals at the University of Miami Library: An Annotated Bibliography.* Madison, WI: Secretariat, Seminar on the Acquisition of Latin American Library Materials, Memorial Library, University of Wisconsin–Madison.

Didion, Joan. 1987. *Miami.* New York, NY: Pocket.

Downing, John. 2001. *Radical Media: Rebellious Communication and Social Movements.* London: Sage.

Easterday, Lois, Diana Papademas, Laura Schoor, and Catherine Valentine. 1982. "The making of a female researcher: Role problems in fieldwork." In *Field Research: A Sourcebook and Field Manual,* ed. Robert G. Burgess, 62–67. London: George Allen and Unwin.

Economist. 2010. "Multikulturell? Wir?" November 13, 35–36.

Elsaesser, Thomas. 1999. "Ethnicity, authenticity and exile: A counterfeit trade? German filmmakers and Hollywood." In *Home, Exile and Homeland. Film, Media and the Politics of Place,* ed. Hamid Naficy, 97–123. London: Routledge.

English, T. J. 2007. *The Havana Mob: Gangsters, Gamblers, Showgirls and Revolutionaries in 1950s Cuba.* Edinburgh: Mainstream.

Federal Communication Commission. 2008. "Low power television (LPTV) service." http://www.fcc.gov/cgb/consumerfacts/lptv.html. Accessed January 13, 2011.

Fernandes, Sujatha. 2006. *Cuba Represent! Cuban Arts, State Power, and the Making of New Revolutionary Cultures.* Durham and London: Duke University Press.

Flores, William V., and Rina Benmayor. 1997. "Introduction: Constructing cultural citi-

References

zenship." In *Latino Cultural Citizenship: Claiming Identity, Space, and Rights*, ed. William V. Flores and Rina Benmayor, 1–23. Boston: Beacon.
Flusser, Vilém. 2002. *Writings: Edited by Andreas Ströhl*. Minneapolis: University of Minnesota Press.
García, Cristina María. 1996. *Havana USA: Cuban Exiles and Cuban Americans in South Florida, 1959–1994*. Berkeley: University of California Press.
García Bedolla, Lisa. 2009. *Latino Politics*. Cambridge, MA: Polity.
Generación Y. http://desdecuba.com/generaciony. Accessed January 30, 2011.
Georgiou, Myria. 2006. *Diaspora, Identity and the Media*. Cresskill, NJ: Hampton.
Gessler, Philipp. 2010. "Der Bundestagsintegrationsbeauftragte." http://taz.de/1/debatte/kommentar/artikel/1/der-bundesintegrationsbeauftragte/. Accessed November 23, 2010.
Ghorashi, Halleh. 2004. "Identities and the sense of belonging: Iranian woman activists in exile." In *Refugees and the Transformation of Societies*, ed. Philomena Essed, Georg Frerks, and Joke Schrijvers, 106–118. New York: Berghahn.
Gillespie, Marie. 1995. *Television, Ethnicity and Cultural Change*. London: Routledge.
Gjelten, Tom. 2008. *Bacardi and the Long Fight for Cuba: The Biography of a Cause*. New York: Viking Penguin.
Gomez, Henry. 2006. "Verdict on Martí moonlighters." http://heraldwatch.blogspot.com/2006/11/verdict-on-mart-moonlighters.html. Accessed January 15, 2009.
Gonzalez, David. 2006. "From Miami, news agency fields reports from Cuba." http://www.nytimes.com/2006/08/04/us/04prensa.html. Accessed August 13, 2009.
González, Edward J. 2007. *Cuban Exiles on the Trade Embargo: Interviews, with a Foreword by Elisabeth C. Aiken*. Jefferson, NC: McFarland.
Gopinath, Gayatri. 2005. *Impossible Desires: Queer Diasporas and South Asian Public Cultures*. Durham and London: Duke University Press.
Granma. http://www.granma.cu. Accessed January 29, 2011.
Grann, David. 2012. "The Yankee comandante: A story of love, revolution, and betrayal." *The Economist*, May 28, 46–71.
Grenier, Guillermo J., and Alex Stepick III, eds. 1992. *Miami Now! Immigration, Ethnicity, and Social Change*. Gainesville: University of Florida Press.
Halbwachs, Maurice. 1992. *On Collective Memory: Edited, Translated and with an Introduction by Lewis A. Coser*. Chicago: University of Chicago Press.
Hall, Stuart. 1991. "The local and the global: Globalization and ethnicity." In *Culture, Globalization and the World System*, ed. Anthony D. King, 19–39. Binghamton: State University of New York Press.
_____. 1992. "The question of cultural identity." In *Modernity and Its Future*, ed. Stuart Hall, David Held, and Tony McGrew, 274–316. Cambridge, MA: Polity.
_____. 1997. "Subjects in history: Making diasporic identities." In *The House That Race Built: Original Essays by Toni Morrison, Angela Y. Davis, Cornel West, and Others on Black Americans and Politics in America Today*, ed. Wahneema Lubiano, 289–99. New York: Pantheon.
Hammersley, Martyn, and Paul Atkinson. 1983. *Ethnography: Principles in Practice*. London: Tavistock.
Haney, Patrick J., and Walt Vanderbush. 2005. *The Cuban Embargo: The Domestic Politics of an American Foreign Policy*. Pittsburgh, PA: University of Pittsburgh Press.
Hartenstein, Elfi. 1999. *Jüdische Frauen im New Yorker Exil: 10 Begegnungen*. Dortmund: Edition Ebersbach.
Harvey, David. 1989. *The Condition of Postmodernity*. Oxford: Blackwell.
Hepp, Andreas. 2010. "Researching 'mediatised worlds': Non-mediacentric media and communication research as a challenge." In *Media and Communication Studies Interventions and Intersections*, ed. Nico Carpentier et al., 37–48. Tartu: Tartu University Press.

References

Herald Watch Blog. "Help Wanted!" http://heraldwatch.blogspot.com/2006/11/verdict-on-mart-moonlighters.html. Accessed January 15, 2009.
Hispanic Fact Pack. 2009. *Annual Guide to Hispanic Marketing and Media*. Chicago, IL: Crain Communication.
Hispanic Online Marketing. 2008. "Yahoo! & Telemundo split is good for Hispanic online marketing." *www.hispaniconlinemarketing.com/2008/11/yahoo-telemundo-split-is-good-for-hispanic-online-marketing/*. Accessed August 5, 2012.
Hoag, Christina. 2006a. "Great ratings intensify upfront sale." *The Miami Herald*, May 14, 1E, 8E.
_____. 2006b. "Newsroom philosophies differ." http://www.miami.com/mld/miami herald/1567634.htm. Accessed October 18, 2006.
Hookway, Nicholas. 2008. "'Entering the blogosphere': Some strategies for using blogs in social research." *Qualitative Research* 8.1: 91–113.
Hoskins, Andrew. 2001. "New Memory: Mediating history." *Historical Journal of Film, Radio and Television* 21.4: 333–46.
Ichikawa, Emilio. http://ei.eichikawa.com. Accessed January 30, 2011.
IMDB. [2009]. "Fuego en la Sangre." http://www.imdb.com/title/tt1159993/. Accessed August 18, 2009.
Infante, Guillermo Cabrera. 2008. *Tres Tristes Tigres*. New York: Primero Edición Rayo.
Juventud Rebelde. http://www.juventudrebelde.cu. Accessed January 29, 2011.
Karim, Karim H. 2003. "Mapping diasporic mediascapes." In *The Media of Diaspora*, ed. Karim H. Karim, 1–18. London: Routledge.
Kitch, Carolyn. 2008. "Placing journalism inside memory and memory studies." *Memory Studies* 1.3: 311–20.
Kleinknecht, William. 1999. "Journalists at risk." *American Journalism Review* 21.10: 32–39.
Kolar-Panov, Dona. 1997. *Video, War and the Diasporic Imagination*. London: Routledge.
Kosnick, Kira. 2007. *Migrant Media: Turkish Broadcasting and Multicultural Politics in Berlin*. Bloomington and Indianapolis: Indiana University Press.
Krispyn, Egbert. 1973. "Exil als Lebensform." In *Exil und Innere Emigration II*, ed. Peter Uwe Hohendahl and Egon Schwarz, 101–118. Frankfurt a.M.: Koch.
Kuhn, Annette. 1992. *An Everyday Magic: Cinema and Cultural Memory*. London: I.B. Tauris.
Kumar, Keval J., Theo Hug and Gebhard Rusch. 2006. "Construction of memory." In *News in Public Memory: An International Study of Media Memories Across Generations*, ed. I. Volkmer, 211–24. New York: Peter Lang.
Landsberg, Alison. 2004. *Prosthetic Memory: The Transformation of American Remembrance in the Age of Mass Culture*. New York: Columbia University Press.
Latell, Brian. 2005. *After Fidel: The Inside Story of Castro's Regime and Cuba's Next Leader*. New York: Palgrave Macmillan.
Lauffer, Kimberley A., Alyse Gotthofer Lancaster, and Sandra Florentin. 2001. "The Feds, the family, the father: The framing of Elián." A paper submitted to the Newspaper Division of the Association for Education in Journalism and Mass Communication for the 2001 Annual Convention in Washington, D.C.
Lavariega Monforti, Jessica, and Lisa García Bedolla. 2006. "Social context and exile politics: A look at Cuban and Cuban-American political attitudes." Unpublished study carried out at the Metropolitan Center at Florida International University; given to the author by an interviewee in June 2006.
Lazo, Rodrigo. 2005. *Writing to Cuba: Filibustering and the Cuban Exiles in the United States*. Chapel Hill: University of North Carolina Press.
Lee, Sarah. 1999. "Private uses in public spaces: A study of an internet café." *New Media and Society* 3.1: 331–350.

References

Lesnik, Max. 2010. "La estefa de los Estefan." http://www.voltairenet.org/article165331.html. Accessed October 3, 2010.
Levine, Robert. 2001. *Secret Missions to Cuba: Fidel Castro, Bernardo Benes and Cuban Miami.* New York: Palgrave Macmillan.
Levine, Robert M., and Moisés Asís. 2000. *Cuban Miami.* New Brunswick: Rutgers University Press.
Library Index. N.d. "Immigration laws and policies since the 1980s—Homeland Security Act of 2002." http://www.libraryindex.com/pages/2414/Immigration-Laws-Policies-Since-1980s-HOMELAND-SECURITY-ACT-2002.html. Accessed March 11, 2009.
Livingstone, Sonia. 2003. "Children's use of the internet: Reflections on the emerging research agenda." *New Media and Society* 5.2: 147–166.
——. 2009. "On the mediation of everything: ICA presidential address 2008." *Journal of Communication* 59.1: 1–18.
Lohmeier, Christine. 2009. "Disclosing the ethnographic self." *M/C Journal* 12.5. http://journal.media-culture.org.au/index.php/mcjournal/article/viewArticle/195. Accessed January 30, 2011.
——. 2013. "Cosmopolitan by default? The significance of place for diasporic identities." In *Communication and Community*, ed. Patricia Moy, 93–108. New York: Hampton.
Lost City. 2005. Directed by Andy García. Lions Gate Entertainment.
Malkki, Liisa H. 1995. *Purity and Exile. Violence, Memory, and National Cosmology Among Hutu Refugees in Tanzania.* Chicago: University of Chicago Press.
Martí, José. 1997. *Versos Sencillos: Simple Verses. Translated, with an introduction, by Manuel A. Tellechea.* Houston, TX: Arte Público.
Massey, Doreen. 2005. *For Space.* London: Sage.
Matheson, Donald. 2004. "Weblogs and the epistemology of the news: some trends in online journalism." *New Media and Society* 6.4: 443–468.
McClatchy Company. 2006. "McClatchy completes acquisition of Knight Ridder." http://www.mcclatchy.com/pressreleases/story/1629.html. Accessed January 14, 2009.
McIntosh, Shawn. 2005. "Blogs: Has their time finally come—or gone?" *Global Media and Communication* 1.3: 385–88.
Medina, Pablo. 2002. *Exiled Memories: A Cuban Childhood.* New York: Persea.
Menéndez, Ana. 2001. *In Cuba I Was a German Shepherd.* New York: Grove.
Miami Herald. 2009. "About US." http://www.miamiherald.com/about_us/. Accessed January 14, 2009.
Miami-Dade County. 2009. "Miami-Dade County Facts 2009: A Compendium of Selected Statistics, edited by the Research Section of the Department and Planning Section of Miami-Dade County." http://www.miamidade.gov/business/library/reports/2009-miami-dade-county-facts.pdf. Accessed November 28, 2010.
Mirabal, Nancy Raquel. 2003. "'Ser de aquí': Beyond the Cuban exile model." *Latino Studies* 1.3: 366–382.
Mishra, Vijay. 2001. *Bollywood Cinema: Temples of Desire.* London: Routledge.
Morley, David. 1991. "Where the global meets the local: Notes from the Sitting Room." *Screen* 32.1: 1–15.
——. 1999. "Bounded realms: Household, family, community, and nation." In *Home, Exile, Homeland: Film, Media and the Politics of Place*, ed. Hamid Naficy, 151–68. London: Routledge.
——. 2000. *Home Territories: Media, Mobility and Identity.* London: Routledge.
Murthy, Dhiraj. 2008. "Digital ethnography: An examination of the use of new technologies for social research." *Sociology* 42.5: 837–855.
Naficy, Hamid. 1993. *The Making of Exile Cultures: Iranian Television in the Los Angeles.* Minneapolis: University of Minnesota Press.

References

———. 2001. *An Accented Cinema: Exilic and Diasporic Filmmaking*. Princeton, NJ: Princeton University Press.

———, ed. 1999. *Home, Exile and Homeland: Film, Media and the Politics of Place*. London: Routledge.

Nespor, Jan. 2000. "Anonymity and place in qualitative inquiry." *Qualitative Inquiry* 6.4: 546–69.

Nielsen Media Research. 2009. "Top TV ratings among Hispanics." http://www.nielsenmedia.com/nc/portal/site/Public/menuitem.43afce2fac27e890311ba0a347a062a0/?show=%2FFilters%2FPublic%2Ftop_tv_ratings%2Famong_hispanics&selOneIndex=4&vgnextoid=9e4df9669fa14010VgnVCM100000880a260aRCRD. Accessed February 12, 2009.

Nielsen Wire. 2009. "Primetime broadcast ratings, February 10, 2009." http://blog.nielsen.com/nielsenwire/tag/fuego-en-la-sangre-tue/. Accessed February 16, 2009.

Nueva Prensa. nuevaprensa.org. Accessed August 20, 2009.

Ogan, Christine. 2001. *Communication and Identity in the Diaspora: Turkish Migrants in Amsterdam and Their Use of Media*. Boston: Lexington.

Okely, Judith. 1992. "Anthropology and autobiography: Participatory experience and embodied knowledge." In *Anthropology and Autobiography*, ed. Judith Okely and Helen Callaway, 1–28. London: Routledge.

———. 1994. "Thinking Through fieldwork." In *Analyzing Qualitative Data*, ed. Alan Bryman and Robert G. Burgess, 1–34. London: Routledge.

O'Reilley Herrera, Andrea, ed. 2001. *ReMembering Cuba: Legacy of a Diaspora*. Austin: University of Texas Press.

Park, Robert E. 1950. *Race and Culture: Essays in the Sociology of Contemporary Man*. London: Free Press.

Passerini, Luisa. 1983. "Report on 'Memory': Final session of International Conference on Oral History. Aix-en-Provence 26. September 1982." *History Workshop Journal* 15: 195–96.

Pérez, Louis A. Jr. 2009. *Intervention, Revolution, and Politics in Cuba: 1913–1921*. Pittsburgh, PA: University of Pittsburgh Press.

Pérez Firmat, Gustavo. 1994. *Life on the Hyphen: The Cuban-American Way*. Austin: University of Texas Press.

———. 1995. *Next Year in Cuba: A Cubano's Coming-of-Age in America*. Houston, TX: Arte Público.

Pérez-Peña, Richard. 2007. "The Times names public editor." http://www.nytimes.com/2007/05/04/business/media/04paper-web.html?_r=2. Accessed January 16, 2009.

Perl, Shoshana. 2006. "Whither Helms Burton? A retrospective on the 10th anniversary." *Jean Monnet/Robert Schuman Paper Series* 6.5: 1–16.

Peters, John Durham. 1999. "Exile, nomadism and diaspora." In *Home, Exile and Homeland: Film, Media and the Politics of Place*, ed. Hamid Naficy, 17–41. London: Routledge.

Portes, Alejandro, and Alex Stepick. 1993. *City on the Edge: The Transformation of Miami*. Berkeley: University of California Press.

Portes, Alejandro, Cristina Escobar, and Renelinda Arana. 2009. "Divided or convergent loyalties? The political incorporation process of Latin American immigrants in the United States." *International Journal of Comparative Sociology* 50.2: 103–36.

Radio-Miami. 2011. http://www.radio-miami.com.

Raíces de Esperanza. http://www.raicesdeesperanza.org/index.php. Accessed December 2, 2010.

Reyes, Gerardo. 2006. "Periodistas despedidos podrán regressar a El Nuevo Herald." http://www.miami.com/mld/elnuevo/15664926.htm. Accessed January 14, 2009.

Rieff, David. 1993. *The Exile: Cuba in the Heart of Miami*. London: Vintage.

References

Río, Esteban del. 2006. "The Latina/o problematic: Categories and questions in media communication research." In *Communication Yearbook 30*, ed. Christina S. Beck, 387–429. Mahwah, NJ: Erlbaum for the International Association of Communication.

Robbins, Bruce. 1995. "Some versions of U.S. internationalism." *Social Text 45* 14.4: 97–123.

Roberts, Brian. 2007. *Getting the Most Out of the Research Experience*. London: Sage.

Robertson, Alexa. 2010. *Mediated Cosmopolitanism*. Malden and Cambridge: Polity.

Robins, Kevin. 2001. "Becoming anybody: Thinking against the nation and through the city." *City* 5.1: 77–90.

Rushdie, Salman. 1991. *Imaginary Homelands: Essays and Criticism 1981–1991*. London: Penguin.

Safran, William. 1991. "Diasporas in modern societies: Myths of homeland and return." *Diaspora* 1.1: 83–99.

Said, Edward. 1984. "The mind of winter: Reflections on life in exile." *Harpers* 269, 49–55.

Samuel, Raphael. 1994. *Theatres of Memory Vol. 1: Past and Present in Contemporary Culture*. London: Verso.

Sandoval, Mercedes C. 1986. *Mariel and Cuban National Identity*. Miami: Edition SIBI.

Saralegui, Cristina. 1998. *Cristina! My Life as a Blonde*. New York: Warner.

Sassen, Saskia. 2001. *The Global City: New York, London, Tokyo*. Princeton: Princeton University Press.

_____. 2006. *Cities in a World Economy*. Thousand Oaks, CA: Pine Forge.

_____. 2007. "A cosmopolitan temptation." *European Journal of Communication* 22.4: 413–426.

_____, ed. 2002. *Global Networks, Linked Cities*. New York: Routledge.

Schlesinger, Philip. 1980. "Between sociology and journalism." In *The Sociology of Journalism and the Press*, ed. Harry Christian, 341–69. Sociological Review Monograph 29. Staffordshire, UK: University of Keele.

Segal, Robert A. 2004. *Myth: A Very Short Introduction*. Oxford: Oxford University Press.

Sheffer, Gabriel. 2003. *Diaspora Politics: At Home Abroad*. New York: Cambridge University Press.

Shulman, Judith H. 1990. "Now you see them, now you don't: Anonymity versus visibility in case studies of teachers." *Educational Researcher* 19.6: 11–15.

Silva, Mark, and Tracy Wilkinson. 2009. "Obama allows unlimited travel to Cuba by relatives." http://articles.latimes.com/2009/apr/14/world/fg-cuba-policy14. Accessed August 13, 2009.

Silverstone, Roger. 1994. *Television and Everyday Life*. London: Routledge.

Sinclair, John. 1999. *Latin American Television: A Global View*. Oxford: Oxford University Press.

_____. 2005. "From Latin Americans to Latinos: Spanish-language television and its audience in the United States." *Telos: Cuadernos De Communicación, Technología y Sociedad* 64: n.p.

_____, and Stuart Cunningham. 2000. "Go with the flow: Diasporas and the media." *Television and New Media* 1.1: 11–31.

Singh, Supriyah. 2001. "Gender and the use of internet at home." *New Media and Society* 3.4: 395–416.

Slade, Christina. 2006. "Perceptions and memories of the media context." In *News in Public Memory: An International Study of Media Memories across Generations*, ed. I. Volkmer, 195–210. New York: Peter Lang.

Smith, Anthony D. 1986. *The Ethnic Origins of Nations*. Oxford: Blackwell.

Sollors, Werner. 1986. *Beyond Ethnicity: Consent and Descent in American Culture*. Oxford: Oxford University Press.

References

Sooryamoorthy, Radhamany, B. Paige Miller, and Wesley Shrum. 2008. "Untangling the technology cluster: Mobile telephony, internet use and the location of social ties." *New Media and Society* 10.5: 729–749.

Soruco, Gonzalo R. 1996. *Cubans and the Mass Media in South Florida*. Gainesville: University Press of Florida.

Stepick, Alex, Guillermo Grenier, Max Castro, and Max Dunn. 2003. *This Land Is Our Land: Immigrants and Power in Miami*. Berkeley: University of California Press.

Stepick, Alex III. 1992. "The refugees nobody wants: Haitians in Miami." In *Miami Now! Immigration, Ethnicity, and Social Change*, ed. Guillermo J. Grenier and Alex Stepick III, 57–82. Gainesville: University of Florida Press.

Strack, Thomas. 1995. "Fritz Lang und das Exil: Rekonstruktion einer Erfahrung mit dem amerikanischen Film." In *Kulturtransfer im Exil*, ed. Claus-Dieter Krohn, Erwin Rotermund, Lutz Winckler, and Wulf Koepke, 184–203. Munich: edition text + kritik.

Strauss, Anselm, Heiner Legewie, and Barbara Schervier-Legewie. 2004. "Research is hard work, it's always a bit suffering: therefore, on the other side research should be fun: Anselm Strauss in conversation with H. Legewie and B. Schervier-Legewie." *Forum: Qualitative Research* 5.3. http://www.qualitative-research.net/index.php/fqs/article/view/562/1218. Accessed June 14, 2009.

Sturken, Marita. 2004. "The aesthetics of absence: Rebuilding Ground Zero." *American Ethnologist* 31.3: 311–25.

———. 2008. "Memory, consumerism and media: Reflections on the emergence of the field." *Memory Studies* 1.1: 73–78.

Telemundo. 2007. Press releases e-mailed to the author.

Thomas, Hugh. 1971. *Cuba, or The Pursuit of Freedom*. London: Eyre and Spottiswoode.

———. 1984. *Castro's Cuba*. Berlin: Siedler Verlag.

Thomson, Denise, Lana Bzdel, Karen Golden-Biddle, Trish Reay, and Carole A. Estabrooks. 2005. "Central questions of anonymization: A case study of secondary use of qualitative data." *FQS—Forum Qualitative Social Research* 6.1: Art. 29.

Thurman, Neil. 2008. "Forums for citizen journalists? Adoption of user-generated content initiatives by online news media." *New Media and Society* 10.1: 139–157.

Till, Karen E. 2006. "Memory studies." *History Workshop Journal* 62: 325–341.

Tölölyan, Khachig. 1991. "The nation-state and its others: In lieu of a preface." *Diaspora* 5.1: 3–36.

———. 1996. "Rethinking diaspora(s): Stateless power in the transnational moment." *Diaspora* 5.1: 3–36.

———. 2007. "The contemporary discourse of diaspora." *Comparative Studies of South Asia, Africa and the Middle East* 27.3: 647–55.

Trenblindado.com. "Exposing the truth about Ché Guevara." http://www.trenblindado.com. Accessed January 30, 2011.

Trommler, Frank. 1995. "Das gelebte und das nicht gelebte Exil des Peter Weiss: Zur Botschaft seiner frühen Bilder." In *Kulturtransfer im Exil*, ed. Claus Dieter Krohn, Erwin Rotermund, Lutz Winckler, and Wulf Koepke, 82–95. Munich: edition text + kritik.

Tsagarousianou, Roza. 2004. "Rethinking the concept of diaspora: Mobility, connectivity and communication in a globalised world." *Westminster Papers in Communication and Culture* 1.1: 52–65.

U.S. Census Bureau. 2004. "Facts for features." http://www.census.gov/Press-Release/www/releases/archives/facts_for_features_special_editions/002270.html. Accessed August 18, 2009.

———. 2006. "Hispanics in the United States." http://www.census.gov/population/www/socdemo/hispanic/files/Internet_Hispanic_in_US_2006.pdf. Accessed March 11, 2009.

References

———. 2007. "American community report—Hispanics: 2004." http://www.census.gov/prod/2007pubs/acs-03.pdf. Accessed July 20, 2009.
Univision. [2007a]. "Univision history." http://www.univision.net/corp/en/history.jsp. Accessed December 11, 2007.
———. [2007b]. "Univision network." http://www.univision.net/corp/en/univision.jsp. Accessed December 11, 2007.
Urry, John. 1995. *Consuming Places*. London: Routledge.
Valdez, Angela. 2009. "Francisco Aguirre Baca, 1920–2008: From the seat of power to the seat of a cab, and back again." http://www.washingtonpost.com/wp-dyn/content/article/2008/12/31/AR2008123102069.html. Accessed January 13, 2009.
Valdivia, Angharad N. 2010. *Latina/os and the Media*. Cambridge, UK: Polity.
———, ed. 2008. *Latina/o Communication Studies Today*. New York: Peter Lang.
Van Dijk, José. 2009. "Mediated memories as amalgamations of mind, matter, and culture." In *The Body Within. Art, Medicine and Visualization*, ed. Renée van der Vall, and Robert Zwijnenberg, 157–72. Leiden: Brill.
Van Hear, Nicholas. 1998. *New Diasporas: The Mass Exodus, Dispersal and Regrouping of Migrant Communities*. London: Taylor and Francis.
Vargas, Lucila. 2009. *Latina Teens, Migration, and Popular Culture*. New York: Peter Lang.
Veciana-Suarez, Ana. 1987. *Hispanic Media, USA: A Narrative Guide to Print and Electronic Hispanic News Media in the United States*. Washington, DC: Media Institute.
Voltaire Network. http://www.voltairenet.org/en. Accessed October 3, 2010.
Voss, Michael. 2008. "Cuba lifts ban on home computers." http://news.bbc.co.uk/1/hi/world/americas/7381646.stm. Accessed May 31, 2009.
———. 2009. "Cuba faces tough U.S. choice." http://news.bbc.co.uk/1/hi/world/americas/7997543.stm. Accessed May 31, 2009.
Waisbord, Silvio. 2000. *Watchdog Journalism in South America: News, Accountability, and Democracy*. New York: Columbia University Press.
———, and Nancy Morris. 2001. "Introduction: Rethinking media globalization and state power." In *Media and Globalization: Why the State Matters*, ed. Nancy Morris, and Silvio Waisbord, vii–xvi. Lanham, Maryland: Rowman and Littlefield.
Walker, Jill. 2005. "Weblog." In *Routledge Encyclopedia of Narrative Theory*, ed. David Herman, Manfred Jahn, and Marie-Laure Ryan. London: Polity.
Walker Rettberg, Jill. 2008. *Blogging*. Cambridge: Polity.
Walsh, Daniel C. 2012. *An Air War with Cuba*. Jefferson, NC: McFarland.
Wiles, Rose, Graham Crow, Sue Heath, and Vikki Charles. 2008. "The management of confidentiality and anonymity in social research." *International Journal of Social Research Methodology* 11.5: 417–28.
Wooffitt, Robin, and Sue Widdicombe. 2006. "Interaction in interviews." In *Talk and Interaction in Social Research Methods*, ed. Paul Drew, Geoffry Raymond, and Darin Weinberg, 28–49. London: Sage.
Yates, Frances A. 1966. *The Art of Memory*. London: Routledge.
Zelizer, Barbie. 2008. "Why memory's work on journalism does not reflect journalism's work on memory." *Memory Studies* 1: 79–87.

Index

A Mano Limpia 98, 112
activism 115–117, 118, 122, 131, 139, 148, 150, 153, 154
African American community 34–35
agenda-setting media 48, 49
agents *see* spies
Aguirre, Alejandro 43, 44, 45–47, 49, 53, 77, 85–86, 101–102
Aguirre, Francisco 44, 48–49
Aguirre, Horacio 43, 44, 45, 48
Aguirre Ferré, Helen 45–47, 58
Alfonso, Pablo 58, 60
American dream 31–32, 34
Anglo community 6, 7, 18, 19, 20, 34–35, 36, 51, 53, 63, 65, 72, 102, 103, 104, 142, 172
anonymity 158–159
anti–Cuban sentiments 36, 72, 133
Aruca, Francisco 78–82
Azcárraga family 87, 90, 91

Balmaseda, Liz 102
Balseros see Rafters
Barciela, Susana 52, 53, 102, 104
Bardach, Ann Louise 54, 75, 81, 82, 100
Barlow, William 69, 78
Batista, Fulgencio 5, 16, 31–32, 43, 75
Bay of Pigs Invasion 6, 30, 151
Beck, Ulrich 16
Benavides, Paul 108, 110–113, 114, 135, 145
bilingualism *see* language
black community *see* African American community
Blaya, Joaquín 88
Bloggers United for Cuban Liberty 110
blogs 107–115, 117, 118, 122, 123, 135, 136, 137, 140, 143, 153
Braziel, Jana Evans 15

Burton, Dan 8
Bush, George W. 57
Bush, Jeb (governor) 167

Calle Ocho see Little Havana
Calzada, Humberto 104
Cancio Isla, Wilfredo 58
Capen, Richard 55
Carey, James 67, 124, 126, 127
Carter, James 79, 80
Casey, Edward 26, 126
Castañega, Carlos 61
Castelló, Humberto 53–54, 60
Castro, Fidel 5, 6, 7, 8, 9, 24, 25, 28, 29, 30, 33, 35, 40, 42, 43, 56, 58, 68, 69, 71, 74, 75, 76, 77, 79, 83, 90, 101, 103, 116, 130, 133, 135, 139, 146, 147, 148, 149, 151, 152, 161, 162, 169, 174
Castro, Raúl 5, 8, 33, 75, 76, 83, 107, 133, 139, 146, 151
Cebrian, Teresa 97, 105
Chicago Tribune 61
CIA 1, 6, 9, 48, 49, 68, 79, 83, 138, 141
circulation 48, 49, 50, 52, 53, 62
Clinton, William 8, 35, 37, 101
CNN en Español 91
Coffey, Amanda 157, 168, 174
Cold War 5, 8, 9, 17, 35, 76, 147, 148, 162
Communism 5, 7, 10, 32, 68, 78, 79, 83, 100, 105, 144, 147
Connor, Olga 58, 61
Corral, Oscar 57–58, 63–64
Cortez, Raúl 86
cosmopolitanism 10, 13, 14, 16, 27, 144, 145
Cuban Adjustment Act 7, 8, 37, 65, 103, 142
Cuban American National Foundation (CANF) 20, 28, 50, 54–56, 65, 74, 85, 116, 152

Index

Cuban Heritage Collection (CHC) 32, 41, 45, 108, 119, 160, 163, 164–165, 169, 174
Cuban Liberty and Democratic Solidarity Act *see* trade embargo
Cuban Missile Crisis 6, 35
Cuban revolution 2, 5, 6, 9, 19, 25, 30, 34, 39, 43, 63, 67, 68, 69, 79, 104, 124, 129, 130, 145, 146–147, 161

Dade County *see* Miami-Dade County
Dallas Morning News 103
debating culture 72, 114, 153
De la Campa, Román 24, 25, 33, 146
De la Torre, Miguel 99
De los Angeles Torres, María 81, 101, 146
Democratic Party 6
De Varona, Esperanza 41, 160, 174
diaspora 2, 10–11, 14, 15, 21, 85, 96, 97, 144, 146
Diáz, Jesús 58
Diáz-Balart, Lincoln 105, 169
Diáz-Balart, Mario 169
digital divide 107
Downing, John 75

Eaton, Tracey 103
Enríquez, Hiram 121
Estefan, Gloria 33, 117
exile (theories of) 1, 11–14, 28, 45
exile mentality 14, 20, 60, 66, 70, 71, 129, 146

Federal Communications Commission (FCC) 84, 87
Flusser, Vilém 13–14
freedom flights 51
Fuego en La Sangre 94–95, 178

García, Andy 19, 31, 33, 117
García, María Cristina 30, 35, 39, 44, 51, 52
Generación Y 117, 137
Georgiou, Myria 15, 27, 157
Ghorashi, Halleh 12–13
globalization (theories of) 14–15, 16
Goizueta, Robert 32–33
Gómez, Andy 103
Gómez, Henry 108–110, 112, 113
Gómez-Rossié, Gladys 164
González, Elián 12–13, 21, 35–36, 85, 99–106
Guevara, Ernesto Ché 1, 146, 161

Haitians 71, 131
Halbwachs, Maurice 124, 125, 126, 127, 128, 134, 139
Hallmark Cards, Inc. 87, 88
hardliners 24, 69, 73, 78, 79, 80, 81, 110, 116, 130, 131, 132–133, 134, 135, 136, 137
Havana 5, 6, 25, 30, 31, 32, 33, 54, 75, 149
Haza, Oscar 98, 112
Helms, Jesse 8
Helms-Burton-Act *see* trade embargo
Hepp, Andreas 156
Herald Watch Blog 108, 109, 110
Hispanic population 4, 17, 18, 19, 36–38, 85, 94, 97, 121
historic exiles (exilio histórico) 6, 7, 30–33, 42, 44, 47, 69–70, 73, 77, 82, 83, 104–105, 107, 129–130, 131, 132, 133, 135, 136, 137, 138, 148, 150, 167
Hombres nuevos (New Men) 145
Hoskins, Andrew 127, 137–138
Hoyt, Clark 60

Ichikawa, Emilio 113
immigration 4, 27, 35, 37, 94, 121, 141–142
Immigration and Naturalization Service (INS) 100
Infante, Guillermo Cabrera 31
Institute for Cuban and Cuban-American Studies (ICCAS) 103, 122–123, 163

journalism ethics 60, 64, 66, 75–76, 114

Kennedy, John F. 6
Kitch, Carolyn 124, 127, 128
Knight-Ridder, Inc. 20, 51–52, 53, 60, 65
Kreuzberger, Mario (Don Francisco) 88
Kuhn, Annette 26, 125, 126

Landsberg, Alison 126, 139
language 36–37, 97, 119–123, 135, 136, 143; bilingualism 52, 77, 96, 119, 121, 168
Lazo, Rodrigo 40–41
Lesnik, Max 78, 81, 82
Little Havana 24–25, 26, 41, 44, 65, 77, 82, 100, 165
Livingstone, Sonia 156
local television 84, 91, 97–99, 105

Index

Lost City 25, 26, 31–34, 148
Lucha (struggle) 21, 68, 74, 106, 110, 119, 141, 143, 144, 153

Malkki, Liisa 12
Mambí Watch Blog 108, 111, 112, 114, 115
Marazul Tours 79, 81
Marcos, Nathalie 115, 118
Mariel boatlift 7, 35, 51, 71–72, 74, 126, 131, 132
Martí, José 25, 26
Martí moonlighter story 56–64, 70, 75, 76, 109
Martís (radio and TV) 9–10, 56–65, 75, 76, 77, 141, 173
Más Canosa, Jorge 54–56
Massey, Doreen 24–25, 149
McClatchy Company 51
McGarrity, Tom 93–94
media management 62
memory (theories of) 124–128
Mesa Redonda (Cuban) 58
Miami-Dade County 6, 7, 30, 31, 34, 50, 51, 53, 68, 71, 111
migration (theories of) 10, 14–15, 144–145
Moas, Raúl 116
Morcate, Daniel 70, 71, 88, 90
Morris, Nancy 27

Naficy, Hamid 12, 13
NBC 92, 95, 178
New York Times 60, 105, 109, 110, 161
New Yorker 1
newsroom philosophy 59, 60, 62, 90
Nicaraguans 6, 20, 43, 44, 48, 86
no-dialogue-policy 24, 134, 151
nostalgia 33, 127, 129, 131, 134, 137, 149
Nueva Prensa Cubana 76

Obama, Barack 9, 170
Okely, Judith 162, 170–171

Pardo, Bernadette 78
Passerini, Luisa 129
Pérez Castellón, Ninoska 73, 74, 76, 98
Pérez-Crespo, Nancy 76
Perez Firmat, Gustavo 23
Pérez-Roura, Armando 74–75, 78
Periodiquitos 41, 107–108, 151
press in Cuba 9
Puerto Ricans 6, 97

Radio Martí *see* Martís
Rafters (*Balseros*) 7–8, 53, 99
Raíces de Esperanza (Roots of Hope) 115–117, 118, 134–135, 143
Reagan, Ronald 78
Réplica 82
Republican Party 6, 37, 170
Richard, Alfredo 92–93, 94
Río, Esteban del 17–18
Roberts, Brian 172
Robertson, Alexa 16
Rodriguez, Silvio 80
Rushdie, Salman 12

Sábado Gigante 88
Said, Edward 12
Salazar, María Elvira 98
Samuel, Raphael 129
Sánchez, Yoani 117, 137, 153
Saralegui, Cristina 42, 87, 88, 89
Saralegui, Francisco 42
Schlesinger, Philip 16, 165
Sheffer, Gabriel 11, 15
El Show de Cristina 88
Sinclair, John 21, 85, 86, 87, 91, 96
Soruco, Gonzalo 67, 68, 69, 77, 84, 87, 88
Soviet Union 5, 6, 7, 33, 147
Spanish Communication Corporation (SICC) 86–87, 90
Spanish Empire 5
Spanish International Network (SIN) 86–87, 90
Spanish Radio Broadcasters Association (SRBA) 87
"special period" 7–8, 147
spies 58–59, 64, 74, 82
state, (nation-)state 14–15, 27–28
Strauss, Anselm 158
Stuart Aguirre, Horacio 45
student organizations 116, 118, 164
Sturken, Marita 25, 124, 127

Televisa 87, 88, 90, 91, 95
Tilson, Donn 159–160, 174
Tölölyan, Khachig 10, 15
trade embargo 8, 24, 28–29, 56, 73, 82, 115, 116, 123, 135
travel to Cuba 8–9, 79, 80, 136, 146, 148
TV Martí *see* Martís

199

Index

unity of Cuba and exile 29, 34
Urry, John 23

Vanidades 9, 42
VanVan 80
Venevision 88
violence 1, 58, 64, 81, 82
Voice of America 9, 57, 78

Waisbord, Silvio 27, 62
Walker Rettberg, Jill 108
"wet foot/dry foot-policy" 8, 103

Yahoo Inc. 92, 121

Zelizer, Barbie 126

www.ingramcontent.com/pod-product-compliance
Ingram Content Group UK Ltd.
Pitfield, Milton Keynes, MK11 3LW, UK
UKHW042005140426
5217IPUK00015B/994

9 780786 468942